For Rosemary Co...
Warm regards

P9-CDX-147

GOOD GRIEF

Rheta Grimsley Johnson

GOOD GRIEF

GRIEF

The Story of
Charles M. Schulz

PHAROS BOOKS
A SCRIPPS HOWARD COMPANY
NEW YORK

Text copyright © 1989 by Rheta Grimsley Johnson

PEANUTS ® Characters: © 1950, 1952, 1958 United Feature Syndicate, Inc.

PEANUTS ® Comic Strips: © 1966, 1976, 1980, 1983, 1985, 1986, 1988, 1989 United Feature Syndicate, Inc.

Cover Photograph © 1989 Cynthia Farah

You're a Good Man, Charlie Brown Lyrics copyright © 1971 Jeremy Music, Inc.

All rights reserved. No part of this book may be reproduced in any form or by any means without permission in writing from the publisher.

First published in 1989

Johnson, Rheta Grimsley,1953-
   Good grief: the story of Charles M. Schulz { i.e. Schulz C/
Rheta Grimsley Johnson.
     p.   cm.
   ISBN 0-88687-553-6 : $16.95
   1. Schulz, Charles M. 2. Cartoonists—United States—Biography.
I. Title.
PN6727.S3Z74 1989
741.5'092—dc20
[B]   89-33732
                                                            CIP

Printed in the United States of America
Pharos Books
A Scripps Howard Company
200 Park Avenue
New York, NY 10166
10   9   8   7   6   5   4   3   2   1

Interior design by Antler & Baldwin, Inc.

For Sarah Constance Crawford

Acknowledgments

*T*his book owes much to hours of conversation with Sparky Schulz; the other cartoonists who know him; his family, staff, and friends. Sparky is a private person, essentially, and at times the subjects we covered were difficult to explore. I thank him for his time and his honesty.

I am indebted as well to my own friends, who brought me food, made trips to the library for me, and listened for hours to my ruminations about the man and his art. They knew when to come and when to stay away. They stuck with me, as they always have.

My husband, cartoonist Jimmy Johnson *(Arlo and Janis),* was uniquely qualified to read, edit, and contribute to this book. His observations and his writing, especially about the evolution of *Peanuts,* the strip's theaters, characters, and themes, added immeasurably to the depth of this study. The book would not have been written without his help, and I am grateful.

Pharos Books editor Sarah Gillespie provided materials and insight and competent, kind guidance. I appreciate her patience.

The emphasis and conclusions about the personality and motivations of Sparky Schulz are mine. Any errors in judgment are mine alone.

I found, through it all, that Charles Schulz is just like we all believed and hoped he would be.

R. G. J.

C**harles Schulz** is not a funny man, not in person, anyway. He does not crack jokes to make you slap your knee; neither does he look funny, all rumpled and ink-stained and pudgy, as a real cartoonist should.

Jimmy Dean, country music singer and sausage purveyor, once said to Schulz: "You don't look like a cartoonist; you look like a druggist." And it is true. His bearing is dignified, stately. There is no flab, no fuss, no trick flower in the lapel.

Sparky Schulz can be outwardly cheerful and charming; inwardly, the man who sees humor in everything is a serious, melancholy fellow, the veteran of a war with depression that has dragged on his entire adult life. He is well-read, quietly religious, firm yet kindly. He chooses his words carefully and talks much like his comic strip characters talk. When someone does something stupid, he is nothing worse than a blockhead. When exasperated, Schulz's strongest oath is "Good grief!"

Tall and lean, he dresses like a vacationing physician, sporting soft, pastel golf sweaters and neat trousers with his remarkably clean tennis shoes. He doesn't own a suit. He does own two tuxedos, which he adores wearing.

He hates barbershop quartets and people without pens who ask him to autograph stuffed animals ("How are you supposed to write on a stuffed animal?"). He doesn't truly hate such things, but he is a no-nonsense man of many peeves who habitually prefaces an endless stream of tiny gripes with "I hate. . ."

In fact, in forty years, he has drawn only one comic strip he regrets, the very first *Peanuts* strip that ever appeared, in which a little boy named Shermy professes to hate Charlie Brown. The children in his gentle strip may get their socks knocked off, but he considers hate an inappropriate emotion.

He loves ice hockey and golf and classical music and cartooning. Both his telephone numbers—office and home—are listed. Sometimes children call him long distance to ask, "Do you really draw Snoopy?"

"Yes. Do your parents know you're calling?" Click.

He is shy and soft-spoken and has a voice that sounds much like Donald Sutherland's. It is cool, polite, and proper.

He does not drink—oh, maybe half a glass of wine with a meal, occasionally. Nor has he ever smoked.

His name is in the dictionary: "Schulz, Charles M. (Monroe) b. 1922—U.S. cartoonist: creator of the comic strip *Peanuts. (The Random House Dictionary of the English Language.)*

A definition he coined—"Happiness is a warm puppy"—is in Bartlett's *Familiar Quotations.*

He is rich and famous, and at the same time shy and anonymous.

One day he answered his telephone to discover Cary Grant on the other end, wanting a certain comic strip original. Schulz obliged but complains he never heard back from Cary Grant.

Another day, Mickey Rooney phoned. "You know that musical *Cats*?" Rooney asked. Yes, Schulz replied, he did.

"Wouldn't it be great to do one called *Dogs*?" Rooney immediately started singing a ditty he thought might be perfect for such a play. He figured Schulz could write the script; Schulz demurred, politely informing Rooney he isn't a playwright. Andy Hardy meets Charlie Brown.

These kinds of things still seem wonderful, almost mystical, to Charles Schulz, who considers himself a behind-the-scenes prompter for Charlie Brown and Snoopy and Lucy and the rest of the *Peanuts* gang, who do the work under the lights.

He still seems genuinely surprised at the perks of his job, the dividends of fame. He cannot completely uproot his image of himself as the awkward kid with a bad complexion who submitted cartoons to the high school annual and waited impatiently to see them published. When the annual was distributed, his drawings were not in it; somewhere along the line they had been rejected.

Rejection is his specialty, losing his area of expertise. He has spent a lifetime perfecting failure.

The man is as gentle as his humor. You never met such a gentle man. While the children in his strip can be bellicose, especially Lucy, they rarely actually strike one another. They don't step on insects and spiders. It is not accidental but—like almost everything about *Peanuts*—a vivid reflection of their creator. A native of the Land of Lakes, exposed all his life to fishing, Schulz can no longer enjoy the sport: "Those fish are down there having a good time."

Barely a high school graduate, he educated himself by reading the classics. A voracious reader, he does not like "funny writing." He prefers serious books by women.

"And I like crime novels if the hero beats up people and shoots them." He surprises you every now and then, this gentle man.

Since the invention of remote control, he has never been able to settle on one television channel. Instead, he flips from station to station. Wishy-washy watching.

He has played golf for fifty years but never made a hole in one. That bugs him. He takes out his own garbage at the studio and takes out his frustrations on the ice-hockey rink.

He is handsome but does not believe it. He took a class in ballroom dancing to please his wife and found he liked to fox-trot.

Forbes magazine rated him one of the nation's ten richest entertainers, estimating his income at $62 million for 1987 and 1988. In 1988 he trailed Michael Jackson, Bill Cosby, Steven Spielberg, Sylvester Stalone, and Eddie Murphy. The magazine's estimate of his income is too high, Schulz insists.

"Nobody makes that much," he says. "*Forbes* never even calls and asks us about it. My people tell me I make about a million a month now, but I don't really know."

For forty years, come 1990, Charles Schulz has given the world daily installments of history's most successful comic strip. It runs in over 2000 newspapers, appears in sixty-eight countries, and has been translated into twenty-six languages. Including Latin. An Italian priest did that. Snoopy became Snupius. Charlie Brown Carolius Niger.

There also have been a thousand books, thirty television specials, and four feature films. Paperback collections of the strip have sold more than 300 million copies. The play *You're a Good Man, Charlie Brown* remains one of the most widely produced musicals in America.

Never have so many little failures added up to such a big success. For faithfully cataloging life's essential hopelessness, Charles Schulz drives Mercedes cars and gets his name in the dictionary. Surely he must laugh all the way to the bank. He really doesn't. To him, life more closely resembles *Peanuts* than his own existence. To explain why is to get into that murky realm of the human psyche where reality isn't necessarily dependent upon physical basis.

It's pure O. Henry. The more miserable he feels, the more heart he pours into his work. The more heart he pours into his work, the more readers love it. The more readers love it, the more successful he becomes.

Perhaps it isn't as unlikely as it seems. In one of history's most hedonistic societies, Schulz's minstrels of misery have attracted millions of followers. He created more than a comic strip when he first dipped his pen and circumscribed the head of Charlie Brown. Schulz tapped into the meaning of life.

1 _____

In the Beginning

*I*t is October 2, 1950. Sixteen inches of snow fell last night in Butte, Montana, where thermometers registered 10 degrees, the lowest in a nation still on the cusp of summer.

Princess Anne is two weeks old.

George Bernard Shaw is a wizened ninety; hard at work on a comedy titled *Why She Would Not*; within a month he will be dead.

William Faulkner is sequestered in Mississippi at shaded Rowan Oak, about to become the Nobel laureate in literature.

There are 2200 drive-in movie theaters in America, twice as many as there were a year ago. Teenagers are flocking to them to not watch Gregory Peck in *The Gunfighter*.

On television tonight, suave Perry Como will host the Fontaine Sisters, and folksy Arthur Godfrey will welcome a tenor, a saxophonist, and a barbershop quartet to *Talent Scouts*.

Last evening the gutsy Philadelphia Phillies clinched the National League pennant—their first since 1915—with a Hollywood

13

home run in the tenth inning by southpaw Dick Sisler that doomed Brooklyn. Ecstatic Philadelphians demonstrate their brotherly love for the Phillies by ripping the clothes and tearing at the hair of the heroes upon their return from Ebbets Field.

The victorious Phillies are featured in large advertisements endorsing Camel cigarettes. Says Willie (Puddin' Head) Jones: "I handle chances in every game, but I don't take chances with my throat. Camels for me—they're mild."

In the World Series, the Phillies will be trounced in four straight by the Yankees.

The newspaper headlines today are ominous and inky: SOUTH KOREAN TROOPS PLUNGE IN FORCE ACROSS 38TH PARALLEL; RED KOREA GIVES NO HINT OF YIELDING.

In Indochina, the French are appealing to the United States for supplies and equipment after taking a beating from the rebels led by Ho Chi Minh.

Chicago's 500-pound gorilla, Bushman, escapes from his cage in the monkey house of Lincoln Park Zoo and remains free for three hours; 500 spectators watch as Bushman ignores bait of muskmelon, avocado, and grapes. Finally a small garter snake and an eighteen-inch-long alligator are used to scare Bushman back into his cage.

J. C. Penney is selling men's gabardine and sharkskin suits for $35. Women's rayon blouses cost a dollar. Boys' wool sports coats are $5.99.

And, in the comics, Mark Trail is dealing sternly with a boatload of evil poachers.

Tough private detective The Saint spurns the seductive efforts of a bottle blonde: "The answer, sweetheart, is NO! I'm sorry, but I think you're something that only the police can deal with."

Slats, of *Abbie an' Slats,* teaches the kids of Crabtree Corners how to kick a football: "Don't try to boot it with the toe, kids. Catch it on the instep."

Joe Palooka is helping a friend who has been forced into a false confession.

In *Steve Canyon,* Cheetah finds herself in an airplane about to run out of gas: "What eef no peoples shoot us down, an' we seenk into sea as petrol geeves out?"

And . . . Shermy and Patty sit curbside, marking the approach of a new kid on the comic block: "Well! Here comes ol' Charlie Brown! Good ol' Charlie Brown. . . . Yes, Sir! Good Ol' Charlie Brown. . . . How I hate him!"

October 2, 1950.

Earlier that year, in a spring fraught with young love and late frost, an earnest, twenty-seven-year-old Charles Schulz boarded the train at St. Paul, Minnesota, with a portfolio of cartoons under one arm. He was bound, with only a passing nod of prior encouragement, for the offices of United Feature Syndicate in New York City.

Forty years later, a plaque at St. Paul's Union Depot honors Schulz, putting him in the company of aviator Charles Lindbergh, author F. Scott Fitzgerald, Senator Hubert Humphrey, and the coach of the 1980 gold-medal U.S. Olympic Hockey Team, Herb Brooks. The five men of the Twin Cities' Walk of Fame.

Forty years later, the denizens of United Feature Syndicate nervously anticipate his every whim when Schulz favors them with a rare visit.

But on that June day in 1950 nobody took much notice of the gangling cartoonist who lived quietly with his father in a tiny apartment over a St. Paul drugstore and worked as an instructor for the art school that had trained him by mail.

He traveled alone.

Schulz's father Carl was a dedicated small businessman, an entirely self-made man who dropped out of school after the third grade and later paid his own way through barber school. For forty-five years he owned and ran The Family Barbershop, as clean as its name, at Snelling and Selby in St. Paul. The shop had three chairs and two other barbers, both of whom Carl somehow managed to keep on during the Great Depression. He overcame the dire times and his own lack of education with metronome work habits.

For he was straight, clean-shaven, and earnest. Daily he braved the obstacles all those of the grim era faced, beating the entrepreneurial odds with determination and countless thirty-five-cent haircuts. He worked six days a week and on his one day of "rest" cleaned the shop.

Carl's relaxation was fishing for sunfish or walleye pike. And his one passion was the funny papers. He loved comics and read them the way some men read box scores or racing forms—with intensity and devotion. He bought four Sunday newspapers every week, for the comics, picking up two local papers on Saturday evening hot off the press.

Carl Schulz's only child—at the age of two days—was nicknamed Sparky, after Barney Google's racehorse Spark Plug. It was an uncle, actually, who suggested "Sparky," but the nickname stuck, a gift to future reporters who inevitably would include that tidbit in endless profiles of a famous cartoonist. A first cousin was similarly dubbed Corky, in tribute to a new comic strip baby in *Gasoline Alley.* It was a family with no artists or writers but one that paid close attention to the comics and their story lines.

Sparky Schulz remembers peering through the windows of the St. Paul Pioneer Press Building, watching as the Sunday comic pages rolled off the huge rotary presses into bins, destined eventually for the living-room floors of the upper Midwest. Entertainment was simpler then, but perhaps more important. Prosperity had not been around any corner the desperate nation turned; escape was the only thing of value the working class could still afford. The comics provided. Lord Plushbottom and Moon Mullins, Skippy, Annie and Daddy Warbucks, Wash Tubbs, Prince Valiant, and Buck Rogers. They were the players. And if entertainment choices were fewer—there were no magic kingdoms or pizza parlors with singing rats, no color televisions or video games—the following for what was available was all the more impassioned.

A barber's love for comics would be his son's legacy. As it turned out, Carl Schulz provided well.

It was quite a revelation for young Sparky when he realized, for the first time, he could draw. "We went to visit my aunt Clara, somewhere out in the country in Wisconsin. She had two sons, and one of them, Reuben, had done a drawing in pencil of a person sitting on a log. And I said, 'That's nice,' when they showed it to me.

But I remember thinking to myself, 'I could do that.' And all through school and even the army I never really met anyone who could draw any better than me."

Sparky's kindergarten teacher may have been the first outside the family to notice his drawing ability, a natural thing that seems to come from the fingers and not the mind and can only be cultivated, never taught or forced. When she passed around fat crayons and butcher paper for drawing, young Sparky took the high road of imagination. His picture of a man shoveling Minnesota snow included a palm tree, exotic flora suggested by letters from relatives in Needles, California.

The teacher took one look at the palm, its fronds free of accumulated ice, its incongruity glaring, and—to her everlasting credit—told him "Someday, Charles, you're going to be an artist." How easily she might have casually observed "Palm trees don't grow where it snows, Sparky." Schulz probably would have gone on to create *Peanuts* anyway, but the teacher's constructive remarks were powerful enough to be remembered today. Young lives pivot on fine points, and Sparky's was no exception.

He was an extremely sensitive child who always worried about improbable things, like what in the world an uncle meant when one day he called Sparky a piker. For days, the child thought about it: "I knew a pike was a fish. And I kept thinking, 'A fish? Is that what he meant? What did he mean?' "

At Richard Gordon Elementary School, Sparky shone academically, even skipping two half-grades. He decorated his notebooks with Mickey Mouse and Popeye, happily oblivious of copyright laws and lawyers. His classmates envied the rodents, sailors, and Schulz's copying skill and prevailed on him to similarly deface their loose-leaf binders. He did.

His school career soured at puberty. He became a shy, skinny kid with pimples and big ears, nearly six feet tall and weighing only 136 pounds. The pretty girls at St. Paul's Central High School never noticed him. He was younger than the other students. After having been advanced the two semesters during his grammar school career because of high marks, his scholarship faltered. In the annual, where they list the extracurricular activities of each student, Sparky had only the annual staff to his credit. He was on the golf team, too, but they forgot to mention that.

He avoided membership in the school art club, the Thumbtack Club, because he was too shy, but when he was a senior, at the invitation of his art teacher, Minette Paro, Sparky did submit a series of cartoons for *The Cehisean* (Central High School Senior Annual).

"I waited and waited for the annual to come out. When it did, my drawings were not in it." He never asked why.

Many years later, however, when Charles Schulz was a household name, Minette Paro would send the cartoonist a copy of an assignment he had completed in her high school illustration class and she had saved.

The assignment was to think up items during the class hour and draw them in triplicate. Twenty-five years later Mrs. Paro returned to her former student his page full of miscellaneous items. There were three barber shears, three caricatures of Hitler, three ink bottles, three golfbags, three light bulbs, three maps of Minnesota, and the like. The young artist even signed his name three times. Schulz was delighted to receive the relic and remembered with pride that his finished assignment included many more items than anyone else's. Within him is a vast emotional archive, capable of retaining with museum quality the obscurest triumphs and the mustiest defeats. This warehouse of woe is as important to his success as his ability to draw.

There were others at the school who openly admired Sparky's talent. "Maybe if I keep at it long enough I'll be as good as you," a girl named Helen wrote in his annual. Nothing has a shorter shelf life than a note in a high school annual, but one can imagine the delight the feminine scrawl gave the bashful boy. Art was his ally, his hope.

It was during his senior year, too, that his mother, Dena, noticed an advertisement in the local newspaper for Federal Schools, a correspondence plan for aspiring artists. The business is still in operation as Art Instruction Schools ("Draw Me"), housed in an imposing building on a downtown Minneapolis corner with the Palmer Writers School and the Bureau of Engraving.

"Do you like to draw?" the advertisement asked. The barber paid the $170 tuition, in installments, for his only son to learn lettering, perspective, and the other basics of cartooning. Think now of all the other young "artists" who enrolled that month, many of them probably never realizing a canvas greater than a cocktail napkin. Nobody keeps statistics on this kind of thing, but Charles Schulz almost certainly has done more with a Draw-Me art education than anyone else in history.

Sparky returned all his lessons by mail, not yet certain enough of his abilities to risk delivering the drawings in person, though the facilities of far-reaching Federal Schools happened to be only a few miles away.

"The truth is, I wasn't a very good student. There were twelve divisions. I remember instructor Frank Wing gave me a C-plus in Division Five."

Division Five was "Drawing of Children."

It was not a good time for the Schulz household. Sparky's mother Dena was gravely ill. The well-oiled routines of the family which were important to every Schulz were necessarily sacrificed to her care. It was a watershed period for the son, abruptly separating what had been from what would be. What had been was security, at least within the family. What would be was something else.

Schulz completed the art course, a little more slowly than what was considered average, and immediately began trying unsuccessfully to sell gag cartoons to magazines.

But it was not time to become a cartoonist yet. The same cold rain that fell on the rest of the world fell on Minnesota and Charles Schulz. In 1943 he was drafted and sent to war. Making it a particularly harsh time in Schulz's life was the fact his mother had finally died after her excruciating bout with cancer just as he was inducted into the army.

Sparky became an infantryman, staff sergeant, and the leader of a machine-gun squad. He was sent to the European theater, but there he saw little combat. Except for a few sketches of army life in a notebook made for him by a bookbinder friend and some doodling for the guys, his art career was suspended for his war years. By V-J

Day he was Stateside again, among the lucky ones, ready to pick up his peacetime life and pen where he had put them down.

Schulz returned determined to draw and sell, but he came close to accepting a job lettering tombstones. Something happened, and the man hiring failed to call back the next day with a solid offer, as he had promised. Again, it is an invitation to imagine: Charles Schulz, on the verge of a welcome retirement, kicked back in his suburban St. Paul den, granite dust on his shoes, chuckling at a comics page without *Peanuts*. It's conceivable, because the Schulz family possessed a strong propensity for settling easily into ruts.

Instead, Schulz made his breakthrough, inauspicious and unrecognized though it was. Roman Baltes, an editor at *Timeless Topix*, a comic magazine owned by the Roman Catholic Church, hired him to letter adventure cartoons already drawn. He lettered in English, French, and Spanish, sometimes without any idea what the balloons he filled were saying. The work was as menial as it could be and still be considered professional cartooning. But that's what it was. The journey of a thousand miles had begun.

Soon he was hired by his alma mater, now labeled Art Instruction Schools, to correct student lessons returned by mail. So his dance card was full, with nights spent lettering Catholic comics and days grading work at the correspondence school. It was a satisfactorily grueling pace for an ambitious young man, a blur of streetcar rides from one job to the next, a good, fundamental dose of daily drawing for Sparky. It was a routine he would never abandon.

Pictures from the time show an agonizingly neat young man, wide collars and dark ties, starched shirts, hair pomaded away from the high forehead, making for almost a perfect heart of a face. It was a face older than its years, a poker face with no real hint of the lively, even jocular mind behind it.

He lived with his father in the depressing upstairs apartment where his mother had died, periodically sharing half of its living space with two women whose husbands were in service. He took meals at nearby Webber's Restaurant and spent his free time at concerts and church activities. There was a girl, but Schulz played second fiddle to her steady boyfriend. He was lonely.

But all was not glum. It was a big churchgoing period in Schulz's life. Owing to events surrounding his mother's death, he had affiliated himself with a Church of God congregation and was quite active as a young adult. All his social life was connected with church or work or sports. He visited often in the home of his minister, sharing ideas about life and cartooning, religion, and the future.

Working at the art school was invigorating for Sparky; it was a place of sharp wits and shared ideas. And the daily drawing was paying off.

With a simple, charming sight gag he broke into the national magazine market and eventually sold fifteen cartoons to *The Saturday Evening Post* between 1948 and 1950. The first successful submission to *The Post* was a drawing of a young boy reading a book while sitting on the very edge of an easy chair, his feet propped on a pointless ottoman.

Not long after he sent the magazine his original drawing a note came through the mail from the cartoon editor, John Bailey: "Check Tuesday for spot drawing of boy on lounge." So used to rejection letters was Schulz that he believed the note meant the cartoon would be in the return mail Tuesday. Instead, they were sending a check for the drawing.

"The usual manner for submitting gag cartoons to magazines was to send maybe ten pencil or pen-and-ink 'roughs,' but I had shown this small drawing in its finished form to Louise Cassidy, who was one of the correspondence school instructors, and when she remarked that she thought it was 'just precious,' I sent it in all by itself. Later, when I began to submit batches of roughs on a regular weekly basis, John Bailey once clipped little notes to each rejected idea, telling me why it wasn't acceptable. This was extremely considerate of him and, of course, was one more reason why he was so well appreciated by cartoonists."

The magazine paid forty dollars for the one-column cartoon. Sparky was ecstatic.

"I wanted to be somebody. All of us want to be somebody, what we are, an individual. I remember so well the first night I was able to say it: 'I am a cartoonist.'

"A group of us had been to a concert, and we came back to somebody's house. There were a dozen or so people around. I was introduced to a stranger, and he asked what I did for a living, you know, just making conversation.

"There just happened to be an issue of *The Saturday Evening Post* on the table that had not one but two of my cartoons in it. That was a grand and glorious feeling."

As he knocked on doors and mailed samples of his work to all the syndicates, Schulz could see he was getting "closer all the time" to selling a strip. For one thing, his drawing was continuing to improve. He worked for a while on a one-panel proposal called *Judy Says*. It featured a Patty-type girl who had a male friend resembling Schroeder in *Peanuts*. The boy did all the talking for Judy in a pseudo-pantomime. Each punch line began with the boy saying "Judy says . . ."

Someone at King Features Syndicate noted *Judy Says*, and thought Schulz's work had potential. "We like what you sent. Do you have another kid feature?"

Carl, of course, encouraged his son's obsession to sell a comic strip. "Dad was so enthusiastic, so well-intentioned. I remember he had a man in the barbershop one day. 'He's interested in what you're trying to do,' Dad told me. 'He wants you to come see him.' So I got my drawings together and went to the bachelor-style rooming house where he was trying to be a writer. We sat there all evening, and he talked nonstop about his writing. It was a total waste.

"I was forever being falsely recommended during that time, or so it seemed."

Schulz persisted, routinely boarding the morning Zephyr to Chicago to peddle his comics. Those rides were social exercises as well as professional ones, for as the train hit the track joints and made the exciting sounds of purpose and good prospects, he occasionally screwed up his courage to speak to another passenger.

"One day on the train I sat down next to a pretty girl who was reading *Marjorie Morningstar*. I asked her if she liked the book. She said she did. I couldn't think of anything else to say, so I got up and left."

During this period he won another important career victory, the sale of a weekly comic feature called *Li'l Folks* to the *St. Paul Pioneer Press.* Not only did it represent his first newspaper sale, it also honed Schulz's talent for pouring important, sophisticated thoughts through small vessels. Little folks—big heads, impressive vocabularies—were the sole inhabitants of the one-panel drawings, quite precocious guys and girls adding a new dimension to sandbox society.

Sparky kept the postman stepping, sending work to this syndicate and that. An editor named Jim Freeman at United Feature Syndicate opened a package from Sparky and was mildly interested, so he held on to the work. He held on so long that Schulz called to see if he should have the package traced. No, no, the syndicate had the work, liked it, and wanted Schulz to come to New York, Freeman assured. In his thirty years with United Feature Syndicate, Freeman received and judged thousands of submissions, both comics and columns, editing such notables as *Nancy, Gordo, Emmy Lou, Ferd'nand*, and columnists Marquis Childs, Norton Mockridge, Amy Vanderbilt, and Grantland Rice. He was no stranger to the sensibilities of creative minds.

"As I recall, I told him we liked the panel—its charm, its characters, its style of humor—but since the market was flooded with panels I asked him to convert it into strip form and try to retain the same attractiveness."

Schulz complied.

"I had already been drawing some strips that were made up of very, very brief incidents, which made them much different from the average, plodding 'What shall we do today?' ideas in the older kid strips. I remember telling a friend that I knew I was really on to something good."

One difference between Schulz and hundreds of other aspiring cartoonists, notes Harry Gilburt, United Feature Syndicate's sales manager at the time, was his willingness to innovate and compromise. Syndicate executives consider such an attitude a sign of maturity and professionalism. "He went along," says Gilburt. "He was smart enough to."

Schulz took the train from St. Paul to New York, armed with

his art, youthful optimism, and a sturdy set of midwestern values. Early on a June morning he left the Roosevelt Hotel and walked through a gray Manhattan drizzle toward the future.

"I loved New York immediately. This was my first trip, and something about being there with the intent to sell a comic strip made it all the more wonderful."

Schulz remembers few other details about the morning he sold *Peanuts.* Just that "a switchboard operator" was the only person at her post when he walked through the intimidating doors of the Big Time. She offered to keep his package of cartoons while he went out for breakfast to kill time. It was raining harder now, and he agreed.

It was Helyn Rippert, the newest hireling of United Feature Syndicate at the time, who first laid eyes on Charles Schulz. She was indeed at the switchboard of the syndicate's office, then located in the old New York Daily News Building on 42nd Street. She looked up from a pile of morning mail to see a tall stranger walking toward her down the narrow hallway.

"In those days, we all did a little bit of everything," she recalls. "Filing. Typing. Manning the switchboard. The editors used to work all hours; it was more of a deadline business then and as a result a lot more exciting. The editors would all come in around ten in the morning and stay until seven at night or so, sometimes coming back for more work after their dinners.

"I had worked for United Press [later United Press International] a year and came to their affiliate United Feature Syndicate as a 'temporary.' Since I was the last hired, I was the one assigned to come in early and sort the mail and field the calls until the office opened.

"It was very early. Probably about nine o'clock. I'll never forget. In walked a tall, slim guy from the elevator. He asked to see an editor. 'You must be from out of town,' I said to him. 'The editors don't come in until ten o'clock or later.' "

"St. Paul," the young visitor replied.

When Sparky returned to the syndicate office that gray morning in 1950, the package left with Mrs. Rippert had been opened and its contents passed around. Everyone who saw it agreed: the strip format was better than the one-panel gags mailed earlier.

Syndicate president Larry Rutman that day outlined the deal—a standard five-year contract offering a fifty-fifty split of profits between syndicate and cartoonist. The syndicate would own the copyright on the new feature, and Schulz would be under contract to provide it. Schulz could take it or leave it. He took it. No ballyhoo or fuss. No way of knowing United Feature Syndicate had just snagged the most popular comic strip ever.

"I remember being happy, but not much else about it," says Schulz. There was a jubilant train ride home—"I ate a steak"—and the pleasure of telling his gratifyingly enthusiastic co-workers at the art school that he had sold his work. "I remember thinking 'Now I'm a cartoonist, not just an instructor at a correspondence school.' "

Euphoria was punctured by the first major syndicate decision. When Schulz got word a short time later that the syndicate had taken it upon itself to name the new feature *Peanuts,* he cringed. The name had no appeal whatsoever to its creator. To him, peanuts meant "insignificant," "unimportant." An appropriate strip, perhaps, to be drawn by a piker.

"Four or five of us suggested names, unbeknownst to one another," says Freeman. "I did. So did Larry Rutman; Harry Gilburt; Jim Hennessy, the business manager, and Bill Anderson, the production manager."

The syndicate was very happy with the suggested name *Peanuts,* which came from Bill Anderson. Nobody seems to remember what the other suggestions were, so content was the syndicate brass with the title it had chosen. To this day, they all defend it. *Li'l Folks,* which Schulz wanted to keep, was too close to a previously copyrighted feature called *Little Folks* by Tack Knight. The name also bore a bothersome resemblance to another United Feature Syndicate property, its most popular one at the time, *Li'l Abner.*

"At a brief staff meeting we went over all the suggestions, and it was decided that *Peanuts* was the most suitable," says Freeman. "It was most descriptive of the all-kids strip. If a small person wasn't called Shorty or Midge or whatever, he was usually tagged with a nickname like Peanut. And, at the time, there was a movement on among publishers to shrink the size of comic strips, and our brand-new *Peanuts* started out shallower than the comics then being marketed. Again, because of its size, *Peanuts* was an apt title. With four frames of equal size and overall four columns wide, the strip could be cut in the middle and carried like a two-column panel."

The syndicate openly used the strip's size and format to sell the new property. The first promotional brochure sent to newspaper editors described the strip as "The Greatest Little Sensation Since Tom Thumb!" Shermy and Charlie Brown, displayed with equal prominence, were on the brochure's cover, standing beneath a sign that says WATCH OUT FOR CHILDREN. Inside, the brochure illustrated the way *Peanuts* could be cut apart and rearranged in a variety of configurations. It also noted that editors could use it "for front, editorial, classified or regular comic pages."

Though the "clever, subtle humor" and "universally appealing characters" were mentioned in passing in the small, rather unimpressive black-and-yellow brochure, the emphasis was definitely on the strip's size and adaptability: "Solves tough make-up problems. Three or 4-column horizontally. One column vertically. Two-column panels."

"Along with my other chores, I also conceived and wrote that first promotional brochure with a staff artist," says editor Freeman. The emphasis on *Peanuts'* size and adaptability, he recalls, was the result of differing opinions among the United Feature Syndicate brass about the inherent merit of Schulz's submission. "Our hands were tied on this brochure, which certainly reflected the enthusiasm, or lack thereof, of some within the UFS management.

"I never doubted the quality of his output, and at this late date I'm not about to say who among our small staff was pessimistic about our new baby."

At first, it looked as if the nay-sayers were right. The new strip did not exactly soar. Seven newspapers subscribed initially and provided the stage for the October debut: *The Washington Post, The Chicago Tribune, The Minneapolis Star-Tribune, The Allentown Call-Chronicle, The Bethlehem Globe-Times, The Denver Post,* and *The Seattle Times.* The Seattle newspaper canceled within three months, Denver in less than a year. There was little additional growth the first year.

"After sales in the first year to only about eighteen or twenty newspapers, I was ready to crawl under the rug," says Freeman. "But I always maintained that any comic worthy of a sales effort should be given at least one year to prove its worth."

"I was catching hell about it from the business office," says sales manager Gilburt. "It just didn't seem to catch on. I felt there were too many characters, and people had trouble remembering who was who." The ensemble cast, small as it was compared to *Peanuts* later, was something very different from anything the editors were accustomed to, says Gilburt.

Gilburt devised a promotional plan, with subscribing newspapers cooperating. The newspaper ran small ads, at no cost to the syndicate, introducing the members of the *Peanuts* cast individually.

"The same ads were offered to new subscribers," says Gilburt. "The promotion expenses were great, but I thought the strip deserving. It had a spark, something almost indefinable. We felt we had to have a hundred subscribers to break even on the expenses. About the second year, it finally started growing. That's when we added the Sunday feature."

Even fellow cartoonist Mort Walker, whose own *Beetle Bailey* began the same year as *Peanuts* and after some adjustment soon won a respectable if not dazzling number of early subscribers, worried about his peer Schulz, whom he had never met.

"I felt sorry for him at first," says Walker. "He ran in the [New York] *World Telegram,* and I saw the strip there. I remember him coming in last in a *World Telegram* readers' poll."

Walker even began a correspondence with Schulz, inviting him to New York "to meet some of the other pros." He fought for Schulz's admission to the National Cartoonists Society, a cliquish organization that then required its initiates to "know someone."

"This guy is a professional," Walker recalls arguing. "His strip is in the newspapers, for heaven's sake." Nobody would have to champion Schulz for long. He joined the NCS, and it wouldn't be many more years before he would never again have to introduce himself to another cartoonist.

Though weak in sales and uncertain of prospect, *Peanuts* survived its first year. By the end of that first year, in fact, there were twenty-seven dailies, and the brand-new Sunday feature had fifteen subscribers. The second year, 1951, was even better; the strip had struggled to its knees. Then, every year after that, growth was fast and constant.

"Fortunately for all of us, *Peanuts* suddenly took off—the rapid development of Schulz's talent in art and comic sense began to pay off and resulted in what the comic strip is today," says Jim Freeman. "Our salesmen eventually didn't have to sell the strip. They merely took orders."

John Selby, editor-in-chief at Rinehart and Company, also saw the new strip in the *World Telegram*. On January 3, 1952, Selby sent a memorandum to his editorial board: "I forgot to say in editorial meeting this morning that I wonder whether we might do a book out of the one comic strip I can read consistently; to wit, *Peanuts* in the *World Telegram*. I can force myself through the whole dreary page and come out stony-faced, but I can always get a chuckle out of *Peanuts*. Is this due to depravity on my part, or is *Peanuts* really as amusing as I think?" To the memo Selby attached samples of the strip, just in case his co-workers were unfamiliar with it. Some were.

Selby first wrote Schulz, suggesting the book, as he put it, "purely on the basis of personal enthusiasm." And at Rinehart he pursued the idea of a book, based less on any readership figures than an editorial intuition, passing the word along to his staff that "Schulz is an extremely decent chap and cooperative in the extreme." To Schulz he wrote: "I first made *Peanuts*' acquaintance late last fall in the *World Telegram,* largely because I like to read *Jacoby on Bridge*, and one day my eye caught your little round-headed people, and I was lost. They are perfectly delightful, and although at this point one has little to go on except a hunch, I have a feeling the book will do well."

The hunch paid off; with the 1952 publication of *Peanuts* the book, there began a healthy comic strip reprint business that virtually pioneered the genre. With the exception of 1953, at least one reprint book has been published every year since.

Meanwhile, the strip was in its creatively formative, fragile months. There were a few editorial directives. Freeman suggested to Schulz that he never call Charlie Brown by less than his whole name —never Charlie or Chuck; however, Schulz already had every intention of doing just that. His instincts were good. Schulz was ready. After being a student of the comics through childhood, the timid young creature of habit had mounted a surprisingly relentless and effective campaign to produce and sell a comic strip. He arrived on the scene with a professional's demeanor and the aptitude of a born cartoonist. It didn't take much adjustment for Schulz to mesh with the grind of syndicate production.

Of course, editors are expected to earn their pay, so there were small things. Freeman recalls occasionally reminding Schulz to draw a horizon line in the background, which the editors felt was needed to provide his characters perspective.

"He misspelled 'weird' once or twice early on, but I can't think of any other grammar or spelling infraction." It was an ironic lapse, considering that "weird" would become a watchword of *Peanuts,* particularly Marcie's constant assessment of her friend Peppermint Patty: "You're weird, sir."

Schulz remembers that Freeman didn't like Snoopy and encouraged him to concentrate on the kids and downplay the beagle. Freeman admits preferring the human members of Schulz's cast— "their charm and captivating conversation" —to Snoopy, whom he felt at first "was a somewhat little nothing." The editor came from a family of ten children, "and for the most part we felt that animals were OK but that they belonged in zoos."

Back in St. Paul, Schulz singlemindedly concentrated on drawing a funny strip, though for a while he kept his job at Art Instruction Schools, too. The important thing was, he had his syndication, the goal of almost every cartoonist with a pen and bottle of ink.

The first installments of the strip with the detestable name were drawn above a corner drugstore in the dreary little apartment.

"I am always asked if I suspected that *Peanuts* would last when I first made the sale," says Schulz. "Sure, I thought it would last. I never intended to draw something that wouldn't last. In fact, when I started out, I thought 'I'll be drawing this the rest of my life.' "

2

Odyssey to Needles

*I*n the winter of 1930 there swept through the small rail-road town of Needles, California, a wonderful rumor: snow in the desert. The citizens of perennially sweltering Needles raced to their cars, drove to the desert, and threw snowballs at one another in a surreal orgy of neighborliness and frivolity. Then, as suddenly as they had come, the good people of Needles heaped piles of snow on top of their automobiles and drove back to town, where the alien snow promptly melted.

Thus went the only interruption of what Charles Schulz remembers as an eerie and eternal summer—the year and a half his family spent in the arid, unlikely world of Needles.

He was six years old when Dena and Carl Schulz loaded all their belongings, themselves, Sparky, and Sparky's Boston bull terrier, Snooky, into a 1928 Ford and joined a family caravan headed west from St. Paul, Minnesota, toward an enclave of relatives living in southeastern California.

The journey was a slow, circuitous one of gravel roads and

crude campsites, a ragtag parade of two cars with tents strapped to their sides, cars that never exceeded forty miles per hour and made frequent and necessary stops. There were makeshift meals cooked over portable camp burners. The trip took forever. Or about two weeks.

Dena Schulz's sister Ella and her husband Bert, known to the family as Frenchy, and their daughter Shirley occupied the second car.

Frenchy was a charmer, a dark-haired jack-of-all-trades who never really settled on a single profession but who—despite his unsettled ways, or perhaps because of them—made an excellent fishing companion and an asset to any such adventure.

Along the way the steady, workaholic Carl Schulz, teamed with the flamboyant Frenchy, sold fountain pens to pay for the gasoline. The pens were not ordinary pens, but pens with novel glass points, which were supposed to be unbreakable.

Schulz remembers: "When we would stop at filling stations or grocery stores, they would try to sell these pens, hoping to get a dollar or two, able to charge that much because the pens were unbreakable. They would prove it by taking the pen and knocking it hard on the countertop. Pen points in those days were normally so fragile.

"Actually they were terrible pens. Glass is so unreliable. Years later, I took some of them to school and sold them for a dollar to some of the kids. I even sold one to a teacher for a dollar."

The curious migration to Needles curls like a live question mark in Schulz's mind today. He has tried repeatedly to figure what the precise plan might have been in the minds of his parents, people presumably settled and with roots in the Twin Cities, certainly not adventurers by nature; surely there was some rosy economic enticement that lured the stable, rather predictable Carl Schulz to sell his barbershop and head west. The son wonders now if it was a desperate move or a hopeful one. He has a vague recollection of Sacramento being mentioned as the ultimate destination, but something must have gone sour, for after the brief stay in Needles the family retraced its steps.

He does not remember the return trip.

"The whole thing is just lost in a fog now to me. I deeply regret that all of those who went are dead now, except Shirley, and I doubt she remembers any more than I. How they were able to convince not one but two families that they should move to Needles is beyond me."

Recollections of the incongruous life there return as snippets today.

He remembers the figure $100 in connection with the sale of the barbershop; rather, the equipment therein. The building itself was leased. A year and a half later, when the family returned to Minnesota, Carl Schulz would reopen the shop and rent a nearby house at 473 Macalister, never again to leave the old neighborhood.

It was his mother's clan that prompted the move. There were nine siblings in all, the children of a Norwegian matriarch named Sophia Halverson, who lived with Schulz's family off and on most of his childhood and whose personal tragedy it was to outlive six of her nine children.

"She was always a very old lady to me. I remember she got an old-age pension of eighteen dollars a month, and occasionally the family had to borrow money from her."

It was grandmother Sophia whom Sparky Schulz drafted as a hockey goalie while he would practice his slap shots in the basement of the house on MacAlister. There was a space of about six feet between the basement stairs and the supporting post, just about right for a makeshift hockey goal. Sophia would take a broom and obligingly stand before the dusty abyss while Sparky blasted tennis balls at her with a hockey stick.

"She made a lot of great saves," Schulz says. The wizened and wrinkled lady loved sports but had trouble understanding them. She once quizzed Sparky about golf: Which score is better, a high one or a low one?

She has come down to posterity as the Van Pelts' offstage grandmother/goalie, noted for her particularly vicious style of play.

It was two of Sophia's sons, Dena Schulz's brothers Silas and Monroe, along with Monroe's young nephew Howard, who moved first to Needles. Howard, a teenager, was thought to have tuberculosis, and the dry climate was recommended for the condition.

Somehow, in the ensuing months Monroe, also a barber, convinced his brother-in-law Carl the move West was desirable.

From a distance it looked good, recalls Schulz.

"I can still remember the day I got my first sight of the mountains. We were at a picnic ground of some kind, and I stood on the picnic table. I was so thrilled; they looked like clouds in the distance."

Somewhere beyond those clouds was Needles, where Silas and Monroe were sitting at a round kitchen table in their undershirts, the ribbed and sleeveless kind, drinking beer and waiting for two sisters and their families, trying to stay cool in the interminable blast furnace that was the eastern Mojave Desert town.

The Schulz residence was to be half a duplex shared with Silas and his pretty wife Lee. The two couples used a garden hose to wash down the filthy walls and ceilings, spraying away spider webs and dirt that had blown in from the desert and collected there undisturbed for years.

Carl immediately went to work in the barbershop with his brother-in-law Monroe on Front Street in downtown Needles, a place distinguished by a nice city park, an active rail yard, and the Harvey House, a 1930s precursor of a Holiday Inn. You could get the news in the *Needles Nugget,* "Voice of the Colorado River Empire," for two dollars a year. White's Lunch was famous for its root beer. There were fresh vegetables and fruits to be had at D. Yoshimoto, general merchandise, and billiards and snooker were offered at The Club. The new Needles Theatre at the corner of Broadway and F Street boasted "the best in talking pictures."

If you needed the police, you called City Hall at MAIN 219 or you could, as the telephone book suggested, "ask the operator to locate an officer for you." Edgar Stout was the mayor, and Warren S. Brown doubled as chief of police and street superintendent. Alfred Williams, the official watch inspector for the Santa Fe Railroad, had the jewelry store. E. M. Nichols's dry goods promoted its "all silk underwear for women." Every day six trains westbound for Los Angeles passed through Needles; six eastbound trains did the same.

Sparky was enrolled in second grade in a shabby wooden

school painted green. The teacher passed out crayons and paper the first day, giving him an immediate chance to strut his stuff. He drew a car going round and round a mountain. He had been impressed by the fact a car cannot climb straight over a mountain to cross it, and he was faithful to fact in his rendering.

"I remember some of the other school projects from that year. One was to draw an igloo and write our spelling words in the blocks of ice making up the igloo."

Evidently Sparky aced igloos, for at the end of the year he and Marie Holland—"a pretty little dark-haired girl"—were the second graders who went to the high school and collected diplomas for being the outstanding students in their class. Dena and her mother, Sophia, took Sparky to the high school that day and sat with him in the back of a cavernous auditorium, waiting for the moment of recognition.

"I remember sitting there, waiting to be called forward. I remember so well several of the high school students coming by and looking down at us. To me, they were grown-ups."

Schulz also recalls one late afternoon, as dusk was overtaking the desert sky, running and playing with Marie outside his home. "It was probably the only time I ever said anything to her."

It was in Needles, too, that he experienced his first Christmas pageant. "We were all lined up, holding letters that spelled out 'Christmas.' Each child would step forward in turn, and say what the letter they held stood for. I had the letter A. I began to notice as it moved on down the line that the other children weren't singing out loud enough, and the teacher was coaching them to sing louder. So I decided when my turn came, I'd sing out."

His turn came. " 'A' STANDS FOR ALL OF US, ALL OF US!" Sparky bleated, and the startled members of the audience, rocked out of their lull, began to chuckle. "It really bothered me. When I got home, I asked my mother why everyone had laughed at me. She said, 'Well, you did sing yours kind of loud and fast.' "

Academic recognition notwithstanding, Schulz remembers Needles as a lonely and miserable place to turn seven.

He impatiently awaited one of those large old tricycles ordered from Montgomery Ward that arrived one evening on the Sante Fe railroad. His parents took him down to the station to get it.

It was to his cousin Howard, one of those high schoolers who seemed grown, that Sparky turned for companionship during the Needles sojourn. He admired the boy and tried to imitate his every move and manner.

"When Howard walked he kept his hands inside the pockets of his sweater—it was a big checkered sweater—and naturally I walked around with my hands in my pockets just like that. He was what we might call today 'cool.' "

Howard was a Western Union delivery boy, a job that provided another dramatic moment in the weird Needles episode.

"None of us had telephones then, but somehow Monte got the word one evening. It seemed Howard, who was off working, had been run over by a train."

Actually, Howard was fine. The Model T Ford he was driving had been, indeed, totally demolished in a switching yard by a run-away boxcar. The boy managed to escape somehow, crawling from beneath the wrecked automobile without a scratch. Schulz to this day keeps a photograph of the mangled car.

Howard proved a cousin of many lives. The tuberculosis he had been diagnosed as having, the impetus for the move of Sophia Halverson's entire family to the desert, somehow mysteriously vanished. Sparky never heard it mentioned again. Howard lived to be a middle-aged man, finally dying of a heart condition.

"I saw him years later; he came to visit me in St. Paul. We didn't have much to talk about. We just stood around and stared at one another."

The brothers Halverson got along well, Schulz says, "as long as they didn't drink." One dark night, in the middle of a desert road, there was a wrestling match between two of them. Monte had quite a temper, and though the night fight is as hazy as the rest of the time in Needles, Schulz suspects Monte was one of those in the swirl of dust.

The time in Needles survives through Snoopy's brother Spike, who lives there among the raucous coyotes and the maddeningly taciturn saguaro cacti—a seedy but appealing little fellow lonely for companionship and cheerful about his limited possibilities of ever finding it.

Needles and the Spike episodes provide a welcome change of pace in the strip, Schulz believes. One of the most purely lovable characters in *Peanuts,* Spike is kept on a short leash, a complement to Snoopy, rarely vying for attention in the same strip. The desert has been a latent, dreamlike inspiration to Schulz, as his entire life has been a distillation of fact to fantasy. Though not deliberate, the wacky, out-of-step life of Spike the beagle seems to reflect Charles Schulz's impression of the blip in his own life that Needles represents.

The modern town of Needles loves the notoriety of being a part of the comic strip and offered Schulz the key to the city along with an invitation to be marshal of an annual parade. He did not go.

The principals from the Needles period seemed predestined for tragedy. Dena Schulz died prematurely of cancer. Monroe was hit by a car. Silas was killed when his own car went over a cliff. Sophia buried them all.

3

The Good Grief

*L*ouie Armstrong singing "What a Wonderful World" is a tonic. Trees of green. Red roses, too. Satchmo's raspy voice covers you like a quilt—just the right weight, a patchwork of color and texture and raw comfort. And, ah, the song's lovely message. Who can argue with watching babies grow?

The lights are dimmed in the upstairs dance studio of what is billed as the world's most beautiful ice arena, the Redwood Empire Ice Arena of Santa Rosa, California. It probably is the most beautiful, too, with wisteria outside and original oil paintings within. Photographic murals of Switzerland surround the rink and set a cool, graceful tone for the skaters' waltz.

In a room above the rink, the Louie Armstrong number signals the cool-down period after a vigorous forty-five-minute aerobics class. Lisa Navarro, aerobics instructor and ice skater, directs five participants to lie on their backs, knees up, palms up, letting the great Satchmo and near-darkness soothe.

The class, three days a week at 8:00 A.M., has been much the same for seven years, the tunes and the exercises altered to keep it interesting and current, the people drifting in and out as schedules allow.

After the workout the participants rise from their Snoopy exercise mats feeling firmer, healthier, happier, fit in their Spandex. Except for one. He is depressed.

Charles Schulz is a tall, athletic-looking man with a high forehead and a thick, handsome shock of silver hair. He looks scholarly even in exercise duds, the Atticus Finch of fitness, slightly out of context bending and reaching, bending and reaching.

His smile looks out of place, too. Sad, somehow. The class was his idea, a bid after quadruple bypass surgery for health and fitness in the bright California tradition.

Yet the class depresses him. "I keep wondering 'Why am I doing this?' " He sighs, a patented sigh pregnant with basic bewilderment about the meaning of everything.

Most things are sad to him, sooner or later. Everything becomes a source of depression. Even music. "I no longer listen to music."

It is a flat, sad admission. The man who made Beethoven's birthday a comic strip holiday denies himself his beloved classical music, unable as he is to bear the weight, the bombardment of such sheer beauty.

He has hockey muscles and organdy sensibilities. His loneliness is not the kind most of us feel when a loved one goes (or passes) away. It is baseless and unrelenting and must be dealt with as a basic bodily function—daily, unremarkably, constantly. And the sad, conspicuous irony is that without this wellspring of grief, there most certainly would not be the humor, the piercingly clear look at human foibles and insecurities, the Charlie Brownness of life that have made the cartoonist rich, famous, and funny.

It is the grief that propels the pen.

Schulz talks about his depression. Not incessantly, but openly, only if you ask. He also talks about the depressing things most of us miss or try to forget, as if he subconsciously catalogues grim trivia.

"Do you know that Leo Tolstoy's wife copied and recopied his manuscripts for *War and Peace* seven and a half times by hand?" Pause. "Later on he divorced her." That piece of poignant trivia eventually found its way into a comic strip gag.

He avoids things: long-distance travel, some public places, strange places. Doctors call it agoraphobia or, simply put, high anxiety.

Joann G. Redding, who has worked with agoraphobia patients at Prairie Village, Kansas, says it is "a marked fear of being alone or in public places from which escape might be difficult or help might not be available in the event of sudden incapacitation—crowded places, tunnels, bridges, on public transportation."

Victims sometimes suffer panic attacks, or worry that they will panic in certain situations or in certain places. The sight of a hotel lobby, for example, puts Schulz in a sweat.

"Just the mention of a hotel makes me turn cold. When I'm in a hotel room alone, I worry about getting so depressed I might jump out of a window."

The literal Greek translation of *agoraphobia* is "fear of the marketplace."

"A better name for it would be phobia-phobia," says Shirley Swede of the Panic Attack Sufferers Support Group in Williamsville, New York. "A person gets a panic attack or finds himself in a state of panic in a certain store, for example. That incident, that moment of stress, makes such an impression in his mind, it occurs with such force, that everything in that environment from then on triggers panic. The very worrying about returning there could cause a drop in the blood sugar level and a physical reaction. The person thinks to himself 'What if I get it again, that horrible panic?' The sufferer keeps avoiding more and more things and places until, in extreme cases, he's confined to the house, or sometimes not just the house but certain rooms in the house. And then sometimes not just a certain room, but, say, the couch."

Common panic-attack symptoms, according to Joann Redding, are difficulty breathing, palpitations, chest pain or discomfort, choking or smothering sensations, dizziness, vertigo, feelings of unreality, sweating, faintness, trembling, fear of dying or going insane, or doing something without control during the attack. Agoraphobia is rarely diagnosed by physicians because complaints about physical symptoms often cause the doctor to look for an organic explanation.

Schulz talks about his own fears with a degree of mild astonishment, as if analyzing the condition of a stepbrother for whom he feels responsibility. He has seen a psychiatrist, but the doctors seem better at diagnosing the problem than curing it. For a man who owns his own ice arena and his own jet and makes enough money to go anywhere and do anything, the situation seems a double shame.

Yet there would not be the money, the trappings of wealth, or —more important—Schulz's unique gift to the world without the sensitivity that so limits his personal life. Those who love him understand that.

"I feel that I'm a lot like him in some ways," says his best professional friend, Lynn Johnston, the Canadian creator of the family strip *For Better or Worse*.

"I have this need to be unhappy every so often. I will get myself into situations almost guaranteed to end in trouble, because I have to be miserable. I think he's like that to a degree. I'm still looking for parents. I think he is, too. It's hard to say 'I'm my own parent.' To take control of your own life. He has this incredible ability to fantasize, to think of his characters as real, to really experience music. He is affected terribly by any loss."

There is such a thing as good grief.

The comic knows that humor springs from sadness, not happiness. Losing is what has kept *Peanuts* living for forty years. Unrequited love is funny; returned love is not. A kid successfully launching a kite is nothing to laugh at; a kid with a kite in a tree is. Charlie Brown being duped season after season into kicking at a football sure to be pulled away is, for some reason, hilarious; a benevolent Lucy would not work. The formula is basic, constant. Losing is funny; winning is not.

"Charlie Brown, I just saw the most unbelievable football game ever played," Linus says one Sunday.

"What a comeback! The home team was behind six-to-nothing with only three seconds to play. They had the ball on their own one-yard line. The quarterback took the ball, faded back behind his own goal posts and threw a perfect pass to the left end, who whirled away from four guys and ran all the way for a touchdown! The fans went wild! You should have seen them! People were jumping up and down, and when they kicked the extra point, thousands of people ran out onto the field laughing and screaming! The fans and the players were so happy they were rolling on the ground and hugging each other and dancing and everything! It was fantastic!"

Asks Charlie Brown: "How did the other team feel?"

"Krazy Kat getting hit on the head by a brick from Ignatz Mouse is funny," Schulz says. "All the sad things that happened to Charlie Chaplin are funny. It's funny because it's not happening to us."

Schulz frets about his work. Not about the relentless press of it, that cartoonists have no vacations so long as newspapers publish seven days a week, every day of the year. No, that's not it. For he is happiest at the drawing board, lettering every word, drawing every line, birthing every idea for every *Peanuts* strip ever done. He doesn't want assistants.

"You don't work all your life to get to do something so that you can have time not to do it," he says.

And Schulz does not worry about quality; he knows he is good. He is modest, sure, but that is more self-protection than anything else. "I don't want to think I'm too good and become another Al Capp." Capp became bitter and belligerent in his last years, taking public snipes at younger cartoonists.

But Sparky Schulz, the highest-paid cartoonist in history, the most popular, cannot simply enjoy the money and the fame and the security that comes with being the best. That would be too easy. He must fret about nothing in particular.

"This is my whole life. I pour my heart into this, every day, and some people don't even read the comics." That is yet another source of melancholy.

Most of all, he hates being alone. He builds mental levees against the loneliness, making specific plans to occupy his time weeks in advance while his energetic wife is away.

"I know he will suffer," says his wife, Jeannie, "and I feel guilty for leaving him."

But anyone would have to leave sometime, and Jeannie's life is full. She is a pilot and poet and has produced a short documentary film. She loves to travel, almost as much as Schulz dislikes it. So coping and cartooning become Schulz's business.

He wrote this about loneliness in a poignant book of essays and strips called *You Don't Look 35, Charlie Brown!:*

There must be different kinds of loneliness, or at least different degrees of loneliness, but the most terrifying loneliness is not experienced by everyone and can be understood by only a few. I compare the panic in this kind of loneliness to the dog we see running frantically down the road pursuing the family car. He is not really being left behind, for the family knows it is to return, but for that moment in his limited understanding, he is being left alone forever, and he has to run and run to survive. It is no wonder that we make terrible choices in our lives to avoid loneliness.

He knew about what he wrote. Doctors say one horrible agoraphobic symptom is the idea some other person, usually a parent or sibling, may die while one is away from home.

The origin of his fundamental sadness remains mostly a mystery to Schulz and to those around him. His mother's death from cancer when she was forty-eight and he was twenty certainly might have triggered it. Schulz carries that memory with him always, fingering its tragic components like a rosary.

At the same time his mother died, Schulz was drafted to serve in World War II. Schulz made a good soldier, but the triple whammy of losing his mother, the security of home, and control of his life may have changed him forever. All the textbooks say the average age of the onset of agoraphobia is twenty-four or twenty-five.

Even today Sparky cannot discuss his mother or look at her photograph without becoming extremely emotional. In a Ray Bradbury essay, a favorite of Sparky's, the author urges the reader to "imagine you have been dead." If you could come back for one minute, what would you do? Sparky's answer: "I'd spend it with my mother."

Schulz, after discovering a name for at least part of his problem, believes his father also suffered from the agoraphobia disorder. "He used his work, the barbershop, as a reason never to travel or do anything. He never went anywhere by himself, either. Even when he went fishing there had to be someone else along.

"He would never have guessed what he was feeling had a name, but I'm convinced that's what it was."

Shirley Swede says a child often inherits the tendency to become agoraphobic, as one might inherit the tendency for high blood pressure. "It doesn't mean you're necessarily going to have high blood pressure if you watch your diet and exercise. Agoraphobia is the same way. You more or less inherit the sensitivity to loss, to stress, that can trigger it. A couple of things would help. One is getting physically fit, so you don't worry so much about heart attacks or that sort of thing. The other is realizing it's not something mysterious, that you first panicked at a time when you were in a weakened condition. That there was traumatic stress, which is normal. Certainly a reaction to a parent's death would occur in almost any sensitive person. But agoraphobics ruminate about the losses; they don't simply grieve and get over it in a year. And they keep remembering the panic attack or attacks they experienced and worrying they will have another."

Those closest to him are at a loss to explain the enduring Schulz depression.

"I cannot figure out what the problem is," says daughter Amy Johnson. "All I know for certain is that it's connected somehow with what makes him the genius he is on paper. And, to me, it seems that he's better now, in this period of his life. He has more friends, and he goes more places now than he has ever before."

His son Monte explains the recurring depression away as "the natural function of an artist." His father, in creating *Peanuts,* is forced to deal continually with the past, he says. "He writes about kids and his past all the time, and his nostalgic sensibilities are always sharp. He looks at stuff that's depressing, and that can be depressing, yes. So many writers and artists are that way.

"But not only does he endure, he prevails. I think I have the same homing instinct he has, the same dislike of leaving. It is a way, I think, of preserving your art, of keeping your mind where it should be."

There have been and are happy times in the life of Charles Schulz, to be sure. Most come wrapped in routine, in familiar places, with familiar faces.

There is a footpath between the cartoonist's studio, where he keeps regular hours five days a week, and the ice arena, where he eats, exercises, and meets his friends. When he walks the road between these two anchors he crosses his own baseball diamond, a field he shares with the general population of Santa Rosa.

He seems happiest there, walking at a brisk clip over the freshly mown baseball field, going from one arena of certainty to another. For he truly lives for his work, something few professionals say after doing the same thing for forty years. And if work can be spaced with a light lunch, a hockey game, some reading, and a quiet dinner with his wife, it helps stave off depression.

Schulz describes what he does as "drawing funny pictures." He seems not to have lost his perspective, remembering that the rudimentary act of dipping pen in ink must come before the animated specials, the licensing products, the honorary degrees, the money. Drawing the funny pictures keeps him sane.

He is not unlike one of his heroes, Ernie Pyle, who also generated big bucks for the Scripps Howard company, which owns the syndicate that distributes *Peanuts.*

The two share a brand of quiet dignity. Pyle's personal grief (stemming from a chronically depressed wife and the tortured love Pyle felt for her) eventually forced his total retreat into work, a solace. Pyle's personal predicament gave the public something it otherwise might not have had.

Schulz even writes somewhat like Pyle, in a clean, honest style. But one man was trapped on the road, the other is chained to a desk.

And there is another major difference between the geniuses. Pyle found comfort in drink, lots of it, and elaborately lewd jokes shared in long letters to close friends.

Schulz has a rigid personal code that prohibits such comforting vices; he has never sworn in his life. "I don't like ugly words."

Charles Schulz lives within a world he has drawn for himself, its outlines dark and indelible.

In 1988 his friend Katherine Crosby moved her annual charity golf tournament from Pebble Beach in northern California to Winston-Salem, North Carolina. Schulz, who loves golf and had traditionally participated, sent a note:

"I really regret that the trip would simply be too much for me. I am not a good traveler and find myself being forced to give up many wonderful opportunities. Pebble Beach was always nice and close and made a perfect vacation. I'm afraid North Carolina is too far for me. . . ."

He stayed home and drew funny pictures instead.

4

"I Suppose We Should Say Good-Bye . . ."

PEPPERMINT PATTY: What do you think security is, Chuck?

CHARLIE BROWN: Security? Security is sleeping in the back seat of the car. When you're a little kid, and you've been somewhere with your mom and dad, and it's night, and you're riding home in the car, you can sleep in the back seat. You don't have to worry about anything. Your mom and dad are in the front seat, and they do all the worrying. They take care of everything.

PEPPERMINT PATTY: That's real neat!

CHARLIE BROWN: But it doesn't last! Suddenly, you're grown up, and it can never be that way again. Suddenly, it's over, and you'll never get to sleep in the back seat again! Never!

PEPPERMINT PATTY: Never?

CHARLIE BROWN: Absolutely never!
PEPPERMINT PATTY: Hold my hand, Chuck!!

World War II clearly marked the end of the beginning for Charles Schulz. The global inferno was an epic backdrop for Sparky's quiet, intensely personal battle against formidable emotions within. His army years represented a sudden, irreversible departure from a sheltered boyhood, a traumatic break that would never quite heal.

Obviously Charles Schulz survived World War II with his life, no sure thing for an infantryman trained to lead a machine-gun squad. In fact, the majority of Schulz's military career consisted of stateside training. His brief time overseas was spent surging across northern Europe in a half-track, trying to catch up with a dwindling war that was always somewhere over the next horizon. He saw only four days of front-line combat against a dispirited enemy. In many ways, Schulz was fortunate.

Of course, it wasn't all gravy. He suffered the homesickness of the young draftee and the oppressive uncertainties of the combat soldier in wartime. From the time he began training, Schulz fully expected to take part in fierce fighting in Europe or maybe even the dreaded invasion of the Japanese homeland. And there was actual danger. That dispirited enemy was shooting real bullets.

Still, Sparky came home intact, largely uncalled upon to do the dreadful things for which he had trained and was willing. Yet he remembers his army days as days of profound loneliness, the source— or at least the beginning—of the nebulous depression that dogs him still.

Many young Americans were changed forever by horrible experiences during World War II, but Schulz's trauma was largely personal, triggered by circumstances apart from the havoc of the times. The most significant thing was the awful death of his mother shortly after his induction into the army.

Through high school Schulz had enjoyed an idyllic family life. An only child, he benefited from a friendly rapport with his parents. Activity centered around the home, and outside diversions always included the close-knit threesome of father, mother, and son. Interests were freely shared, including the love of newspaper comics. Carl and Dena Schulz took pride in their son's talents and encouraged him.

Carl Schulz the barber was a tireless provider, and the St. Paul neighborhood was, for little Sparky Schulz, a rock of stability. Through the entire Great Depression, the Schulz household survived modestly on thousands of haircuts, and Sparky was out of high school and taking art lessons before it dawned on him that ends did not always meet for Carl's family. Dena Schulz regularly prepared a dinner of pancakes, a favorite of young Sparky's. The boy thought his family must be well-to-do indeed to afford such delicious fare, when in reality Mrs. Schulz was economizing.

The household was a blend of reserve and warmth, where countless little routines were readily established and faithfully observed. Today Schulz wistfully recalls its sights and particularly its sounds.

"The first thing I would hear every morning would be our dog Spike yawning in the hall. That's where he slept, in a clothes basket under a blanket. I could hear him tumble out of the basket and walk into the kitchen to take up his place for the day, under the stove.

"The next thing I would hear would be my mother. Every morning she would say the same thing: 'Sparky, it's time to get up.' She would say it in sort of a soft singsong, almost a whisper.

"I can hear that voice now."

Every morning his father would have the same thing for breakfast, coffee and toast. Every weekend the family would walk to the movies. Once they took a whispered vote and all agreed to leave in the middle of a film to return home and hear *Amos 'n' Andy* on the radio; it was as impetuous as the Schulz family got.

Many summer weekends they traveled north to Mille Lacs, "a tremendously large lake where it was always cold in the morning. We never had a motor, so we'd row out, my mother, Dad, and I, and troll for walleye. It didn't seem to be my idea of fun, unless the fish just happened to be biting." As Sparky grew older, the fishing expeditions grew more ambitious. They often tried for sunfish on the St. Croix River. Fishing never became Sparky's passion as it was Carl's.

Though today he refuses to fish at all, in those days it was part of the family's precious routine, a part of things close and familiar.

About the time Sparky graduated from high school things changed. He remembers other sounds. Late-night sounds. The cries of his beloved mother as cancer and its pain killed her over a long two years. The family moved from its house on Macalister to an apartment over a drugstore at the corner of Snelling and Selby so the pharmacist could climb the stairs and administer daily shots of pain-killing drugs.

In February 1943, Charles Schulz was drafted. For a few days he was quartered at an induction center at Fort Snelling in Minneapolis. He was given a weekend pass to visit his critically ill mother across the Mississippi River in the old St. Paul neighborhood. On Sunday night, as he prepared to return to Fort Snelling, he went in to say good-bye to her.

"Yes," she said, "I suppose we should say good-bye, because we probably never will see each other again." She died the next day.

Schulz's father drove Sparky back to Fort Snelling after his mother's funeral. He stepped out of Carl's familiar 1934 Ford into a foot of snow, and before the day had ended he shipped out to Camp Campbell, Kentucky. The teeming troop train passed over his neighborhood, the sandlots where he had played ball, the ponds he had skated, the past. Schulz was not simply leaving a wonderful home; he was facing the fact it really no longer existed.

"I remember crying in my bunk that evening."

Schulz and hundreds of other young men were being sent to Camp Campbell to be melded into a new division, the 20th Armored. Schulz would spend almost two years there, maneuvering around the hills of southern Kentucky and northern Tennessee, mastering .30- and .50-caliber machine guns. He applied himself to this odd new trade with diligence and eventually would become a staff sergeant and squad leader.

Sparky had not been in camp long when he came down with a stomach virus. In the barracks latrine, his misery compounded by the knowledge he was supposed to stand guard duty shortly, Schulz made a friend for life. Elmer Hagemeyer, a fellow draftee from St.

Louis, discovered Schulz's predicament and took it upon himself to intercede with the first sergeant: it didn't hurt that Sarge was also from St. Louie, and Schulz was relieved from duty.

Ten years Sparky's senior, Hagemeyer had been a policeman until he was drafted. Older and a lot more happy-go-lucky than Schulz, Hagemeyer initially fit into army life better. As they got to know one another, the insouciant Hagemeyer began to assume something of an older-brother role to Schulz.

"When they grabbed me, I had been a policeman for three years already," says Hagemeyer, who lives in St. Louis today, now retired from the police force. "I had been around that type of work, taking and giving orders. Charlie was often depressed, always shy, a loner-type of fellow.

"It was a time when you needed a friend, more than you did in civilian life. He would get depressed, but I just wasn't the type to get depressed. So I'd get him out, to a movie or something. He loved to go to the show. At first, I just went along; eventually, I came to like it, too. He'd always ask the rest of us fellows if we wanted to buy some popcorn. Nobody ever did, but he would. Then we'd all eat off Charlie."

To most of the platoon and to Hagemeyer, Schulz was "Charlie." Hagemeyer and Schulz still visit by telephone, and Sparky is still Charlie. "I can't get used to this Sparky business."

For a dime the pals could see new movies at the comfortable service club, often before the films were in many of the civilian theaters. If he saw a good one, Hagemeyer would recommend it to his wife back in St. Louis.

"Elmer would write to me to go see such-and-such a movie," Margaret Hagemeyer recalls, "but I could never find the ones he mentioned." Hagemeyer is dyslexic, the couple eventually decided, and he was getting the titles all mixed up.

Hagemeyer had a car, and he would often return home on leave. ("Driving back and forth to St. Louis was probably the most dangerous thing I did in the war.") Soon his buddy Charlie was accompanying him. Margaret and Elmer had been married two and a half years when he was drafted, and she had returned to her parents' home for the duration. Schulz became attached to Margaret's family, the Habenicts. At their house, he always stayed in a finished attic flat where he soon felt comfortable and secure.

"Sparky loved it," says Margaret. "He didn't have to make his bed."

When the soldiers invaded St. Louis, they always wanted to go to "the nicest place in town" for dancing and dining, Margaret says. She remembers a dinner at a fancy hotel where she sat next to Schulz, who was dateless, as usual:

"Some of the fellows ordered Scotch. Sparky said, pointing at the Scotch, 'I've tasted better medicine.' " (He was twenty-three before he actually ordered a drink for himself—a Daiquiri, which he did not finish.) That night in St. Louis, Schulz and Margaret danced. He let her know in a whispered confidence that he had never danced before.

As he remembers it, Schulz had never been very popular as a youth, particularly as a teenager, mostly because of his palpable shyness. As a raw young soldier, this reticence was the basis for much of his misery. Stripped of the compensating warmth of his home and family—forever, tragically—Schulz felt desperately isolated in the midst of the boiling humanity that was wartime Camp Campbell. His association with the Hagemeyers was a great relief, a touch of normalcy and family, although Sparky never managed to shake a sense of being alone. Today, the sought-after Schulz remains the victim of an indecipherable loneliness he traces to that period of his life.

Actually, the army itself offered Schulz some good experience. Slowly, his almost crippling shyness was overcome by martial necessity, and he began to develop a working confidence. The young man who had never liked summer camp surprised himself and others by becoming a good soldier. Discipline, hard work, a desire to excel, all traits that would serve him well later, emerged in the young man.

A recruit can feel alone in an army barracks, but it's an intimate environment where it is almost impossible to actually be alone.

"When you lived together like that, you got to know a group of fellows, what a person stood for," explains Hagemeyer. "You also

knew pretty soon if a person had an ability. Charlie's was cartooning. He drew some training aids and pictures of life in the barracks."

The soldiers soon were asking Sparky to decorate their letters
home with cartoon sketches of army life. The Hagemeyers have
eighteen envelopes with Sparky's sketches, including one that jokingly prevailed upon Margaret to send some other cake besides coconut. "No, thanks," a cartoon Sparky is saying to a cartoon Elmer,
who is holding a cake. "I hate coconut."

"He was always oriented to comic strips. He idolized *Krazy Kat*.
He mentioned he would like to have a comic strip some day, but he
never made a big deal about it."

Mrs. Hagemeyer has appeared in *Peanuts* in two capacities. Hagemeyer is the married name of Linus's teacher/goddess Miss Othmar and the name of Marcie's organ teacher. The real Margaret Hagemeyer is an organist who sometimes plays at the St. Paul United
Methodist church in St. Louis.

Early in 1945, the division embarked for Europe. In February
Schulz's squad arrived at the town of Croisy sur Andelle in northern
France, and Sparky's squad was billeted at a chateau, where they expected to be temporarily. There, the famous army directive "Hurry
up and wait" took effect, and the warriors spent a lot of their time
playing softball. More ubiquitous than softball was army scuttlebutt.
In ancient military tradition, there was endless rumor, gossip, and
speculation; everyone quickly learned so much that no one knew
anything.

But again, still, when Schulz thinks of his time at the chateau,
loneliness is the overriding distinction.

Carl Schulz wrote his son every day he was overseas.

"He had these little writing tablets, and all the letters read
about the same. He would always talk about the weather in St. Paul,
and then, end it like this: 'Well, it's time to take the dog out for a
walk,' " Schulz says with a smile. "But I appreciated it so much."

A cartoon rendition of the soldiers' chateau would appear on
American television many years later in the special, *What Have We
Learned, Charlie Brown?*, the ambitious animated *Peanuts* tribute to
the Allied invasion of Fortress Europe, and in the movies as the *Châ-*

teau Malvoisin (The Chateau of the Bad Neighbor) in *Bon Voyage, Charlie Brown.*

In *What Have We Learned, Charlie Brown?,* the country house was headquarters for the *Peanuts* cast as it toured the Normandy battlefields. The production was a bold creative effort for Schulz and the producer of his animated specials, Lee Mendelson, for they didn't want to trivialize the somber subject matter while treating it with comic characters. Schulz thinks they pulled it off and takes pride in the fact few other cartoon casts are "real" enough to do it.

Schulz and his squad left the chateau April 1. Finally, five weeks before V-E Day, Sparky was unleashed on Hitler.

In a half-track named Sparky, Schulz and his men began a 600-mile tear across war torn northern France.

"Everything was bombed out, crushed; every building shot up; bullet holes were everyplace," Schulz remembers.

Every day they rode, getting closer to the enemy, "but what we usually ran into was a bunch of GIs sitting on porches."

The German army had long since been driven out of France when they set out; in fact, advance patrols from the American and Soviet armies were already bumping into each other in the heart of Nazi Germany. The green 20th Armored Division was attached to the Seventh Army, which had landed on the French Riviera in August and fought up the Rhone River to link up with the thrust from Normandy, giving the Allies a continuous front.

Sparky the half-track crossed the Rhine into Germany on a pontoon bridge at Remagen, where the famous Ludendorff Bridge had already collapsed. Thinking back, Schulz remembers being struck by how clean the German forests were, especially compared to those in France.

Once in Germany, Schulz the invader personally spared one life:

"We had just pulled into a little village—I'm not sure where it was in Germany—but we had just pulled into it, and one of the German soldiers had been wounded. My friend Sergeant Hagemeyer and some others were over attending to him. Our half-track moved down a ways through the village and stopped.

"I jumped down out of the half-track and ran down by myself to the end of the village, where I came across a large artillery emplacement. I didn't see anybody around, but then I noticed near the emplacement a stairway that ran down to a small wooden building which appeared to be, perhaps, a barracks where the people tending the place might have been living.

"The door to this barracks, which incidentally was painted all black and looked rather awesome, was open, and I was about to go down the stairs into the barracks when I thought that wouldn't be a very good idea. I had no way of knowing who was in there.

"So I took a concussion grenade off my belt, and I was about to toss it down through the doorway and follow it in. Just as I took it off, a small dog came trotting along, ignoring me completely. He trotted down the stairway into the building and disappeared.

"I thought, well, why hurt the poor dog? He seemed innocent enough. I put the grenade back on my belt and went back to the half-track where the rest of the squad was, and that was the end of the incident."

Perhaps the Head Beagle remembered.

When his squad began to catch up with the war, the Seventh Army was rolling south and bearing down on Munich, birthplace of the Nazi party. It had linked up with the right wing of Patton's Third Army and both were driving hard in the direction of Austria.

Sparky's squad was one day behind the liberation of the concentration camp at Dachau. He and his men slept in foxholes that night, and the next day their half-track was met by four concentration-camp survivors stumbling down the road, hugging the American armor.

The Wehrmacht had all but collapsed totally, and one of the Allies' major concerns was the processing of hundreds of thousands of German prisoners.

"People would come down the road surrendering," says Schulz. "It was surprising how little anybody cared."

Sparky was getting his wish. He wanted to survive the war—not only for the obvious reasons but also to see how it all turned out. Would Hitler be captured alive? Why had Rudolf Hess really flown to England?

In the final days, the Seventh Army crossed the Danube. On April 30, elements of the Seventh took Munich. On May 4, they took Berchtesgaden.

The exploits of Charles Schulz and his men are documented thusly in *Crusade in Europe* by Dwight Eisenhower: "Other troops occupied Salzburg."

He was there, in Salzburg, Austria, when the war against Germany ended.

It turned out that the fresh division indeed had been slated for the invasion of Japan.

"None of us liked the idea of traveling clear across the Pacific," says Schulz, as if the journey would be the true ordeal, not the millions of fanatical natives waiting to fight him to the death when he arrived.

"When we found out we weren't going," recalls Hagemeyer, "it was the best news any of us ever had."

After returning from Europe, the 20th Armored spent two months in California. Margaret followed, living with Elmer in a motel off base. Sparky stayed on base, but on weekends the three would drive the 150 miles or so to Santa Ana, where the Hagemeyers called on friends and Sparky visited his hockey-playing grandmother, Sophia Halverson, who had taken root near there, a transplant of the Needles sojourn.

Facing discharge, Schulz actually began to get sentimental about his army years, remembering the good times and forgetting the bad. He thought about reenlisting, but didn't.

Almost exactly three years after his mother died, Schulz returned to St. Paul a civilian, took the streetcar to his father's barbershop, walked in, and in Schulz-family fashion said simply, "Well, that's it."

5

Wisteria and Warm Puppies

*S*chulz begins his day at 7:30 A.M., before the world of shopping malls and day care and dentist appointments has rolled its impatient commerce onto the sunny byways of California's northern wine country.

It is his quiet time. He starts with a cup of coffee at the ice arena, in the Warm Puppy snack bar, sitting always at the same table in a plastic-and-chrome chair by a window looking out on the redwoods and wisteria. The first order of business is reading about the state of the world, beyond the soothing influence of wisteria and warm puppies. His source: *The San Francisco Chronicle.*

On the rink skaters glide by, taking advantage of early-morning instruction, each grim young face a study in unadulterated physical ambition. The skaters are learning forward sizzles and snow-plow stops and forward spirals, and, to them, Snoopy's creator is just another adult getting a slow start on the day.

To others at the picturesque arena he is a touchstone, a constant.

"You can set your clock by Sparky," notes Karen Kresge, a former Ice Follies star who teaches skating at Schulz's rink. Like many of the denizens of the ice arena, Karen is Sparky's friend and confidante, a fellow traveler in one of the rare realms where the cartoonist feels perfectly at home.

"I tell him he looks like Douglas Fairbanks, Jr." She laughs. It is Karen, too, who obligingly rounds up a gang for a trip into San Francisco when his wife Jeannie is out of town and Sparky is fending off the inevitable loneliness.

Possibly, but not probably, Schulz will glean a gag idea from his morning newspaper.

"I'd be more likely to get an idea from *The New Yorker.* But ideas rarely come that directly anyway. When people ask where ideas come from they really want to know if you get them from the *Reader's Digest* or something. They don't understand the creative process. Besides, I'm too proud to use anyone else's idea."

At 8:00 A.M. three days a week he dutifully bounces through his forty-five minutes of aerobics upstairs in the arena's dance studio. Aerobics or not, by 9:00 A.M. any weekday work begins across the street and two short blocks away at One Snoopy Place, home of Creative Associates and Schulz's studio. Creative Associates is the company Schulz formed in 1970 to help handle his complicated business affairs and leave him free to concentrate on the strip. Schulz steadfastly refuses to call what he does work. It is, he says, "drawing funny pictures, the best job in the world."

The office is a single-story, stone-and-redwood building with attractively landscaped grounds, not unlike a lot of other office buildings in the burgeoning town of Santa Rosa, population approximately 100,000. Except, of course, for its distinctive address. Located at the end of a short private street, it is purposely tasteful and functional.

"I shied away from anything that looked too arty or pretentious."

Inside, the novelty of this Santa Rosa business cannot be hidden as easily. When you open the door you know you have stumbled into a never-never land of marketable imagination. It appears, at first, as if a couple of secretaries have invaded a toy store, setting up desks in the midst of much fun and frivolity. Snoopy and his cartoon cohorts are stamped onto every conceivable toy and product, book and record. Toothbrushes to typewriters. Snoopy sewing machines and sleeping bags. Joe Cool parkas. Everything the serious aficionado and casual collector could seriously or casually want.

The books on the shelves have international titles: *L'Has Feta Bona, Charlie Brown! La Vita E Sogne, Charlie Brown! Gu-gu-gu Snoopy, Snobben och Rode Baronen, Schröder—oder: Beethoven, Du bist der Grosste!*

The walls are hung with posters featuring Snoopy and Charlie Brown. Busts of Ludwig van Beethoven crop up now and then on a bookcase or an end table. It is a place any *Peanuts* enthusiast would understand and feel comfortable visiting. Yet there is a crisp, businesslike atmosphere, a tone set by Schulz himself.

The sample products at One Snoopy Place are not for sale. However, the *Peanuts* fiefdom in Santa Rosa is completed by Snoopy's Gallery and Gifts, a modern two-story shop next door to the ice arena on West Steele Lane. A stained-glass window of a skating Snoopy adorns the building. Inside, a small staff presides over another array of *Peanuts* paraphernalia on the first floor and a museum of artifacts relating to Charles Schulz and his famous works on the second. The colorful assorted bric-a-brac at Snoopy's Gallery and Gifts is indeed for sale to a steady stream of tourists and fans. In the museum are photographs of Schulz, original comic strips by Sparky and other artists, and odds and ends from a long and celebrated cartooning career. The retail store and museum serve a practical function beyond turning a few more bucks. It is a place to route the well-meaning pilgrims who turn up on the doorstep of Schulz's studio. Their homage could easily play havoc with day-to-day production of *Peanuts,* with each tourist wanting "only five minutes" of the cartoonist's time.

Much has changed since he drew *Peanuts* on the kitchen table of his father's rented apartment. The purity of the simple profession —the cartoonist really needs only imagination, pen, ink, and paper —has been somewhat diluted by phenomenal success. The transformation is not lost on Sparky. He may have foreseen success when he began, but he did not envision its trappings. Although he is doing exactly the same work, most of the modern office essentials he and his staff rely upon had not even been invented in 1950. Photocopying machines, fax machines, computers, and electric typewriters compose the support system for a rudimentary enterprise that a thirteenth-century scribe could comprehend instantly.

In the studio itself things are reasonably orderly, like the man. A Keith Christie sculpture, "Lincoln's Vision," adorns one tabletop. "I deliberated for weeks before I bought it."

There are a rather dated bright-blue shag carpet and a modest executive desk sporting few adornments, one being a plastic elephant gewgaw for holding notes. Next to the desk is Schulz's drawing board, and across from it a couch and massive coffee table piled high with comic strip reprint books and calendars, most of them by other cartoonists. On the couch is a stuffed Cathy doll. He keeps supplies in a white cabinet with Schroeder and his piano painted on it.

There are a few plaques on the wall, but self-congratulatory items are at a minimum. His interior decorating seems to match his philosophy about awards. When he accepted the local Boy Scouts' award as Sonoma County's citizen of the year, he quoted them Luke 6:26: "Woe unto you when all men speak well of you."

Mostly what fills his walls are color photographs of his five children, his grandchildren, and wife Jeannie.

His oldest daughter, Meredith, and her husband run a mule ranch in Colorado. Elder son Monte is in Santa Barbara, where he is an aspiring novelist. Craig, who lives near his father in Santa Rosa, is quiet and calm, perfectly cast as a charter jet pilot. Amy is married and lives in Provo, Utah, with her husband and four children; she converted to Mormonism and once went to Europe as a Mormon missionary. Jill is an actress living in Los Angeles, as gregarious as Craig is quiet; she moonlights as a paid emissary for Roller-Blade (a brand of skates with tiny rollers set in blades, like ice skates, but for use on asphalt, hardwood, or concrete) and auditions endlessly while waiting for the Big Break.

On a prominent counter in the studio is an antique hand-cranked record player. The old phonograph is the cartoonist's failed attempt to "give this office some character, like Bill Melendez's place." Melendez is the animator of the *Peanuts* television specials and has an undeniably interesting office in Los Angeles, much of the interest derived from the spectacular mess. It is not a look Schulz could copy, try as he may; he is about as sloppy as a German surgeon.

Before the drawing of *Peanuts* can begin, Schulz sits across his desk from Pat Lytle, a secretary recruited fifteen years ago from a Methodist Sunday school class he taught for ten years. He dictates—in articulate, complete sentences—short replies to most of the letters and requests that come in with fierce regularity. The office receives more than a hundred letters a day. All are answered promptly.

"Everybody wants something." Schulz has a bit of an edge to his voice this morning. But then, the codger is gone, and in his place appears a gentle man who wants everyone to like him. Despite many unreasonable requests on his time and talent, he begins in earnest trying to oblige.

It is a constant problem, really, being almost entirely accessible, as he insists on being, and still getting the work done. Why doesn't he just hang a DO NOT DISTURB sign on his doorknob a few hours each day while drawing?

"I would, but I never know when the ideas are going to come. Besides, that way you must depend on someone to have the judgment to let a call from the President through."

He laughs. But it probably is one of his most persistent problems. His natural inclination is to talk to each person as if it will be the only phone call he receives all day, not always because he wants to but to be polite. That policy keeps him on the telephone, off and on, constantly.

The mail on a typical day: A musician sends his recent recording on tape cassette. Schulz expresses appropriate thanks but does not listen.

"Although I try to be as accommodating as possible with all the special requests that come in the mail, the one place I draw the line is listening to tapes. I absolutely refuse to do this and regard them as a real intrusion. Of course, now that videos have become so popular, they have been added to the refusal list."

Pat scribbles furiously in her notebook as Sparky continues to dig through a stack of mail.

"Hmmmm. This guy wants a Schroeder. I'll do a felt-pen drawing for him." He employs a felt-tip pen for such quick, informal sketches. Schroeder is harder to draw, he says. "But I can bat out Snoopy with my eyes closed."

Charlie Brown remains the hardest of all the *Peanuts* characters to draw because of the round head of the world's most famous round-headed kid.

There are letters from aspiring cartoonists, sending their work to the master for his critique. He complains that most have no sense of cartooning history, no appreciation of strip artists gone before. What's more, they have no talent.

"I've yet to have anybody send me anything good. I feel like saying 'I'm not running a correspondence school.' "

Yet there are stories like this one: Bill Holbrook was a twenty-two-year-old staff artist for an Atlanta newspaper, unhappily drawing charts and pie graphs and whatever else was assigned him.

"I thought about drawing a strip now and then, but the odds were daunting; I put the idea on a back burner."

Then Bill happened to visit family in California. An aunt and uncle there surprised him by arranging a meeting with Schulz. It was just the kind of favor Schulz might consider an imposition, nervy strangers expecting him to freely distribute his valuable time upon request. But, as usual, he did it.

"He was in the ice rink, waiting in the coffee shop," remembers Holbrook. "I didn't even have any samples of my work with me, though if I had only known ahead of time I would be there, I would have loaded him down. He was very inspiring.

"His basic advice was to keep plugging, to keep trying to find myself. Never give up. On the airplane ride home I thought 'I'm going to try this!' I just needed a kick in the pants to get me to buck the odds, and Sparky gave it to me."

Holbrook met Schulz April 3, 1982; in July of the next year, King Features Syndicate introduced Holbrook's new comic strip *On The Fastrack* in twenty-four newspapers. In 1989 Holbrook's strip about the employees of Fastrack, Inc., had enlisted some 150 news-papers and Holbrook was launching a second feature for The Washington Post Writers' Group, a strip called *Safe Havens,* set at a day-care center.

Schulz was first in line at a Santa Rosa autograph party for Chicago cartoonist Nicole Hollander, creator of the offbeat *Sylvia* and author of *Never Take Your Cat to a Salad Bar.* Later he escorted the visiting cartoonist to lunch.

Despite his protestations, he inevitably finds time to help young talent.

"You'd be surprised how many working cartoonists are around now who say they received a reply to a letter they wrote to Charles Schulz when they were youngsters, an event that encouraged them to try to be cartoonists," says Lynn Johnston.

For Schulz there is always a variety of peripheral business: a foreword to write for hot new cartoonist Bill Watterson's second collection of *Calvin and Hobbes,* a promotional video to tape for licensing products in Japan. The interruptions will continue throughout the day, mostly in the form of the constant telephone calls.

Some are requests for interviews; they average about fifteen per month. "I accommodate the newspapers first, then radio and television when I can. After all, it's newspapers I make my living from."

Schulz is increasingly less generous with personal appearances outside northern California. In fact, he has gotten downright stingy. In 1988 he readily turned down invitations to address graduation exercises at Princeton and Harvard. The same year, however, he seriously considered an invitation to keynote the graduation ceremony at the Piney Woods Country Life School in rural Mississippi. A historic, impoverished little academy founded to give black country children a basic education at the turn of the century, Piney Woods School intrigued Schulz—not enough, however, to overcome his increasing distaste for travel. But it all illustrates the point he has reached. Prestige and money cannot sway him as readily as his own whims and curiosity. He can afford to do the things he wants to do and avoid the things he doesn't (the latter category being the larger).

"I used to get a phone call and a request to speak at this or that and feel obligated to go. I ran around giving chalk talks at men's church groups, making a fool of myself." Now he limits such appearances and concentrates more on the strip itself.

He has never charged for his rare talks. "That would be immoral."

On this particular day, April 3, 1988, reporters want his comment on the death of fellow cartoonist Milton Caniff, creator of *Terry and the Pirates.* So telephone traffic is even heavier than usual.

Most would agree that with Caniff's death the mantle of dean of professional cartoonists has passed to the trim, athletic Schulz.

"Milton Caniff probably did more to elevate the art of drawing comic strips than any other individual," says Schulz to an *Editor and Publisher* writer. Schulz has, after all these years, mastered the interview, giving reporters just as much as he deems appropriate. No more. No less. He calls them by name and proceeds, as he puts it, "to charm their socks off."

He generally will address any subject and often is asked to—from a vague request to describe "the drama of the political conventions" to today's more specific questions about Caniff's contributions to the art.

"No, no, not just Caniff's intricate drawing." (Always make sure the reporters understand what you are saying.) "He did much to give the profession dignity."

Schulz has been blessed with good press over the years, an inordinate number of national magazine covers, and a minimum of controversy, even the unforeseeable pecadilloes that threaten to drive most cartoonists insane. ("What did you mean, sir, when you referred in your strip to 'Irish' potatoes?")

Early on, Schulz taught himself to speak properly and succinctly. It was part of his overall self-improvement impetus in younger days, while in the service and later as a teacher at Art Instruction Schools, as if he were preparing all along for the public role he now must play, doing television interviews and meeting assorted dignitaries.

"I was very earnest when I was probably about eighteen or

nineteen, in learning more about how to do things right. As a bonus in the correspondence school, we got a couple of books. One was how to write proper business letters. I think another was called *Business Etiquette.* I wanted to know how to eat properly, how to speak properly, how to write properly." Sparky devoured his bonus books as eagerly as the art lessons they accompanied.

"I tell my children there'll come a time when they'll be sitting down to eat with a governor or a book editor, and they'll want to know how to do things right. This doesn't mean that I've conquered things. I often feel out of place, so I want to tell young people 'There'll be a time when you wish you knew better words, and you wish you had a better way of expressing yourself. It'll happen.' "

The advice is excellent, of course, but it comes partly from Schulz's vague inner fear that he doesn't fit in, that he will do something stupid and embarrassing, that everyone else is privy to a secret he doesn't share.

There are welcome distractions during the work day of Charles Schulz, too. Calls come from friends—famous pal Billie Jean King or unknown Santa Rosa little-theater actress Mollie Boice. Mollie wows Schulz with her Katharine Hepburn imitation, and they frequently have lunch or walk to the nearby bookstore together. He buys her books he thinks she might enjoy.

Finally. After the preliminary prancing and pawing, the extracurricular duties that can completely sap a creative person's strength and time if permitted, Schulz is ready to draw.

Sometimes he comes armed with an idea, sometimes not. But each and every weekday he draws, or tries to. He is a strong believer in routine and regular hours, unlike many peers whose hair-raising tales of deadline production are legend.

The muse punches a time clock, Schulz firmly believes. So he stays as much as ten weeks ahead of his syndicate's deadline on the Sunday strip, six weeks ahead on the daily, which would make him an editor's darling even if *Peanuts* were not the greatest financial success story in the industry. Though he works very far ahead, he compares staying there to running up a glass hill. "It may take me six months to gain a two- or three-week lead, but it seems to take only a few minutes for that lead to disappear." Any comic strip artist would readily attest to that truism.

He also is adamant about spelling and factual accuracy. If a strip makes a musical reference, Schulz has done his homework, copying exact scores for authenticity. Same goes for medicine, law, sports, or religion. He inspires praise, generally, from professionals in each field.

His office bookshelves are filled with reference aids that collect no dust: *The Interpreter's Dictionary of the Bible, Surgical Diagnosis and Treatment, Clinical Cardiology, Save Your Stomach, Eisenhower: The Inside Story, The Complete Poems of Carl Sandburg, Lewis Carroll: The Annotated Alice.* Periodicals, too, play their part in making sure the exchanges among the conversationally precocious *Peanuts* gang are on the money before they are on the page.

He is equally faithful to artistic detail and practices what he has called "mental drawing." He has described the process as a true burden.

"While I am carrying on a conversation with someone, I find that I am drawing with my eyes. I find myself observing how his shirt collar comes around from behind his neck and perhaps casts a slight shadow on one side. I observe how the wrinkles in his sleeve form and how his arm may be resting on the edge of the chair. I observe how the features on his face move back and forth in perspective as he rotates his head. It actually is a form of sketching, and I believe that it is the next best thing to drawing itself. But I sometimes feel it is obsessive, like people who click their teeth and find that they have to do it in even numbers, or people who cannot resist counting telephone poles. It may even be some kind of neurosis, but at least it accomplishes something for me."

If his attention to detail and punctuality are not enough to please the insatiable syndicate, there is his penchant for tackling sensitive topics without being offensive: religion, love, old age, new math, war, and psychiatry. Rarely does he fool with politics, except in the broadest, philosophical sense.

"I feel a great responsibility to keep from offending people."

Schulz submitted roughs for only two or three weeks after *Pea-*

nuts began its long run. "Roughs" are exactly that: preliminary pencil sketches of the finished drawing to come. They are routinely used by magazine cartoonists to sell an editor on a single cartoon idea, and they are often required of new comic strip artists by nervous editors less than confident in their untried novice. Rough sketches give the syndicate editors a chance to veto or amend an idea.

"I discovered I couldn't do the work twice. Very seldom do they [the syndicate] fight me on anything, mainly because I'm more aware of their responsibility to the newspaper editors than they are."

One notable exception was the introduction in 1968 of Franklin, the black child in *Peanuts.* On his initial appearance, Franklin was invited home with Charlie Brown. A worried syndicate executive didn't really object to Franklin's inclusion so much, but: did Charlie Brown have to invite him directly into his home? Schulz persisted, and Franklin came to dinner with little ado. Such displays of front-office spinelessness are lore among syndicated cartoonists, but the truth is that syndicates are quite color-blind. To them, everything is green. It must be admitted, however, that Franklin remains the only black *Peanuts* player and has never developed into much more than a token.

Peanuts is the one area where Schulz is unassailably secure. As the strip has grown to mammoth scale, his confidence in his singular ability to interpret and present his own little universe has grown with it. Latter-day employees of United Feature Syndicate live in awe of the West Coast superstar and must wonder sometimes what happened to the acquiescent and compromising Minnesotan who worked so closely with sales manager Harry Gilburt back in 1950.

Some well-meaning minions through the years have arbitrarily changed things, causing him great pain.

"Once I had Charlie Brown saying 'I can't even hope good.' Someone corrected the grammar, changing 'good' to 'well.' Anyone knows 'I can't even hope well' doesn't have the same sense to it as the other."

Schulz ranted and drew his deadliest weapon; he threatened to quit. The culprit, a hapless new employee scared witless at the thought she had "lost" the syndicate its heavy hitter, cried. Nobody arbitrarily changes things anymore.

Back at the office. An idea eventually comes from who-knows-where, and it is time to draw his funny pictures. Schulz does it all, including the tedious lettering, a skill he perfected early, hand-lettering *Timeless Topix* comic books. Every idea. Every drawing. Unlike many successful cartoonists, he pays no assistants to do the dull work.

He uses a 914 Radio penpoint, which (he cheerfully points out) is no longer being made. "I bought all they had left."

Lynn Johnston once lost sleep over Schulz's penpoints:

"The first time I visited him, he told me about buying up all of the points. He would quit drawing *Peanuts,* he said, when he ran out of points. He seemed very depressed. I worried and worried about it. The next time I visited, I anxiously asked him about his supply of points. He laughed and showed me boxes and boxes."

"I have millions," Schulz confirms.

Lynn found out later Schulz has all sorts of "quitting times" planned. Upon observing a scuffed, well-worn patch in the center of Schulz's drawing board, Lynn asked her friend "What is that from?" He looked at her a moment, she says, "as if I were a bit daffy," and then said: "It's from hard work. When I can see all the way through to the floor, that's when I'll quit."

When her *For Better or Worse* was nearing its thousandth sale, Lynn jokingly bragged to Sparky, "I'm catching up with you."

"When you catch up with me, that's when I quit," deadpanned Schulz.

Schulz prefers R. Esterbrook penstaffs. In the beginning he worked for a while with a brush, but he has long since gone exclusively to a pen. To warm up, he often makes sketches, which are in some ways better than the finished drawing, he insists, because of their spontaneity. The final version is drawn on Strathmore three-ply, high-surface Bristol paper.

Whatever the tools, the drawing is as important as the writing. "Far more important than most people think. The drawing must charm, interest. But, most importantly, you must draw funny."

He admires James Thurber's crude cartoons immensely. They are good, Schulz says, simply because they are funny. Perspective and detail become unimportant if the reader knows a table is a table and that table is funny to look at.

"I have trouble with things like garden tools and furniture. I've never been satisfied with my drawings of those kinds of things. And if you can't draw it, you can't cartoon it."

It is as if he has successfully adopted the philosophy of Archibald MacLeish's *Ars Poetica,* with its perfect rule for simple, poetic symbolism: "For all the history of grief/An empty doorway and a maple leaf."

He admires the skillful drawing of Roy Crane *(Captain Easy, Wash Tubbs,* and *Buz Sawyer)* and George Herriman *(Krazy Kat).* As a child Schulz studied the characters and styles of Elzie C. Segar *(Popeye)* and Percy Crosby *(Skippy).* He calls the classic *Popeye*—that is, the strip before its hero was modernized and softened up—"the perfect strip." Yet it would be virtually impossible to narrow down three or two or even one direct influence on his personal drawing style. The uniqueness of *Peanuts* has set it apart for years, and imitators of Schulz are hardly even recognizable as such. That one-of-a-kind quality permeates every aspect of the strip and very clearly extends to the drawing. It is purely his with no clear forerunners and no subsequent pretenders.

Practice has made Schulz reasonably swift. He can draw a daily strip in an hour. He prefers not to draw six strips in one day, although he has done it many times. He ideally finishes six daily strips in two days and then turns his attention to the Sunday page, to which an entire workday is devoted.

"I always keep the door to my workroom in the studio closed, because when I am bent over the drawing board concentrating on a pen line, I hate being suddenly startled by someone who has come quietly into the room without my knowing it. This is also why my drawing board faces the door. I don't mind people coming in without knocking as long as I can hear the door open. In spite of all this, I sometimes am startled when someone comes in too quietly and suddenly speaks."

He breaks for lunch, dining at "his" table at the ice arena. The fare generally is light, a bowl of vegetable soup or a tuna melt. Sometimes he indulges in a marshmallow sundae.

He is exceedingly comfortable dining at the rink, where friends either surround him for casual conversation or leave him entirely alone, depending on the signals he emits. He can get downright rhapsodic about the rinkside banter.

"This is what I like, you know, talking and joking with people who know me. I never was one for standing around the golf course or clubhouse and making small talk. But I like conversation like we have at the arena. It's one of the great joys of life."

The process of the drawing itself, for Sparky, begins with doodling, drawing one of his characters in some odd or funny stance until the words for the action become, to him, apparent. "He writes and draws at the same time," observes Lynn Johnston. "I have to do the writing first. Sparky does the two things simultaneously. But who knows where the idea comes from? It's the most elusive thing, when you're sitting there. It all depends on what mood you're in, whether you are in the real world or some fantasy world at the time. It could be the smell of bacon cooking or when something funny happens. . . The characters are actors, but on paper."

Schulz usually calls it quits about four, sometimes returning to the arena for a game of hockey or meeting Jeannie for dinner at a local restaurant. One of his favorite haunts is the quiet restaurant at Los Robles Lodge, where he knows the staff and they know him. His routine is constant, simple, exactly as he likes it.

"It never has mattered that much to me where I live. I could live in New York City if I had an apartment and a good studio. I never worried much about having a grand vista at my studio. The plainer the better, really. Less of a distraction."

At day's end, he gets into a sporty, burgundy 560SL Mercedes with a customized license plate—WDSTK-1—and drives the eighteen minutes home to the hills overlooking Sonoma Valley's breathtaking wine country. His is a nice house, not huge or ostentatious, an unobtrusive nest in the gentle rise above the distant, diffused lights of Santa Rosa. The most impressive thing about the home is the view—

which is constantly changing with the weather and the position of the California sun—and the isolation, which is part illusion. There are neighbors, but their homes, too, are built neatly within the natural scheme of things and are only brief interruptions in the lush landscape that rolls and folds like green velvet. There is a feeling of privacy and wonderful aloneness that nearly always comes with elevation, and the Schulz estate is spectacular in that sense alone.

The only apparent security precaution at the Schulz home is a single strand of tinkling bells strung through the yard about belly high, meant to keep the deer away from the flowers. Paralleling the driveway is an unfinished stone wall, not unlike the one Charlie Brown and Linus stand behind when contemplating life. Originally, the gang sat on a street curb to philosophize, but as his own children came of age the cartoonist became safety conscious. He didn't want Charlie Brown grazed by a car. Thus the wall.

Schulz started the real-life wall himself years ago but is constantly saying he doubts if he'll ever finish it.

The only valuables in evidence at the Schulz home are intensely personal ones: a small wall hanging woven from the hair of Jeannie's late and beloved Samoyed hound Sasha, several flamboyant wildlife paintings by Walter J. Wilwerding, a former co-worker of Sparky's from Art Instruction Schools. When Wilwerding died, the estate contacted Schulz first, and he bought a lot of the art.

There are also sketches by Andrew Wyeth and dozens of original cartoon strips by Sparky's favorite comic strip artists. Photographs of an active family—hiking, mountain-climbing, skating—adorn the walls; it is a house in which you cannot imagine a formal gathering taking place—it is too friendly for that. Schulz has a spacious studio at home but rarely uses it. He prefers to make the drive to Snoopy Place, keeping his work and home environments separate.

There are a couple of dogs at the Schulz home; one is a golden retriever named Dropshot, the other a mixed-breed from the animal shelter, Andy. As is the case with most families with lots of children, there has been a succession of family dogs, some of them more memorable than others. There was a St. Bernard named Lucy, and, yes, there has been a beagle named Snoopy. Charles Schulz actually gave Snoopy away, to a man who brought a load of shale for the driveway. None, until the orphan Andy, has captivated Schulz like his own childhood dog Spike, the inspiration for Snoopy. Spike was a black-and-white pointer who appeared in Sparky's first published drawing, in 1937, in the newspaper feature *Ripley's Believe It or Not!* There, along with a seventy-five-year-old petrified apple and a champion cigar smoker was "a hunting dog that eats pins, tacks and razor blades." (Sparky swears it's true.) Spike's garbage disposal of a stomach was the least of his fascinating qualities. He could fetch potatoes from the basement and knew when it was nine o'clock on Saturday night and time to go out for a newspaper.

Andy the mutt is personable and loyal, says Schulz. "He's the only dog I've had since Spike who'll come up to you when you sit down and put his head in your lap." Requited love.

At home, Schulz might watch a little television. *Cheers,* the situation comedy set in a bar, is one of his favorite programs. He likes the fact that the show's love interest is never resolved. Reading is a nightly ritual for Schulz. Before the lights are doused, he has read something.

Around ten o'clock he starts thinking about turning in. And tomorrow, well tomorrow, the grind begins again, if you can describe a world of wisteria and warm puppies as a grind.

6

Twelve Devices

*T*he first comic strip character in history was a bald, round-headed little boy in a distinctive shirt. The fantastic popularity of R. F. Outcault's *Yellow Kid* inspired *The Katzenjammer Kids*, which in turn begat a host of imitators. So Charles M. Schulz did not exactly invent the kid strip.

So-called creative people understand better than most that there is nothing new under the sun. Working with boulders of granite, with empty stages, with blank paper, they are credited with making something out of nothing, but that isn't exactly what they do. All art is derived from what is in actuality a remarkably finite human experience. Whatever the medium, the creative person's task is to interpret an essentially unchanging reality, a dog-eared reality pondered by Homer and Mel Brooks and everyone in between. The artist succeeds if he or she can present something familiar from an unfamiliar angle.

Schulz intuitively understands this. It is the basis of his stock advice to aspiring cartoonists: eschew the obvious gag; think three, four times; is a fresher, funnier cartoon being overlooked? It is this imaginative quest for something original that has separated *Peanuts* from a seemingly unrelated horde of generic kid strips.

"Where do you get your ideas?" is by far the most commonly asked question of any cartoonist, and for most it is a continual source of consternation. It's like asking a carpenter "Where did you get that house?" He can either respond with the obvious ("I built it") or with the intricate ("Well, I went down to the hardware store and got some nails and wood . . . "). Both replies would be equally accurate and unenlightening. But no one would ask a carpenter that, because they can see where the house came from.

In truth, what goes into a good house goes into a good cartoon. Skill, thought, and hard work. Yet because it all occurs between the cartoonist's ears, it seems more like magic. The good cartoonist looks at the same thing as everybody else and then produces a drawing of something nobody else saw.

When asked for the millionth time "Where do you get your ideas?," cartoonists must bite their tongues to keep from blurting out "That's the stupidest, most insulting thing you could ask!" The good cartoonists, who work so hard to produce a worthwhile gag, can easily forget the admiration behind the innocent question. Aware that he would starve in the cartoonist's shoes, the questioner is really expressing awe of the ability to write a joke on demand, a joke good enough to be sold for money. The good cartoonist works so hard to kindle his innate spark that he is amazed when reminded his doodles don't necessarily reflect all that hard work. Of course, the bad cartoonist simply thinks he's a genius.

A more precise question would be "How do you do it?" Equally difficult to answer, perhaps, but at least the cartoonist might reply "It's my gift, and I've worked hard to develop it."

For forty years Schulz has worked hard, and he has his routine about nailed down. He doesn't worry, as his father did in the early days, that he won't continue to come up with a new gag every day. If he has a professional anxiety, it is that his originality will fail him, that he will never come up with another innovative device that will catch the readers' imaginations and set *Peanuts* apart from the pack.

Schulz identifies twelve such devices that have worked so well he is willing to attribute to them his strip's historic popularity. He is particularly proud of the ideas, for they are products of his unique intellect, things no one else would have thought of. Or at least no one did. To Schulz, the twelve things that helped make *Peanuts* are:

The kite-eating tree. "Something has to happen. Something has to catch on for a strip to really soar," Schulz says. "One of the first things that really worked for me was Charlie Brown getting that dumb kite caught in the tree. He was standing there all week long, looking at it. And people loved it."

Besides being the first of the twelve devices Charles Schulz considers indispensable to the popularity of his creation, the introduction of the kite-eating tree was one of the first *Peanuts* series, consecutive strips on one subject building to a resolution. For one agonizing week, Charlie Brown stood with his kite hung in a tree as one by one the cast came by to make sardonic observations on his ineptness.

The tree is a living symbol of Charlie Brown's ineffectiveness. Its appearance coincided with the emergence of his wishy-washiness. Although the put-upon persona of Good Ol' Charlie Brown was to become the bedrock of *Peanuts,* he was in the beginning a little wise guy with uncharacteristic verve. That was before kite-eating trees.

Schroeder's music. Schroeder was introduced in 1951, the second new player added to the original cast, after Violet. Though a toddler in infant jammies at the time, he quickly established himself as a musical prodigy, playing the toy piano before he could talk. His idol, of course, was Beethoven, and the classical scores he tickled out of his little piano were painstakingly copied by Schulz from real sheet music. Authenticity needn't imply reverence, however. Schroeder's scores have proven a bonanza of visual humor: other characters bump into them, birds sit on them, and Charlie Brown's kite even gets tangled in them.

"The piano idea actually came from a small toy piano we had bought for our three-year-old daughter Meredith," says Sparky.

Schroeder was not the first musician in *Peanuts.* That distinction belongs to none other than Good Ol' Charlie Brown himself. In the strip's first year he was afflicted with violin lessons. At Schulz's suggestion, Charlie Brown's violin was omitted from the first book of *Peanuts* reprints in 1952. By then Schroeder's talent was progressing, and it so pleased Schulz that he did not want to dilute its impact. In fact, it was Schroeder's music in the strip, particularly Schulz's faithful rendition of musical scores, that caught the attention of editor John Selby at Rinehart in New York and first caused him to approach United Feature Syndicate and Schulz about the book.

After forty years, Schroeder's music blends into the expansive tapestry Schulz has woven, but in the first decade Schroeder's music had a direct impact. Many gags about Schroeder, his piano, and Beethoven helped carry the strip along. It was as close as a newspaper comic can come to having theme music.

Linus's blanket. Closely akin in many ways to Schroeder's music is the security blanket. The first character in *Peanuts* to drag a blanket around was Charlie Brown. But that, too, soon fell to another newcomer. Lucy and her little brother Linus were introduced into the strip in 1952, and, like Schroeder, Linus premiered as an infant. He grew fast if not far, and he retreated not to music but to a blue flannel blanket that he dragged everywhere. Like the music, the blanket inspired countless gags, fostered many plots, and attracted a lot of attention to the strip in its first ten years. It came to define poor Linus, who is in some ways the most sagacious principal in *Peanuts.* He plays a pretty good second base and displays a genius for origami but has various troubles with certain holidays.

The blanket has been another wellhead of visual humor. Linus wields it like a whip, folds it into improbable shapes, and wages titanic struggles with Snoopy for it. The regenerating blanket has been cut up, ripped, stomped on, tailored into sports coats, and nearly incinerated. Linus's blanket came to life in 1965 and chased the human characters in one of the very few *Peanuts* episodes ever rejected by United Feature Syndicate. Former syndicate president Larry Rutman called it "monster stuff" and prevailed on Schulz to replace the gags.

Linus's unflagging resistance to outside pressure to give up his blanket has characterized the theme. In the strip he never yields, but in reality he has. Schulz admits that Linus has outgrown the blanket, and he seldom draws Linus with it anymore. But he has never overtly renounced it, and he never will.

Schulz takes credit for contributing the term *security blanket* to the American lexicon.

Lucy's psychiatry booth. When Schulz introduced Lucy's sidewalk ruminate stand in 1959, his readers thought "Hmmm, I wonder what he meant by that."

Much, perhaps a little too much, has been made of the exploration of the psyche in *Peanuts.* Happily for the brooding, instrospective Schulz, the timing of his new comic strip coincided perfectly with an explosive expansion in the field of behavioral science. For his exploration of such timeless conditions as loneliness, insecurity, and depression he was regarded as thoroughly hip. Adherents of the avante garde hailed Schulz, and conversely he was derided by mossbacks who thought his unrealistic children didn't steal enough cookies or break enough windows.

In Al Capp's *Li'l Abner,* Charles Schulz the creator of *Peanuts* was parodied mercilessly as "Good Old Bedly Damp, the creator of *PeeWee.*" In the parody, syndicate moguls are greatly upset that Bedly Damp's wildly lucrative strip has suddenly changed drastically.

"Can't you see what's wrong with *PeeWee?*" they ask.

"Frankly, no!" replies Damp. "At last the kids are talking like kids, and the dog [Croopy] is barking—like dogs do."

"But your readers don't understand real kids—and they're scared of real dogs," Damp is told by his syndicate bosses. It turns out Damp's neighbor, a psychiatrist, has moved away, and without his influence the characters in *PeeWee* no longer "talk like cute li'l psychiatrists"—to Damp's relief and the syndicate's horror. Damp is fired, and the psychiatrist is hired to write *PeeWee.* A quick talent search launched to find someone who draws as *badly* as Good Old Bedly Damp unearths none other than Li'l Abner.

Others have unabashedly grouped Schulz with Socrates, Aristotle, Freud, and Jung for his "uncanny ability to condense the most

sophisticated psychological concepts into a few cartoon frames."
That was the way Dr. Abraham J. Twerski put it in the introduction
to his book *When Do the Good Things Start?* The entire book is an
exploration of basic psychiatric principles as illustrated by *Peanuts*
comic strips.

Undeniably, the cartoonist is an astute pupil of human nature.
As such, he is sympathetic to psychiatrists and their endeavors, but
he doesn't shill for them. His layman's pragmatism might be illustrated by the advice Lucy gives a Charlie Brown who wonders why
he likes to be alone at times and at other times he feels so lonesome:
"Try to live in between. Five cents, please."

So what did Charles Schulz mean when he put Lucy behind
that booth? Only one thing is certain. He thought it would be funny.

"The booth really was a take-off on the lemonade stands that
appeared for years in other kid strips," explains Schulz.

Also certain in retrospect is that it created a lot of attention for
Peanuts.

Like the music and the blanket, the booth remains, institution-
alized, but Schulz has slowly moved away from the unrelenting con-
templation that earned the strip much of its first serious recognition.
It is mellower, more subtle today, and with the addition of Peppermint Patty and Marcie, more active than passive.

Snoopy's doghouse. In the beginning, Snoopy actually slept in
his doghouse, and a three-quarter view that worked in perspective
was the readers' most familiar angle. Snoopy would languish inside,
his head drooping out the door—just like a real dog. But Snoopy is
more than a real dog.

The studious reader understands that the metamorphosis from
doghouse to amphitheater of the surreal is closely related to the tran-
scendence of *Peanuts* itself from a traditional kid strip to a solitary
benchmark of the cartooning craft. The vehicle of Snoopy's imagination soared (literally as a Sopwith Camel) in the early 1960s, but in
reality it was Schulz's imagination that soared, boldly riding any current that led somewhere funny.

Gags about the doghouse go all the way back to the very beginning, but the early strips involving the doghouse reflected Schulz's

Li'l Folks motif: the kicker for a conversation between Charlie Brown and Shermy about the proliferation of air conditioners in the suburbs is a three-quarter drawing of the doghouse complete with portable air conditioner. At one time it sat against the Browns' house, where it was crushed by a giant icicle at the end of a suspenseful sequence.

The emergence of Snoopy's doghouse as Grand Device centered not on actual depictions of the humble abode but on allusions to its fantastic contents. Readers never see its interior, but there is said to be, among other things, a Joni James album collection, a pool table, and paintings by Andrew Wyeth and Van Gogh. When Schulz and his young family lived in the town of Sebastopol, near Santa Rosa, his combination office and guest house was destroyed by fire. The incident inspired a 1966 *Peanuts* sequence wherein Snoopy's doghouse burned—along with his Van Gogh. AAUUGH!

About the same time readers were becoming aware of the opulence of Snoopy's digs, he abandoned them for an ascetic existence on the roof. And the only view the reader is ever given is a left side view. Yet as its graphic depiction became severely restricted, its function became limitless. The doghouse has been wrapped by kinetic artist Christo, the birds play dominoes in it, and it is the terminus for an endless stream of awful manuscripts.

Snoopy himself. Snuffy Smith did it to Barney Google; Dagwood did it to Blondie; Mike Nomad did it to Steve Roper, who had done it to someone named Chief Wahoo. And Snoopy has done it to his own master. Conceived as the protagonist of *Peanuts,* Charlie Brown remains the eccentric hub around which all the action wobbles. He is the only player to ever get billing: *Peanuts, featuring Good Ol' Charlie Brown.* But face it, Charlie Brown, Snoopy has stolen the show. He is the figure most readily identified with the strip—or without the strip—and Schulz concedes that *Peanuts* reached the height of its popularity on Snoopy's bi-wings.

Schulz consciously works to maintain an ensemble cast and to prevent Snoopy in particular from dominating *Peanuts,* but he takes great pride in Snoopy's superstardom.

"Some comic strip characters, just like in other media, sort of rise above what they are," says Schulz. "Popeye is a perfect example. Popeye is immortal. Mickey Mouse is immortal. Charlie Chaplin. Jack Benny. You can't remember anything funny Jack Benny said, but mention Jack Benny and you immediately know what I'm talking about. I think Snoopy has done that, too."

United Feature Syndicate pins avaricious hopes on Snoopy's immortality. The syndicate believes that after Schulz ceases to produce original *Peanuts* strips, Snoopy products will endure, much like the teddy bear.

To document Snoopy's contribution to *Peanuts* would take volumes, every word of it unnecessary. Suffice it to say he started as an ordinary pet dog, but beginning in the late 1950s, Snoopy almost single-handedly delivered *Peanuts* from a nondescript neighborhood to an original world of its own.

The Red Baron. The strips featuring Snoopy and the Red Baron were the most popular *Peanuts* episodes ever, Schulz acknowledges. Readers loved *Peanuts* before; they love it now. But in October 1965, Snoopy the World War I Flying Ace was introduced and they went *crazy* for *Peanuts.* The strip caught fire and became that frightening, all-consuming beast, the Pop Phenomenon.

Today it seems that everybody and his sister are famous, but few in any field truly experience the worldwide attention lavished on the man from Minnesota and his comic strip during the latter half of the sixties. *Peanuts* was inducted into Americana, and Charlie Brown the loser was universally loved.

But such white-hot adulation never lasts, and when it inevitably subsides the onus falls on its object. Today Charles Schulz hears and reads things like "*Peanuts* just isn't as good as it used to be." It hurts, because he works as diligently as ever to make the strip as good as he possibly can. He has never rested on his laurels and hardly pauses to enjoy his staggering rewards. What such critics mean is that *Peanuts* isn't as popular as it once was, which is to say it doesn't hold the world spellbound. It isn't enough that it is still the most popular comic strip there is or ever was.

So to the Red Baron episodes falls the bittersweet distinction of being the pinnacle of *Peanuts.* It worked beautifully, so beautifully that nothing can be expected to duplicate it.

Schulz abandoned the theme as the fury of the Vietnam War increased: "It reached a point where war just didn't seem funny."

He later resumed the adventures of the World War I Flying Ace, but with more emphasis on love and loneliness than on crashing and burning.

Son Monte takes credit for giving his dad the idea for the Red Baron sequences; he was collecting models of World War I aircraft at the time they began. Schulz bristles and says just because he was looking at the planes and then thought up the Red Baron stuff doesn't mean Monte gave him the idea. But then he concedes that maybe Monte can have a little of the credit.

Woodstock. To be a totally effective comedian, Snoopy needed a second banana, so along came the small and yellow Woodstock.

More than ten years prior to Woodstock's introduction by name in 1970, birds were flittering in and out of *Peanuts* with regularity. Linus caused a minor scandal by patting the birds on the head. They loved it, but he finally was pressured to quit, because "No one else does it." However, the birds really liked to hang around with Snoopy. A neighborly rapport was naturally established as the birds fluttered about Snoopy on top of his doghouse. Soon they were pals, and the birds' indecipherable chatter became Snoopy's Greek chorus.

Snoopy was flying so high in his increasingly incredible world of fantasy that it took the birds to bring him back to earth; they helped maintain a connection with reality, albeit a strange reality. Snoopy wasn't insane after all. Or if he was, at least he wasn't alone.

In 1967, three years before the introduction of Woodstock by name, Snoopy is visited briefly by a "bird hippie."

"I don't see why he gets so upset," concludes Snoopy. "No one understands my generation either." Youth has always been restless, but there had never been anything in America quite like the Age of Aquarius ("the age of aquariums," according to Sally Brown). Schulz at the time sported a crew cut and a highly visible stamp of approval from the establishment. Yet the exchange between the "bird hippie" and Snoopy represented a gentle and worthwhile observation at a time when many other established cartoonists were taking cruel and surface potshots at the flower children. Such instances where outside events are directly reflected in *Peanuts* are rare.

The name Woodstock was taken from the rural New York rock concert that is remembered as a high-water mark of the restless sixties, but Schulz says this has no significance. He just thought it a good name for a bird.

"Woodstock demonstrates perfectly my constant contention that the drawing is vitally important," says Schulz. "Until I developed the cartoon figure to that certain point, Woodstock could not function. Now, all the birds look alike but are 'cartooned,' so they can express emotions."

Actually, the character of Woodstock was well in place before he was named: the drawing of the bird that would be called Woodstock was copyrighted in 1965. His nominal recognition somewhat formalized the feathered rabble that had been hovering around the doghouse for so long. From there, he went on to play Laurel to Snoopy's Hardy.

The baseball games. The baseball strips are about baseball as *Peanuts* is about children. Peripherally.

Baseball was first used casually in *Peanuts,* whenever a glove or a bat could be a useful prop. Within the first decade, however, the baseball theme had coalesced and was probably the hardest-working device Schulz employed.

The games have generated some marvelous visual humor—Charlie Brown getting his shoes knocked off by a line drive, Snoopy making a grab with his mouth, Lucy ignoring a lazy pop fly. More important, the deliberate pace of baseball made it a natural setting for the outlandish discussions and acerbic exchanges that are so common among the characters. There have been some epic Sunday pages where the players discuss Mother's Day, real estate development, lots of theology—almost anything but baseball.

In its heyday, the baseball diamond was an anthill of activity, a showcase for the lavishly cast *Peanuts.* It was the only place to look for such lost souls as Violet, Shermy, and Patty, players scratched from the starting roster of the everyday strip. In later years, baseball episodes have come to consist mainly of Charlie Brown and his recalcitrant outfielder Lucy.

The indispensable element of the baseball gimmick is the losing, of course. Besides Snoopy, probably nothing has come to typify *Peanuts* more than Charlie Brown going down in flames on his pitcher's mound one more time. The team, which has no name really, is usually on the short end of a lopsided score, and on the rare occasion when victory is near the goat in Charlie Brown loses the day. Charlie Brown wants it so bad. He tries so hard. He never wins. It is something every reader who happens to be human can understand. It is one of those natural orders of the *Peanuts* universe, and it cannot change.

Schulz prefers golf and tennis to watching baseball. He draws on his childhood experiences with sandlot ball as the inspiration for the games within *Peanuts.* Snoopy's chase of the home-run record paralleled Hank Aaron's, but the strip owes little to modern major league ball. While golfers, skaters, tennis players, and gymnasts often get mention, players of team sports are seldom given a cameo in *Peanuts.* When they are, they're often vintage players such as Joe Di-Maggio or Joe Garagiola.

The football episodes. Football in *Peanuts* comes and goes with the autumn leaves, but it has never enjoyed the place baseball assumed. Its shining moment, of course, is the place-kicking gag, when Lucy pulls the football away from Charlie Brown. It has been going on for thirty-two years and is a perfect example of what *Peanuts* is all about: losing, losing again, losing some more, losing the next year. It isn't a happy thought, really, but it is a universal dread. Those who think a comic strip should be more positive don't really understand humor—or life, for that matter.

Besides losing, the running (and falling) gag is a pure example of another element that has worked so well for Schulz: repetition. One newspaper editor canceled *Peanuts,* complaining that the author did the same things over and over. He was forced to reinstate the comic strip, with an apology, when his disappointed readers set up a postal howl.

Nothing else in *Peanuts* is so mechanically repetitious as the football joke. Every year it gets harder to think of a fresh gag involving the same stunt, but it must be drawn. Each time Charlie Brown falls and Lucy triumphs the strip is reinforced.

A few years back, Ronald Reagan told Schulz the gag was his favorite. "I'm easily flattered into continuing something," Schulz says.

The Great Pumpkin. Like the football-kicking episodes, the Great Pumpkin is an annual event. Linus is the most intellectual of the *Peanuts* characters, but he also is the most guileless. A dangerous combination in anybody. He is the most likely to grow up and join a far-out cult. In fact, he has joined one already. Despite his yearly dose of reality, he never forsakes his mistaken notion that something called the Great Pumpkin is going to bring him gifts.

Conceived as a roundabout statement on Santa Claus and the commercialization of Christmas, Schulz takes pride in this concept, because he thinks it is an invention that has outgrown the strip. People, he likes to believe, talk about the Great Pumpkin, are aware of the Great Pumpkin, without necessarily knowing where it came from—like Al Capp's Sadie Hawkins Day.

The little red-haired girl. Hank Williams's plaintive ballad "I Can't Help It If I'm Still in Love with You" spurred the inclusion of the little red-haired girl in *Peanuts.* After listening to the song over and over again, Schulz was inspired to include in his cast of characters the unrequiting lover. Since loss is the underpinning of *Peanuts,* a futile love interest was demanded. The little red-haired girl filled the niche admirably, providing more versatility than a successful but seasonal gimmick already in use—Charlie Brown's empty valentine box.

The little red-haired girl has never been depicted (Schulz does not count the animated version), and he believes she never will be. She is best worshiped from afar. Love remains aloof. The football is never kicked. The Great Pumpkin never comes. The winning run is never scored.

7

The Little Red-haired Girl

She is real. The little red-haired girl, Charlie Brown's elusive love, lives and breathes and bounces grandbabies on her knee in Minneapolis.

Donna Wold is sixty years old. She shares her split-level home with an ancient black cat called Iggy and a fireman named Al, her husband of thirty-nine years. Her hair, which once was bright red, is now a soft white-gray, cut short in a friendly bob. Her blue eyes shine from behind trim eyeglasses. She bowls on Wednesday and adores airports and routinely travels to visit with her seven grandchildren. She is a small woman, still pretty, her Swedish ancestry apparent. Yet time has exacted its inevitable toll on her unassuming life, most all of it spent within a few square miles of Minneapolis. A diabetic, she takes insulin shots twice daily and carefully polices her diet. Her son Dan, the oldest of four children, died from diabetic complications, ultimately heart failure, in 1984. She misses him.

Once upon a time, forty years ago, Donna Mae Johnson was in

love with two men. One, a handsome Navy veteran named Al, lived conveniently next door to her Lutheran Church, Holy Trinity. They had known each other since eighth grade, where both of them stood out in the student population because of their red heads. Soon after he returned from service, Al watched the vibrant redhead singing in the choir one Sunday morning; he suddenly saw her with new eyes and impulsively asked the man sitting in the pew beside him if he knew Donna Johnson's telephone number. Al's seatmate just happened to be dating Donna's sister and, without hesitation, rattled off the number. Donna and Al became a couple.

The other love of Donna's young life was an art instructor at the correspondence art school where she began working in the accounting department after her 1947 high school graduation. He was seven years her senior, born a Lutheran but now a deeply religious member of another denomination, the Church of God. Those two differences—age and religion—gave Donna's mother pause. And the mother, in turn, gave Donna grief.

Donna called him Sparky.

The romance was slow to build, taking the demure half steps of a more mincing and subtle age. The two of them, Sparky and Donna, tiptoed toward full-scale courtship. She delivered an apple a day and an occasional poem to his third-floor desk, running the gauntlet of stares from his co-workers. He passed by her second-floor post and jotted notes on her desk calendar. Not athletic, she nonetheless joined the Art Instruction School's softball team, the Bureaucats; he was the coach. After the games, Sparky would offer the players rides home in his car; Donna's house at the corner of Longfellow and 33rd was always his last stop.

Seeking to better herself, Donna enrolled in a shorthand course at the Minnesota School of Business. Sparky walked her from the offices of Art Instruction to her classes. "Usually he talked me out of attending," she says, laughing. "He was a pretty good convincer. He's the reason I'm a failure and never was a great executive secretary or whatever. Ha!"

The shorthand soon fell by the wayside, an inside joke between the lovesick pair. Sparky sometimes penned gibberish "shorthand" notes at the top of serious and heartfelt letters, a lover's code of scratches and slashes, much like Woodstock's "conversation" would look years later in the comic strip yet to be born.

The little red-haired girl of the strips is like Beethoven's Immortal Beloved and Shakespeare's Dark Lady of the Sonnets. An unknown quantity, a faceless angel. Only, for Schulz, there is definitely a face to go with the most famous of his offstage characters. And there is a residue of remorse about it all:

"I can think of no more emotionally damaging loss than to be turned down by someone whom you love very much," he says. "A person who not only turns you down, but almost immediately will marry the victor. What a bitter blow that is. It is a blow to everything that you are. Your appearance. Your personality."

Today, Donna Wold sits at her kitchen table in a cozy middle-class home, remembering. She surveys her precious keepsakes, reminders of that bittersweet time when two sought her favors and life stretched before her like a banquet. There are the cartoons Sparky carefully affixed to the top of a box of candy on St. Patrick's Day. "Good morning!" the note says. The little girl he drew looks identical to the character Patty, who debuted in *Peanuts,* one of the original four characters. Even her dress is the same. Except Sparky had taken a brush and put a swipe of red wash across the hair of Donna's picture; the first Patty in *Peanuts* is a blonde.

There is a tiny silver replica of a hope chest—"I never had a charm bracelet to put it on"—and a gilded box topped with rhinestones designed to hold a miniature lipstick, powder, and perfume, which Sparky bought at the Roosevelt Hotel in New York during his successful trip to sell *Peanuts.*

Sparky would remember the gift as simply a pin, but Donna knows better. She has examined it countless times, closely.

There are letters from Sparky, which Donna keeps private except for one, which she is willing to share: "If the test of absence is the best test, then I am more sure than ever. Last night I kept thinking of you all the time. . ."

Snow is deep and clean outside on the deck where the birds of winter convene. Her husband Al thoughtfully keeps the birdbath water heated.

"When our daughter Peggy was home over the holidays, she couldn't believe the same father who used to fuss about turning the lights off was heating the water in the birdbath," says Donna, laughing. She has an easy laugh and is the kind of woman who would appreciate watching birds.

Also on the table among the mementos is her desk calendar from Art Instruction, its days filled with penciled notations from several months in 1950 when the romance raged. She used the calendar as an abbreviated diary, a way to keep track of the active social life she suddenly was leading. The conflict of her heart was clear, in the dates she recorded in code. Sparky was CS. Al was Al. She had been dating Al, although not steadily, since 1948. There were other, minor players. One was George Smith, a good dancer, but he was a Catholic and therefore not a serious prospect for the devout Lutheran Donna. Her first official date with Sparky, March 2, 1950, came on a Thursday:

CS. Ice Capades. NICE!!

Monday, March 6, 1950, was typical:

downtown with CS. Steak. "Intruder In The Dust" at the World. Walking/ in and talked. left at 10:45. Al called twice. Came over twice.

On March 16 she wrote Schulz's last name at the top of the page. First, she spelled it with a *t,* then erased her mistake and spelled the name correctly. At the bottom of the page she wrote his address: 170 N. Snelling, Apartment 2, St. Paul.

On March 22, she stayed home from work, sick. Roses came from CS. March 23: "Hockey game, CS. St. Paul, 1, versus Minneapolis, 3. Al called 8, 9, 10. Mad at me!"

On their third date, Donna remembers Sparky saying: "I wish I had a diamond ring in my pocket to give you right now." It was a busy spring for Donna, juggling her two suitors and trying to come to terms with her own feelings. "How will you ever decide?" she asked herself on Monday, May 8, in her neat, slanted, calendar prose.

Meanwhile, she made her choir practices, took long walks with both Sparky and Al, played cards with the gang from Art Instruction and went roller-skating with her friends from the Lutheran League. She gave blood on Good Friday, got a new bedroom suite, collected newspapers for a church paper sale, went to a Lakers game and a Mother—Daughter banquet. All duly noted. She got to know Sparky's Aunt Marion and Marion's husband, a trumpet player named Bus. They all played cards together, and Sparky showed her how to play a game called Prediction. She met Sparky's father. Sparky came for lunch at her house, and the dubious Mrs. Johnson cooperated by fixing pancakes especially for Sparky; they were his favorite. The downtown World Theater offered a discount for those buying tickets before 5:00 P.M., and Donna and Sparky often rushed from Art Instruction to take advantage of the price break, seeing *The Third Man* and *The Red Shoes* and other current movies. Donna dreamed of becoming a florist; Sparky talked about selling a strip.

Sparky drew mixed reviews from Donna's family. He came calling frequently during those intense few months, sometimes wearing a pale gray shirt with a black zigzag around it not unlike Charlie Brown's trademark shirt. "It was his favorite," says Donna fondly. "He had another one just like it, except different colors. Pale green with a dark green zigzag, I want to say."

Her one sister adored him. "She claims he was the one boyfriend I had who was nice to her."

Donna's father reacted to Sparky Schulz the same way he reacted to all of her boyfriends. Though Donna begged him not to, he asked that staple question of skilled inquisitors disguised as doting fathers: "Did you play football?" For Sparky, of course, the answer was "No."

The mother kept her eyebrows raised about the cartoonist and his prospects, prompting Donna, on at least one occasion, to suggest an elopement. "I always talked her out of it," says Sparky, "because we didn't want to hurt the family. That's what I get for being a nice guy."

When Sparky returned from New York on June 15, he called Donna at 10:40 P.M. to tell her he had at long last sold the comic strip. "He gave me a little white cat, curled up and sleeping, complete with directions. When I was ready to get married I was to put the cat on his desk at work, when he was away from his desk, a signal that I had made up my mind. . . I kept the cat in my desk drawer—handy—just in case."

The picnic both remember as a benchmark in the romance was spread on Saturday, June 24, 1950, at Taylor's Falls near Minneapolis. Donna mixed a glass jar full of pancake batter to surprise her beau. They cooked them in a skillet over an open fire. That evening they made it to the Highland Theater in time to see *My Foolish Heart,* starring Dana Andrews and Susan Hayward.

"I think about it now, or hear the score, and it just about breaks my heart," says Schulz. For years he remembered wrongly that Anne Baxter, not Susan Hayward, had been in the film he and Donna saw. The sight of Anne Baxter on the screen would fill him with a nostalgic longing. Then, one day, a friend set him straight: for years his depression had been triggered by the wrong image. Of course, he got a gag from the mix-up, a Sunday strip where Charlie Brown relates a similar experience that supposedly happened to his dad.

Only the cars have changed. The old Minneapolis neighborhood is still flanked by spacious parks and a generous allotment of trees and evergreenery. Donna Wold drives slowly by the Highland Theater, which still stands. A motorist behind her impatiently pats his accelerator, revving his motor, but she takes her time anyway. The theater exterior is exactly the same, she says. The name is all done up in neon, and there are other fiftyish touches—geometrical blocks of aqua and peach. Only, now playing are *Ernest Saves Christmas* and *Who Framed Roger Rabbit,* not the stuff of classic romance.

On that Saturday in June 1950, everything, but everything, reeked of romance. After the syrup on the pancakes and the syrup on the silver screen, sweet talk probably was inevitable. Sparky and

Donna sat in his car. "I never did tell Sparky that when I went home that night my mother said 'I thought you'd run off to Iowa and gotten married.' We didn't, of course." Iowa was where people from Minnesota went in those days for quickie weddings. But for two conscientious and religious sweethearts like Donna and Sparky, Iowa was at least a million miles away.

Though there are a few more entries concerning CS on Donna Johnson's desk calendar, the trip to Taylor's Falls seemed to mark an impasse.

"It was a terrible thing, really, caring for two people like that," she says. "Al proposed July first, and I realized I would soon have to make decisions. I love Al, and I loved Sparky, and up to the last minute it was the most difficult decision."

About that time Sparky wrote her a note on his typewriter at Art Instruction: "I am so sorry for the sadness that I have caused you. It's because you are so good that you feel all these things so deeply, which is another reason why I love you. . . ."

Religion played a part in the decision. Though the difference in their denominations mattered more to her parents than to her, Donna was not the type to disregard parental preference altogether. She had visited with Sparky at his Church of God, "where he seemed to have so many dear friends." Sparky was devoted to his new faith, not his old.

Who can say what finally tips the scales toward one relationship over another? Donna cannot. Sparky certainly doesn't know. For whatever reason or reasons, the romance ended abruptly when Donna informed Sparky of her engagement to Al.

"On an afternoon in late July, I told Sparky it was going to be Al. I was home sewing. As usual, I had the ironing board set up in the kitchen. We sat outside on the back steps for a long time. He drove away. I went inside and cried. He came back about thirty minutes later and said 'I thought maybe you changed your mind.' It was close!"

Donna's calendar page from Thursday, July 13, 1950, says this: "Home. Sewed. Ironed. Talked to Al—asked me over to see TV tonight and tomorrow. CS came over at 9:10—11: I didn't go to Al's."

Donna Mae Johnson married Al Wold at Holy Trinity Lutheran Church October 21, 1950, when the strip *Peanuts* was nineteen days old. She already had quit her job at Art Instruction, "because I thought it would just be too hard, too awkward, with Sparky working there and me marrying somebody else."

By 1956, when Charles Schulz was signing autographs at a downtown Minneapolis bookstore, he was married, a father, and beginning to ascend to that pinnacle of fame few ever reach. Donna, pregnant with her second child, waited in a long line to ask for his autograph. "The lady in front of me was saying 'I'm his biggest fan.' And I thought 'Oh, no, you're not!' "

Sparky signed Donna's book with a rather generic inscription that bothers her slightly, even today: "For Donna, with sincere best wishes. . . ." Later he gave her a ride to her parked car.

During those early years of the strip, when Schulz lived in a rather prestigious house in Minneapolis, the home of a former Minnesota governor, replete with a red-tile roof and gleaming stucco walls, Donna wheeled her baby carriage by to check out the address the newspaper had listed. By Schulz's own account, "I was already successful beyond my wildest dreams" in the mid-fifties. He remembers paying $32,000 for a house in Minneapolis, a sum that impressed his friends, his father, and himself. "Everyone was astounded I could make so much cartooning."

By 1958, when he moved his young family to California, he was making about $50,000 a year.

"I saw pictures of his wife in the newspaper; she looked very pretty," says Donna. She read the newsmagazine accounts of his California digs and marveled that her unassuming Sparky had a four-hole golf course and an artificial waterfall. Years later, on a trip through California with Al, she stopped at the ice arena on the chance Sparky would be there. He wasn't. "Al was good about it. He sat in the car in case I got a chance to talk to him."

"I think I'm the luckiest person in the world," she states when asked about any regrets. "I'm happy. I have enjoyed being a housewife. There's nothing I have missed."

And Al? How does he feel about it all, about his Donna being the little red-haired girl? "It's fine with him. He doesn't mind. It's just one more thing that makes him feel lucky," says Donna sweetly.

"I just am glad that a hometown boy made good," Al says with conviction. He is a smart, extraordinarily polite man who would hold the door for a burglar. Or heat the water for the birds.

The first time Donna saw a reference to the little red-haired girl in the strip, she knew. "At first, I thought it must be a composite of all his girlfriends. He had other girlfriends. Not just me. And then, after seeing some of the jokes, I knew he meant me. It was like reading an old love letter. It was so very nice to be remembered. But, really, I just happened to be there.

"And then there was that television special that showed the little red-haired girl and called her by a name. Heather. I decided again that the character wasn't me, exactly. Heather is such a good composite name."

She told only her immediate family about her inclusion in the famous *Peanuts* lineup. "Other people would have thought me crazy if I said, 'That's me. I'm the little red-haired girl.' " Donna's mother, ironically, was proudest of the fact. "She told everybody. All her friends."

"It took her a while to convince me she was the little red-haired girl," says Al, winking. He is a district fire chief now, called out for the major fires, not the smaller ones. He has made a success in his own field and seems self-assured and anything but jealous.

"How could anyone be jealous about something that happened that long ago, anyway?" wonders Donna.

Al does tease his wife about the romance. "Why did I have to do away with all my love letters and souvenirs when you still keep yours?"

Held together carefully with rubber bands, there are hundreds of strips clipped from *The Minneapolis Star-Tribune* that Donna has saved through the years, beginning in 1950. Many of them are about the little red-haired girl; she has saved every last one of those. Some are simply favorites featuring other characters. She owns no originals other than the sketches Schulz made for her in 1950. Her favorite collection of reprints: *You're in Love, Charlie Brown.*

Donna never left that world they inhabited, the cartoonist and the little red-haired girl. As she drives, she points out the places they walked and talked and ate. There is genuine affection in her voice, too, when she turns the tables and asks questions about Sparky the man and what he is like today.

"When he dies, I'll know. The whole world will know. If I die first, he'll never even know. Unless I can get Al to write him a little note. . . ."

8

Doomed Romances

Requested, the pleasure of your company.

It was March, 1952, when curvaceous Daisy Mae Scragg and reluctant Abner Yokum exchanged marriage vows in Dogpatch, U.S.A., at a simple $1.35 ceremony performed by Marryin' Sam and witnessed by a nation.

The courtship had been a long one. Seventeen years. Daisy Mae's earnest efforts to catch Li'l Abner had inspired an American institution. Schools and communities across the United States added Sadie Hawkins Day to their November calendars. It was a turnabout day when girls openly chased boys, asking them to dances or carrying their books. Sadie Hawkins Day was Al Capp's invention, an annual footrace in Dogpatch where terrified bachelors were given a head start over desperate spinsters. If caught by a woman, Dogpatch law required a man to, oh horror, oh black day, oh pit of pits, *marry* her.

For years, a comely and incredibly lovesick Daisy Mae schemed to catch disdainful Li'l Abner, but fate conspired against her at every turn. It was a perennial comic strip ritual. She never caught him in the race, but finally Li'l Abner did marry Daisy Mae. He consented, because his role model Fearless Fosdick — hero of the comic strip within a comic strip — married sweetheart Prudence Pimpleton. Daisy Mae was happy. Mammy and Pappy Yokum were ecstatic: "At last our dreams an' th' dreams o' billyuns o' other decent people has come true!!" Americans were delighted. The Scragg—Yokum nuptials were considered so important they made the cover of *Life* magazine.

"It was the biggest mistake in comic strip history," says Charles Schulz matter-of-factly. "People always wanted Li'l Abner to straighten up and for Daisy Mae to catch him. Once it happened, the bottom dropped out of the strip.

"There was a streak there for about twenty years where a lot of comic heroes were getting married. Buz Sawyer even got married. The romance immediately goes out of the strip."

It's worth noting that the imaginary creators of "Fearless Fosdick" agreed with Schulz; they decided it was a horrible idea for Fosdick to marry and made it all a dream. Li'l Abner thought he, too, was off the hook until Mammy Yokum explained it to him:

"But, son, try to unnerstan', yore marriage warn't no dream. It don't matter no more whut Fosdick done done or whut Fosdick didn't done done, yo' is married, hopelessly, permanently married."

What Schulz understands is the power of unrequited love on both an artistic and personal level. For him, the little red-haired girl is not just an effective offstage comic strip character. She is, instead, the unattainable, the ethereal, the love never to be kissed, married, or forgotten.

Or drawn, for that matter.

On the comic pages, the little red-haired girl will never know Charlie Brown is alive, no matter if he watches her from afar until her red hair grows gray. She will never even appear in the strip, because some things are best imagined.

Linus will never willingly admit to being Sally's Sweet Baboo, no, not even in his most insecure moment; the blanket will remain his main squeeze.

Schroeder will always prefer Beethoven and a musical monk-ishness to big-mouthed Lucy, who, in her vanity, will never be able to fathom it.

Marcie and Peppermint Patty will forever jockey for something more than a platonic relationship with Charlie Brown.

The golden retriever will always get the French poodle for whom poor Snoopy pants.

Celibacy is the comic ticket. If, in a weak moment, the cartoon-ist succumbs to the desires of his doodlings, the plot is gone, the mission accomplished. It's back to the ol' drawing board, for no realized love is half as interesting as one that might be.

So, as the dean of comics sees it, Li'l Abner never should have married Daisy Mae. Brenda Starr should have remained a gleam in her Mystery Man's eye. The Phantom, Ghost Who Walks, should have kept on walking. Joe Palooka shouldn't have answered the bells. Better Prince Valiant had unchivalrously left Princess Aleta at the altar. Kerry Drake and Juliet Jones and Phil Finn and Steve Canyon and Mary Perkins and Smilin' Jack, Jr. — all of them would have been better off if they had remained single.

It is amazing how many comic strip characters have lost their mates along the way—never by divorce, for heaven's sake, but by a bizarre array of contrivances—as cartoonists have struggled to put some excitement and freedom back into their strips. A wedding has always been a quick fix, a surefire ratings-builder, but the comic strip marriage for the long haul is something else altogether. A few have managed, the most obvious example being the Bumsteads, Blondie and Dagwood, but even when such a marriage does take, a cartoonist must be prepared for a thorough change of emphasis and appeal. The difference between a comic strip wedding and marriage is, well, the difference between a real wedding and marriage. One is festive and happy, while the other is uncertain, hard work, and if people are going to pay to watch, they'd rather watch the wedding, thank you very much. The humorous strips do seem to pull it off a little better, because they invite readers to laugh at themselves, but wedding bells can be the death knell of an adventure strip that must thrive on excitement and romance.

Still, Schulz does not intend to take any chances. Losing at love is one of the most traumatic and common losses of all, so it isn't surprising that unrequited love is such an important and pervasive element of *Peanuts*. It certainly is something the cartoonist feels comfortable writing about. He renders a virtuoso score of love and all its accidental notes — rejection, longing, loss, jealousy.

To Schulz, it all approaches the very essence of life.

"I hate it when people ask 'Do you ever deal in social issues, you know, like *Doonesbury*?' And I always say, 'I deal in more social issues in one month than *Doonesbury* deals in all year. I deal in issues that are much more important than drawing four pictures of the White House.' "

Unfulfilled love interests each and every one of us, Schulz contends. "You want to get somebody talking, all you have to do is stir that pot. Everyone's gone through it. I suppose a lot of it, too, has to do with how you deal with loss. Some people can get over loss very quickly; then there are people who can remember every golf match or tennis match, or any loss. They never get over it. Maybe I've been somewhat like that."

For him there was Donna, of course. Two marriages and forty years later, it hurts. He has amazing recall for details from the relatively short time he spent with her.

"I remember the dress she was wearing when a group of young adults from our church went over to her church and gave the service. We all played volleyball down in their gym afterwards. She had on a violet dress. I still remember the feeling I had just looking at her. . . .

"Having her turn me down was like losing on the eighteenth hole." To Schulz, losing is losing.

His first model for romance was the same one most of us have — that of his parents. Carl and Dena Schulz, for the most part, seemed to their son like a happy, loving couple. There were never any memorable fights, no scenes from *Bringing Up Father.*

"I did, however, sense in later years some restlessness. My mother and I started going to the movies on Sunday evenings. She was collecting the free dishes they gave away.

"I remember when my father started saying 'I can't afford it,' and Mom and I would go without him. It only cost twenty cents. It was a bad sign and a real mystery to me.

"I didn't worry about it, though; I became tied up in my own activities, and then Mom got sick and that was that."

Carl and Dena were both the offspring of immigrants and hard-scrabble farmers; Carl's parents came to America from Germany, Dena's from Norway. In fact, Carl, one of four children, was born in Germany while his parents revisited their homeland on what apparently was an extended stay. The adults weren't U.S. citizens; therefore Carl wasn't either.

"Dad became an American citizen when I was sixteen," recalls Sparky. "I helped him with his study of American history for his citizenship test." Sparky did not, however, attend Carl's naturalization ceremony, and he still regrets that. "We do so many thoughtless things when we are young."

Sparky's paternal grandparents settled and farmed in upstate New York. In their last years they had a small truck farm and raised vegetables, which they peddled to nearby towns. Sparky only vaguely remembers his grandmother Emma — "She was big, robust, very German" — and doesn't remember his grandfather, the senior Carl Schulz, at all; he made only one trip to their farm with his parents when still a toddler. Carl was able to decipher his father's letters, all written in German, but was unable to write back in the native tongue.

Dena Halverson had eight siblings and was reared in the Wisconsin countryside. Sparky never met his maternal grandfather, Tom Halverson, either, but Dena's mother Sophia, the beloved, hockey-playing grandmother, lived with the Schulz family off and on throughout Sparky's childhood. She was the only grandparent he really knew or remembers.

"She was one of those unfortunate older people who always had to depend on her children for everything. She had one daughter in Pennsylvania, children in two different places in California, and then our family in Minnesota. She'd rotate between the families and their homes. She was always lonely for the children she was not with.

"I remember going with my parents down to the train depot many, many times to put her on the train. She would be off to Pennsylvania or off to California."

Sophia Halverson routinely helped with the daily domestic chores wherever she landed, doing a share of the washing and cooking and cleaning, and, at the Schulz residence, eventually nursing her sick daughter Dena. For a while, when he was small, Sparky shared a room and a bed with his grandmother. "She snored a lot," he remembers.

So nomadic was Sophia's lifestyle as she traipsed back and forth between her scattered children, she had few material possessions and certainly never a home of her own. She did have her faith. "I remember she loved to listen to a radio program called *Slim Jim,*" says Sparky, "because it ended with a hymn."

Sophia's daughter Dena and the ambitious barber Carl met in a Minneapolis restaurant when both of them were still quite young. Dena was a waitress and Carl a regular customer. Carl ducked in each morning for a breakfast of Cream of Wheat. Always Cream of Wheat. The barber was convinced he had ulcers and soothed his mind with a few warm words from the attractive waitress and his stomach with a warm bowl of cereal.

"He had horrible stomach problems, which at one time were so bad he ate nothing but Cream of Wheat, every meal, for an entire year. Absolutely nothing else.

"She was concerned about him. It turned out he didn't have ulcers, but he always continued to like Cream of Wheat and eat a lot of it."

Carl married the kind waitress who had brought him his Cream of Wheat.

On November 26, 1922, their only child was born at home in Minneapolis. While he was an infant, the family moved to the twin city of St. Paul. One of Sparky's earliest memories is of his mother pulling him on a sled through deep snow toward the hospital to see his father. Carl had undergone surgery; Schulz is not certain but thinks it might have been an appendectomy.

Theirs was a workaday world without much room for romance. The visitors in the Schulz household were almost always relatives. Uncle Harris Halverson and family were a social fixture every Friday night, with Sparky and his cousin playing soldiers or cowboys in one room while the adults played a card game called Five Hundred in the next.

After Dena's death, Carl Schulz eventually was remarried to a sweet woman named Annabelle. Carl purposely waited, though, until his son, the twenty-eight-year-old war veteran, also got married, "because he didn't want to leave me alone," says Sparky. Father and son cleared out the old corner apartment where Dena had died and said "I do" within a few weeks of one another.

Immediately after the devastating rejection by Donna Johnson, Sparky had begun to see Joyce Halverson (no relation to the Halversons in Schulz's family), the pretty sister of a co-worker at Art Instruction Schools. The courtship was swift. They were married in April, 1951. For a few months, the two sets of newlyweds, Carl and Annabelle, Sparky and Joyce, lived in Carl's roomy, newly rented house in St. Paul. Sparky drew *Peanuts* on a card table in the basement.

Sparky's first marriage of twenty-one years and five children ended unhappily. Ex-wife Joyce was "like a surgeon," he says, "while I was more a doctor of internal medicine."

She acted. He deliberated. They divorced in 1972.

It was Joyce's idea to move from the Twin Cities, first to Colorado Springs in 1951 for a short, nervous stay and then to a sprawling horse ranch in Sebastopol, California. In Colorado Springs, Schulz felt the only serious professional doubts he has ever experienced since the sale of *Peanuts*; the comic strip was two years old, and he teetered on the shaky, solitary trapeze of creativity that can send one soaring or crashing.

"I'm surprised I survived that period, really. At first I tried working at home. But if the idea didn't come, I'd go out and cut the grass. It just wasn't working." It was not the lack of solitude that bothered the cartoonist. His oldest daughter, Meredith, was a baby, and his mother-in-law periodically lived with the young family, but those distractions were not the problem. There was simply no sense of being at work, of professional constraints that Sparky found he would forevermore need to make himself think.

"It was my mother-in-law who suggested I get an office. She was visiting with us at the time. So I rented a little room in the downtown business section of Colorado Springs. I had no telephone, no help of any kind. I even cut up the cardboard to put around my cartoons to mail them to the syndicate. Often, I went out and had lunch alone. I did a lot of reading. It was lonely."

Fortunately, the year passed, as all years do, and the Schulz family returned to the Twin Cities, to Minneapolis, and bought a home. Six years later, in 1958, they moved to California, where they settled for good. Once there, it was Joyce who oversaw various stages of improvement at a twenty-eight-acre horse ranch they whimsically named Coffee Grounds. It was on Coffee Lane in Sebastopol, famous for its apple orchards and about twenty minutes from Santa Rosa. She instigated construction of a swimming pool and tennis courts and a four-hole golf course for Sparky.

In 1966, the family compound was brushed by misfortune, when the original residence burned to the ground. Joyce, undaunted, raised a miniature golf course on the dwelling's foundation.

At the time of the fire, Schulz and Joyce were already living in a new house, and the old house had been renovated as a studio and living quarters for a secretary and for Joyce's mother. Sparky made a point to rescue the six strips he had just finished and left out on his desk; since that day he has never left finished work lying about.

The family's lifestyle on the playful estate received a lot of ink in the sixties, when Schulz and *Peanuts* began to generate tons of publicity. There were countless photographs of pony carts and children, which accurately captured the frenetic, storybook lives of the five little Schulzes, whose happiness was quietly underwritten by a prosperous father's peculiar profession.

"When I tell people now about the place where I grew up, it sounds like Disneyland or something," says daughter Amy. "Mom likes to build things."

In some ways, the years at Coffee Grounds were among

Schulz's best. Professionally, he approached and reached his peak of popularity. He wouldn't say he did his best work there, necessarily, but he did see his comic strip reach fruition, its material largess growing to what was already beyond his wildest dreams.

His children grew up around him, going through the prepubescent stage he had elevated to an art form. Not a man who adores children but rather one who identifies with them, Schulz naturally fell into a friendly, involved relationship with his own offspring.

Fathering has always been the solitary thing in Schulz's life that could make cartooning just a job in comparison. When his sons were young and knew only that they needed a catcher for a ballgame and that, hey, Dad was handy, Sparky would put down his pen and pick up a baseball mitt in the middle of the workday. It was perhaps the only way he has ever taken full advantage of the working flexibility that is one of the most rewarding aspects of being a syndicated cartoonist. He liked that the children felt free to come to him, not in the least awestruck by his importance, or what others would tell them later was their father's unparalleled "genius."

Probably no middle-aged housewife ever felt so alone in her empty nest as did Sparky when his children grew up and left home. He complains about it every so often, ruing the days his children left and dreading the one when they may not need him at all.

One day over the Pacific, years after Coffee Grounds, Sparky studied for the longest time his son Craig, who at the time was busy at the controls of the jet. Suddenly it seemed too much for Sparky to comprehend that now his son was a responsible adult — the adult responsible, in fact, for keeping the jet out of the ocean: "It upsets me the kids have to grow up and be so big," he said sadly. "Once they become adults, it's like they've died."

Not the type to coo or chuck a baby's chin, Sparky treats his grandchildren like small adults. Maybe he expects them to talk back like Linus or Charlie Brown.

Craig's young son Bryan saw his grandfather with a package of M&Ms and asked for some. He got this deadpan response: "I don't share. You know I don't share." Then Bryan got some M&Ms.

Although his life and residence now are dramatically quieter and simpler, the Coffee Grounds period was a good one, he says, conducive to both children and cartooning. "There were many good times there."

There were tribulations at Coffee Grounds as well. In 1966, Carl and Annabelle Schulz drove from Minnesota to California to pay his son a visit. On the third night of the visit, Sparky heard his stepmother crying out in alarm from the guest quarters. Carl, sixty-nine, who suffered from angina, had struggled to find his nitroglycerin tablets but died before anyone or anything could help him.

And Charles Schulz was not happy in his marriage.

"I was seventeen when they divorced," recalls Amy, "and there really never was any great trauma. Mom and Dad never spoke badly of one another, and they both remarried within a month of one another.

"It seems perfectly normal the way it is now. The only surprising thing to me is that they stayed together so long, or that they married at all. They are nothing alike."

It was Joyce who designed the fabulous ice arena and oversaw its construction. She even commissioned a photographer to visit Switzerland and shoot pastoral murals to hang on the walls encircling the rink.

If there was no external trauma, or if it was hidden from the children, there must have been internal upheaval; Schulz doesn't like to talk about his divorce and views his first marriage as something of a personal failure. He says he still feels some guilt.

"I was thinking the other day about the rings Joyce and I had when we got married. Inside was engraved the word *Forever.* It turned out it wasn't forever; it was twenty-one years."

Like many another newly divorced person, Schulz was lonely and adrift. He lived for a while in his studio that Joyce previously had decorated, sleeping on a hideaway bed, buying plastic bowls from the grocery store for his morning cereal. Starting over. Taking things a day at a time.

When he met Jeannie Forsyth, at the ice arena naturally, her gregarious nature and energy soon engulfed him, and new friendships were less of a problem than they might have been otherwise. Jeannie had a boxcar-load of friends and a full agenda.

She is a small, independent woman who looks a little like the actress Jane Wyatt, who played Margaret Anderson on *Father Knows Best.* She plays tennis, jogs, hikes, kayaks, and—to rest—rides a stationary bicycle while watching television.

Sparky and Jeannie were married in 1974. Friends say she is the ballast for the unsteady Schulz; the perfect complement, they rave. Schulz says they avoid talking politics to avoid arguments; Jeannie's views are more liberal than his own. The energetic Jeannie loves to travel and generally must do so without her husband. Yet she seems to retain her own identity, a strong one at that, and is defensive of Sparky while exceedingly careful not to take credit for his accomplishments. She has her own.

In 1987 Jeannie Schulz produced a documentary called *What a Difference a Dog Makes,* a film extolling the value of Canine Companions, an organization begun in Santa Rosa to train dogs to help the handicapped. The powerful documentary follows the two weeks of dog "boot camp," when the canines learn eighty-nine different commands, including turning on and off lights, pulling wheelchairs and punching buttons in elevators. The documentary was nominated for an Academy Award.

When Jeannie flies in the Schulz airplane, she sits up front with the pilot. She has her single-engine license but covets the additional knowledge that would let her fly the jet. Flying is not a new hobby; it runs in her family. In fact, Jeannie's mother, septuagenarian Pam Vanderlinden, has been piloting her own airplane for more than a quarter of a century.

Jeannie writes poetry, sometimes dedicating the verse to her children from her first marriage, Lisa and Brooke:

> In the bird kingdom
> A juvenile specimen may be deceiving
> While a parent
> Is always apparent.

> *—The Sharp-Eyed Observer*

Sparky's cartoons did not suffer during his divorce and the inevitable transition, he says; the change was simply more grist for the mill.

For love's befuddlements are funny. At least on paper.

"Isn't it one of the first, great, interesting things in life, this search for the perfect mate? It runs through all of literature, doesn't it? It is the backbone of all of our stories. With whom are we going to marry and live happily ever after? Nothing much is interesting once that is settled."

Thus he carefully cultivates doomed romance for almost every one of his comic strip characters. They are all smitten, sooner or later, but with few positive results.

"The romances all fail for different reasons, don't they? Schroeder obviously can't like this obnoxious, dark-haired girl with her forward ways. And the little red-haired girl probably doesn't even know Charlie Brown exists. He can't even get near her."

Schulz has never thought much about how the little red-haired girl would look drawn. "I've never even tried. She has been in the animated shows. We gave in there, but the animators drew her. I didn't. Somehow you always sell out for a cheap victory somewhere along the way."

The animated little red-haired girl was Heather the homecoming queen in *It's Your First Kiss, Charlie Brown*. Schulz broke another of his own cardinal rules and gave Charlie Brown and his fans a cheap thrill, a kiss. And simultaneously, so he couldn't possibly enjoy it, he gave Charlie Brown a stomach ache. Don't look for a repeat performance on the comic pages.

"I think it would be wrong to draw her. Once you have gone so far, you should never try to come back. People visualize her much better. They'd be disappointed if I ever drew her."

For the little red-haired girl exists in a womb of a time and a place, a warm, protected chamber that cannot be disturbed and cannot be reproduced. She doesn't really live in Charlie Brown's neighborhood, for all his mooning about after her. She lives in the past.

9 _____

"I Want to Meet Lee Remick . . ."

*I*t is a warm Santa Rosa twilight at historic Railroad Square. The best of an old part of town has been spared orchestrated demolition and even time's haphazard ravages.

This evening the street's glory repays the preservationists. Neon and night come alive to compete for predominance on this avenue lined with upscale automobiles and stylish eateries, most of them—cars and restaurants—new.

The name of the place Schulz chooses is Polka Dots, some interior decorator's salute to the 1930s, tapping that decade's rich vein of connotative value, the art deco, glass bricks, the chrome and clean line suggesting, however subliminally, simpler lives and wider spaces.

Santa Rosa's young professionals populate the place, having ordered the house chili or a specialty dessert, all to be brought around by neat waitresses in buttoned-down, Oxford-cloth shirts, waitresses who look like they do not really wait on tables for a living. The customers—tanned, toned, informed, and prone to wax metaphysical — rest their scuffed Topsiders beneath tables covered with clean butcher paper. Pens are handy in a cup on each table. Good food takes time; so does doodling.

The paper beneath Schulz's elbows is clean. Blank. Accusing. Perhaps it looks too much like the beginning of his workday.

"I can't ever think of anything to draw," he sighs.

He is serious. The man whose comic strip appears in more newspapers than any other cartoonist's, who has given the world the most celebrated chump of all times, cannot think of anything to draw.

He leaves the restaurant, its walls hung with the noble efforts of rookie artists, his own place setting a clean slate.

There is no polite way around saying this: Charlie Brown learned a lot about losing from Charles Schulz. Schulz has problems with confidence. Problems with everyday life. Problems with relationships. Schulz is a loser, of the vulnerable, lovable, Charlie Brown variety.

His life sounds like a cleaned-up Rodney Dangerfield routine. No respect.

"I remember when I used to go into my father's barbershop for a haircut. If a paying customer came in while I was in the chair, I'd have to step down and wait for my father to cut his hair. There I would sit, with half a haircut, feeling ridiculous." The significance of such a small, long-ago incident, understandable from the boy's and the father's perspective, is not so much that it happened but that Schulz remembers it. He still feels the self-conscious embarrassment of the half-shorn little boy.

No respect. Consider the evolution of that barbershop in St. Paul. Somebody who thinks of these things tried to start the ball rolling to have the barbershop listed on the National Register of Historic Places, the real-life shop of "Charlie Brown's" father. But the ball got lost in the tall weeds of bureaucracy. The Minnesota Historical Society wouldn't pursue placing Carl Schulz's shop on the National Register. The Register, said a spokesman for the organization, requires that its landmarks be associated with dead people, preferably good and dead, say fifty years.

"Fifty years allows time to put things into perspective. Someone's popularity might be more fleeting than historic." Sigh.

The site now is part of a popular watering hole called O'Gara's, a fact unsettling in its own right, since Schulz does not drink and looks somewhat askance at those who do. Computer games and pinball machines fill the tile-floored room where Sparky's hair used to fall. The original barber pole is gone; the scars of the bracket that once held it still mar the outside wall. The pole itself is up the street now, at one of those new unisex hair salons.

When Schulz was included in the Twin Cities' Walk of Fame, which was dedicated at the old Union Depot in St. Paul, he asked an old high school friend to accept the honor in his place. "When it came time for my friend to speak, he just said, simply, 'Thanks.' That was it. The end. I had expected him to prepare a little speech." The rest of the honorees were represented with more eloquent acceptance speeches. Naturally.

In 1965, the Central High School class Schulz graduated with was planning its twenty-fifth reunion in St. Paul. His name popped up on the list of people the reunion organizers did not know what happened to. By 1965 Schulz had won two of the National Cartoonists Society's prestigious Reuben awards, an Emmy for the animated special *A Charlie Brown Christmas,* and *Peanuts* had been featured on the cover of *Time* magazine. He was a millionaire several times over.

Five years ago, a smart new restaurant at Santa Rosa's Sheraton Hotel, the Round Barn Inn, refused to seat Schulz and his companions because they were not wearing the coats and ties the restaurant required. The hostess was haughtily unaware she was turning away Santa Rosa's most famous son, a man who does not own a business suit but prefers to dress with fastidious care in golf sweaters and neat slacks.

The man with a household name does have an amazingly pale

presence, almost an aura of anonymity. If you listen to him and observe him in action, you will find yourself feeling sorry for him.

Waitresses foul up his order. He asks for grilled swordfish; they bring him salmon. He asks for salmon; they are fresh out. He orders salad; they forget to serve it.

Of course, these are the things that happen to everyone, really, but his acute awareness of them has allowed him to create a make-believe fiefdom of frustration that speaks to us all.

"When I was little, I was so convinced that I had a very plain face that I was surprised when anyone recognized me," Schulz once wrote. Thus his rendering of Charlie Brown, the plainest kid on the comic strip block, with the parts no more remarkable than the whole.

Schulz is a walking American Express commercial. You know his name but not necessarily his face.

In fact, one day while shopping in a posh Hollywood men's store, Schulz handed over his American Express card, and the clerk said: "*The* Charles Schulz? The one who draws Snoopy?" She squealed and otherwise raved and Schulz acknowledged her flattery by sketching a quick Snoopy. Then the clerk matter-of-factly demanded some identification.

The children of his St. Paul neighborhood knew him as Sparky, the kid whose sandlot baseball team once lost 40—0. (Lucy once admonished Charlie Brown: "Don't let your team down by showing up.")

In the ninth grade, Sparky Schulz flunked algebra, Latin, English, and physics all at the same time, a grand slam. He was tortured by insecurity and a bad complexion. "Whatever happened to pimples?" he muses today, free to think about it now behind a stockade of years. "That doesn't seem to be the problem it once was." Maybe not to a man in his sixties.

Even now he sometimes dreams of the popular girls in his high school class, the ones he could not speak to and who, he is convinced, never knew he was alive. "I remember one girl came up excitedly to me one day and told me, a nobody, she was going to a party that Friday night. And I thought, 'Why is she telling me? I won't be going.' "

In 1950, when he sold *Peanuts* to a syndicate and it made its modest debut with only seven newspapers, Sparky and a companion went around Minneapolis, visiting each and every newsstand, hunting for newspapers with the strip in it.

"Hey, mister, you got any newspapers with *Peanuts* in it?"

"Nope, and I don't have any with popcorn in them either."

There are lots of photographs of Sparky from around this time. The syndicate took some for promotional uses. In one, a friend notes, he looks particularly handsome. "It was probably retouched," says Sparky.

Once, while attending a cartoonists' function at the posh Beverly Hills Hotel, one of the other participants noticed Sparky Schulz sitting by himself in the ritzy foyer as she went in for breakfast. After having coffee, a grapefruit half, and reading the morning newspaper, she left the hotel restaurant only to discover Sparky Schulz was still sitting in the foyer. Still alone. "Still by yourself, I see," she remarked.

"I thought if I sat here long enough I'd see somebody famous," replied Sparky.

There is something about the man that cries out for protection. And the people of his geographically intimate Santa Rosa circle—the doctors, the journalists, the clerks, the retired Midwesterners moved to California for its sun—know him and protect him with their loyalty and their silence. They keep his secrets and observe his space. His is a tight but democratic roster of friends.

It would seem a pleasant sort of fame to have, actually, not gaudy and busy like that of a sports or rock star. More like a local television weatherman's: localized, compact. His friends are fiercely devoted, not anxious to talk about him without his nodding them on.

Schulz walks the sidewalks of Santa Rosa routinely—several times a day from the studio to his ice arena, often to a nearby shopping mall, Coddingtown, that houses a favorite bookstore. He covets the exercise and seems oblivious to the constant stream of automobiles that makes every trip by foot an adventure, California style. He thinks as he walks: about his next strip, his next film, his next word. It is a preoccupation that pays.

It is spring. Early afternoon. The clematis and larkspur are sprouting with abandon in the brief median and bank lawns kept lush with sprinkler systems. Schulz talks as he walks. About places he would like to go, people he would like to meet.

"I want to meet Lee Remick, but I never will."

It is a strange statement coming from a man whose life is chock-full of celebrities who are as near as his little black book. Would Phyllis George have coffee on your patio?

The Apollo Ten astronauts borrowed the names of his creations, after all, when paving the way to the moon. Their command module was Charlie Brown. The Lunar Excursion Module was Snoopy. All America sat anxiously waiting for the historic separation of the two spacecraft on the dark side of the moon. Any blockhead ignorant of the characters—there might have been two or three at the time—became educated that day.

Schulz rode as grand marshal of the Tournament of Roses Parade, that most florid of pop spectacles. He shared a couch with Jimmy Stewart on *The Johnny Carson Show.* What could be headier, what credentials more impressive?

This is a man who has daily tributes and celebrity pop calls paid him. Nancy Reagan had her limousine drop her by his studio just so she might say hello.

Carol Channing waited in her car in the studio parking lot while her son, who wanted to be a cartoonist, asked Schulz's advice. The son, Chan Lowe, did become an editorial cartoonist.

Not to mention that Schulz was named a California Father of the Year, the same year as Ronald Reagan and Pat Boone. They obviously weren't taking just any old dads.

Rubbing elbows with the stars does not seem to allay the basic Charlie Brownness in Schulz. "I never can talk to my good friends Peggy Fleming and Billie Jean King, really. I'm so afraid I'll say something wrong, and Billie Jean King won't like me."

"He has expressed that to me," says King, who adores him. "I don't think he has any idea how very good he is at what he does. Like all artists, there will always be that insecurity."

Honors and honorary degrees fall like Oregon rain, frequently but softly, without the kind of tiresome ballyhoo that fast wearies the public of a celebrity. His is a more retiring fame, of a gentler, longer-lasting variety.

But the honors have come so often and for so long that one might suspect the self-deprecation is calculated. When he talks about his failures—with women, with work, with life—is his insecurity being worked overtime, fighting pretension and immodesty, purposely keeping him in a Charlie Brown frame of mind? It is no act. It is the way he feels, and any sophomore psychologist can tell us that innermost attitudes need have nothing to do with reality.

We are at age thirty, at forty, at sixty the same person, essentially, we were at ten years old. Inside us, for better or worse, is the same core being who first stepped off the school bus or raced down the street after the ice cream man. As shy, as bold, as confident, as wary. As honest or as mean. However we are molded by the time we are three years old is about it, the social scientists say; our hearts and souls don't grow larger and lower like waistlines and voices. The gist of our personality is there, and only the shell that protects it changes much afterward.

The amazing thing about school reunions, for instance, is not how much everyone has changed; the amazing thing is how much the same everyone remains. The take-charge types from high school organize the reunion to begin with, don't they? And let's face it: the beauty queens still look good and know it; the eggheads may have more to show for their studious introspection, but they remain just as uninteresting to the popular crowd as ever.

The difference between sixteen and sixty is most of us eventually become comfortable with ourselves, hang the rest of the Class of 1940. Most of us.

"One day I was behind the desk at the Art Instruction Schools. It had been a long time since I had had any dates of any kind with anybody, and I was very lonely. This pretty young girl would come up every day with some letters to be signed. I was only about twenty-six at the time.

"I watched her walking around the room, day after day. Finally, I worked up my nerve and said 'Would you be interested in going out for dinner and a movie?,' and she said 'Aren't you kind of old for me?' Boy oh boy, it would have been better if she had just reached over and punched me in the nose."

Things have not improved much.

In 1988, a seventeen-year-old South Carolina student interviewed him for her school newspaper. "How old are you?" she asked.

"Sixty-five."

"Wow!"

He expects the worst. He has to leave the room for something. He comes back. "You're still here!" he says excitedly to a female reporter interviewing him. "Often when I come back, the woman is gone." Now, surely Charles Schulz doesn't have a real problem with female visitors literally ducking out on him at the first opportunity, but he seems to think he does. Is he joking? Of course he is. Sort of. But not really. It all gets jumbled up, somehow, in an emotional Big Bang that produces the world's most famous comic strip.

There is the loser's mantle to be worn. He worries about his universal fraternity, those people, as songwriter Janis Ian wrote, "whose names are never called, when picking sides for basketball."

"I was lurking around his studio one day, and he invited me to sit in on a business meeting," remembers cartoonist Lynn Johnston. "It involved people from Determined Productions (one of the first *Peanuts* licensees) who all sat there and conducted their business very matter-of-factly, very much to the point. Then they got all fired up about a costume contest they had envisioned for the schools, with children designing the clothes for stuffed Snoopys. The idea was the children would buy a Snoopy, make the clothes, and then take the doll to a shopping mall or some other place where the dolls could be judged, and the best costume would win. Then the local winners would compete, and the national winners would get to go to the Smithsonian, where the winning dolls would be on display.

"All the time this talk was going on about winners, winners, winners, Sparky sat, looking at the floor. Suddenly he said 'What about the losers?' "

There is, too, the irritating matter of the hole in one. While he shoots a respectable golf game, he has never shot a hole in one. "I came close to one when I first took up the game and then never came close again for years. Wouldn't you think the golfing gods would grant me one after fifty years?"

No hole in one? Perhaps he is a little whiny. Certainly, these are Texas League catastrophes in a major league world of war and famine and disease. They are merely sand in the suntan oil of life. Yet they are incalculably important to the work of Schulz, who has based his strip on the constant curves, the little insults life hurls at us. If his own existence was too perfect, too appreciated, too high-and-mighty, if he did not have a propensity for losing at the little things, *Peanuts* might not have lasted. It might not even have been born.

Not to worry. Schulz will never forget his loser's roots and become a self-confident, suave winner. No matter how successful the comic strip, life will continue to pull away his football. It is the way of things.

"I really never make appearances in classrooms, because I don't feel that I am especially good at that sort of thing. And I've always had the theory that cartoonists shouldn't venture out in public too much, talking. They should stay at home and sit behind the drawing board, drawing. But recently I relented as a special favor to a close friend and found myself in front of a kindergarten class. The teacher asked me to draw a Snoopy on the chalkboard.

"Now all my life I've always liked to draw on the chalkboard— you had to stand up there in front of the class and make a fool out of yourself doing geometry on it, but you never got to draw. This was my chance to draw on a beautiful, big, green chalkboard. So I drew one of my great Snoopys, turned around and said 'Well, what do you think?' One little kid stood up and said, 'Can't you draw a better one than that?' "

10

Voyage of the Beagle

*E*verybody knows the cast of *Peanuts* is made up of children and other beasts.

Children and their activities have been the relentless vehicles of Schulz's creativity since he returned from World War II to begin his career as a paid cartoonist. It was to be a career that would include remarkably little wasted time or motion, for *Peanuts* is the product of an unfaltering evolutionary process that practically began when Schulz did.

The first gag cartoon he sold to *The Saturday Evening Post* in 1948 featured a solitary little boy, and the succeeding sales typically featured a visual joke with no dialogue (a "sight gag," in cartooning parlance) that involved the activities of small children. Indeed, cartoon pantomimes of youngsters engaged in absurd sporting pursuits were the hallmark of Schulz's *Saturday Evening Post* period. The whimsical drawing of two small boys in hockey paraphernalia facing off on the frozen surface of a birdbath certainly presaged a ton.

Within these early cartoons was the basis, both technical and philosophical, for much of what was to follow over the next forty years. When *Peanuts* first began to get national attention in the mid-fifties, a lot was made of its "sophistication," its intelligent conversation and passive introspection, yet Charles Schulz adheres religiously to the definition of a cartoonist as "someone who draws funny pictures." He will argue that the drawing within a comic strip is more important than the writing. It is, he insists, what makes a cartoonist a cartoonist. If Schulz feels *Peanuts* is getting too wordy, or if he is having trouble writing a good joke, or if it just hasn't been up to standard of late, he will deliberately return to slapstick, depicting a visual absurdity that's simply fun to look at. Simply fun to look at. That is the common denominator of all successful comic strips, believes Charles Schulz—and that includes one so sophisticated as his own.

Schulz can feel justified in his opinion. He caught their attention with his subtle, spoken witticisms, but he made them stand up and cheer when Snoopy flew his doghouse into the wild blue yonder in search of the Red Baron.

This fealty to his visual medium was evident in Schulz's early magazine gags. Also apparent was his knack for exaggeration, his appreciation of outlandish humor for its own sake. This grasp of burlesque was to be a critical facet of the cartoonist's future success, but it sometimes has been underrated by fans in their desire to give Schulz his due for the intellectual appeal of *Peanuts*. However, it freely characterized his formative work; absent were the intimate repartee and analytical black humor that would be so important later.

The Saturday Evening Post was the only major magazine Schulz managed to crack in the late forties, but those sales undoubtedly added much pizzazz to the young Minnesotan's portfolio, giving him entree to the newspaper syndicates in Chicago and New York and the confidence to exploit it. But possibly the most important step had already been taken right there in St. Paul.

Li'l Folks was a cartoon feature developed in 1947 by Schulz for his hometown newspaper, *The St. Paul Pioneer Press*. Practically, it was *Peanuts.* Running every Sunday in the women's section, an installment of *Li'l Folks* consisted of three or four single-panel cartoons, all featuring children. There was the original Patty; there was a young piano student who concentrated on Beethoven; there was a dog identical to the first version of Snoopy. There was even a boy named Charlie Brown.

There were words in *Li'l Folks,* quite a few of them, although because of the single-panel format there was none of the give-and-take dialogue that Schulz considers so important to *Peanuts.* There was some of the spark that would eventually distinguish the strip (a near-Charlie Brown, with his arm around a near-Snoopy, tells a near-Patty: "My buddy and I like to think of ourselves as being successful products of this new postwar world!"). There was also something skewed about Schulz's little folks; they were sometimes capable of being keenly sarcastic and even downright cynical.

But many of the gags were conventional. The tiny musician, forerunner of Schroeder, resented practicing and wasn't very good. Childish mischief was common, giving the feature an adult perspective although the players were all children. Baseball was a game, not a metaphor for life.

Success breeds success, but not always directly. After doing the feature for almost two years, Schulz asked the editor of the *Pioneer Press* for daily exposure in a better spot in the paper and more than the initial ten dollars per week that he was still receiving. The editor said no, and a wounded young cartoonist tendered his resignation. To Schulz's chagrin and amazement, it was readily accepted.

So Schulz's major avenue of cartoon creativity had been closed. His space in *The St. Paul Pioneer Press* was gone, and his market for almost 200 cartoons yearly had collapsed to a handful of magazine sales. However, because of *Li'l Folks,* Schulz's talent progressed, enabling him to make that first *Post* sale. He also had been showing *Li'l Folks* around the newspaper syndicate offices, where he had received mild encouragement. Despite a cosmic interruption of his little industry, the planets were already in fortuitous line.

The next year a major syndicate bought *Li'l Folks.* Although a name change would be needed and a strip format was decided upon, it was the weekly feature from the St. Paul daily newspaper that Schulz sold to United Feature Syndicate.

The decision to make *Li'l Folks* a strip probably was one of the most monumental in the history of the comic strip trade. It was made rather casually the morning Schulz sold the feature. His sample portfolio consisted of several *Li'l Folks* panels and some unpublished strips Schulz had been experimenting with. The syndicate officers liked the strips, partly because they perceived a glut of panels on the market at that time. Everyone, including Schulz, agreed the four-panel strip format had more potential. They weren't wrong. Regardless of the commercial success it might have attained, it is hard to argue seriously that *Peanuts* could have approached its present scope as a one-panel cartoon.

If Schulz didn't recognize this in 1950, he did soon. In a 1974 essay he wrote:

> One of the most delightful aspects of life is conversation. Talking with a new friend, discovering new ideas and learning about each other can be one of the great experiences of life.
>
> Good writers know this and make use of it in other media. I have been trying to introduce this into the *Peanuts* strip for the past several years, because I feel it is an area that has not been well cultivated.

If the name of the new strip wasn't the most monumental decision in comics history, it certainly has been one of the most talked-about. Charles M. Schulz's distaste for the title *Peanuts* is well documented. He didn't like it when it was suggested, and he doesn't like it now. However, his latter-day objections aren't rooted so much in genuine disappointment with the seven-letter word as in the loss of control, the personal defeat it represents.

The name had no appeal to Schulz in 1950; it seemed frivolous and unrelated. It came out of an informal committee in New York with little input from Schulz (who was also at a loss for a decent title). But there is nothing so helpless as a young artist at the mercies of those with the power and the money. The syndicate decided to go with *Peanuts,* and though the incident never deteriorated to the point it had to be spelled out, Schulz knew he had two choices, accept such decisions or walk—and for Sparky Schulz the latter was really no choice at all.

Actually, *Peanuts* is an excellent name. It doesn't highlight any one player in a strip whose strength is a large, well-defined cast. As intended, it does convey an impression of physical diminutiveness but in an imaginative, esoteric sort of way, not in pedestrian fashion like, well, *Li'l Folks.* True, for the first ten or fifteen years, it was not unusual to hear a casual reader refer to Charlie Brown as "Peanut," but the title and Schulz's good work eventually married. Mention *Peanuts* today and most people will think of a comic strip, not a leguminous herb.

Forty years later, it is impossible to imagine how the strip could have been any more successful with another title, but Schulz continues gently to grouse about it. He still seems to find it hard to believe someone else was allowed to name *his* comic strip, and he was powerless to prevent it.

That's the real rub. It certainly wouldn't happen today. As already mentioned, Schulz earned an early reputation around the syndicate as a reasonable, adaptable young artist. This reputation arose, however, not from a pliable personality but from a calculated willingness to swallow whatever was necessary to reach his goal.

The oft-told episode is more than an anecdote; it is an insight into the tenacity, the competitiveness, and the attention to detail that have gotten him where he is. He simply does not like to lose. And Charles Schulz does not forget.

Countless grains of sand are similarly festering within the cartoonist's shell, and eventually the world will be favored with a pearl.

But *Peanuts* it was to be, and the strip got started with four children and a dog.

The inexorable progression of Schulz's art and career continued with the debut in the fall of 1950. The comic strip picked up where *Li'l Folks* left off. There were more of the sight gags, there were gags about sports, and there was the same smart-aleck banter among the players.

Furthermore, there was an established cast. While its physical resemblance to the *Li'l Folks* players was close, the repertory brought a continuity and a familiarity that would have been difficult to achieve within the abandoned format. With characters, meticulous character development could begin. Also, the strip format gave the new characters room to roam, to converse, and it allowed nuance. Solid characterizations and complex, subtle wit would become the heart and soul of the strip's immense appeal.

As it began to gain attention, *Peanuts* became known as the comic strip starring kids only, the comic strip without adults.

To say *Peanuts* is about children is to say *Huckleberry Finn* is about boating. There is an essence of human truth in *Peanuts* that is the core of its appeal, but the characters, especially the original troupe, are not very realistic children. To the kids in the strip, childhood is more like a profession than a stage of development. Instead of gathering at the coffee machine to wax philosophical, they congregate at the pitcher's mound. Charlie Brown no longer enjoys his kite but feels obligated to fly on, in the face of certain humiliation and hopelessness. Many readers must have jobs like that. The kids (Schulz often refers to them as "the kids") are articulate and literate. They have a capacity for reflection and abstraction far beyond most children—or most adults, for that matter.

Yet an even bigger mistake (and one that often gets made) is to think of the *Peanuts* kids as "little adults." Schulz certainly doesn't think of them that way. They have the naivety and charm of children. Charles Schulz's creations are innocent as lambs. They do not even have the carnal awareness of children, much less adults. They exhibit not so much a maturity beyond their years as an intelligence. They are beings with the ability to turn the cognitive power of adults on the problems of kids, and, lo! we discover, or remember, that those problems are as real as any.

This all gives *Peanuts* a marvelous versatility that allows Schulz creative latitude. Each character is capable of reaching great depth but is free to float at any level therein, as the situation demands.

The confused chronology of *Peanuts* is a reflection of the cartoonist himself. He is capable of sitting at his drawing board and recalling, in all earnest, a disappointment experienced in high school; not just remembering it, but feeling it. His own emotional jurisdiction is immense. For him personally, there are no significant boundaries between adulthood and childhood, not in terms of what's just, what thrills, and what hurts. Especially what hurts. The man who has built a comic empire around the skeleton of his own life is not a man to look back and laugh.

After forty years *Peanuts* is as devoid of adults as ever, but the impression has faded; it is a testament to the integrity of Schulz's creation that people now tend to think of "the world of *Peanuts*," a domain complete unto itself where nothing is obviously missing.

In the early strips, the children's mothers had voices; Linus's teacher was a significant, offstage player with a name, Miss Othmar; parents were routinely referred to and addressed, giving them a tangible, hovering presence. As *Peanuts* evolved, however, adults were given less practical purpose, and more and more their doings became hearsay and allegory.

For some reason, the most family interaction has always seemed to occur in the Van Pelt household. If a gag involves the presence of a parent, Linus and Lucy often get the call, perhaps because Linus is in such obvious need of outside intervention to protect him from his crabby sister. The introduction of their infant brother Rerun in 1972 was certainly a reminder that the adults are out there somewhere doing something. He wasn't the first infant sibling born into the cast, but he has been the only one to come along since the comic strip reached full flower.

Poor Rerun. There's not much left in *Peanuts* for an infant. Even his name is a foreboding of his precarious status in the strip. His close physical resemblance to his brother Linus doesn't help. Rerun's main assignment is to sit terrified on the back of his mother's bicycle, giving her one of the modern strip's few concrete adult roles. Another one, of course, would be Marcie's and Peppermint Patty's teacher. Her name, Miss Tenure, is seldom used.

There have been countless cameo mentions of adult celebrities, almost always sports figures or artists admired by Schulz. They're too numerous to list, but recurring names include Billie Jean King,

Bill Mauldin, and Peggy Fleming. And, of course, there is Charlie Brown's hero, the mediocre and fictitious minor leaguer Joe Shlabotnik.

Charlie Brown and his sister Sally don't seem to be as closely supervised as their neighbors the Van Pelts. In fact, there is something almost sad and orphanlike in the independence of the Brown children. Yet probably the most important adult character in *Peanuts* is their father the barber.

Charlie Brown's dad is an imaginative blend of Schulz's own father and himself. He appears almost exclusively through Charlie Brown's soliloquies. Charlie Brown will relate something his father told him that is invariably an unvarnished memory or emotion of Schulz himself ("Well, years ago my dad owned a black, 1934, two-door sedan"). Such strips are often very real and very poignant.

In recent years, stories have sometimes been attributed by Charlie Brown to his "grandfather." It is still Schulz talking, but his experiences and reflections have a generational quality that nowadays would be more suited to a man older than Charlie Brown's father. It is one of the very few accommodations to the passage of time within *Peanuts.*

Charlie Brown always speaks of his father with respect and understanding. He is portrayed as a simple, hardworking, gentle sage, as Schulz remembers his father.

Of course, none of these adults is actually drawn in the strip.

If the bust of Ludwig van Beethoven is discounted, *Peanuts* has been violated by the depiction of adults only one time. They were spectators at a golf tournament in which Lucy was playing. It was one of the earlier Sunday strips.

"I don't know why I did that. I regret it," says Schulz.

11

Blessed Assurance

In one of Sparky's *Li'l Folks* cartoons, a boy and a girl are standing almost back to back. Unbeknownst to the boy, his empty mitten, draping from his coat sleeve on a long string, has somehow found its way over her shoulder and is resting on the breast of her coat. Indignant, she admonishes him: "Please!" It is as dirty as Charles Schulz gets. When he was a teenage cartoonist, Schulz's own mother helpfully suggested, "Maybe your cartoons aren't smutty enough."

Charles Schulz does not worry about being considered a prude. Instead, he casually admits it: "I suppose in a way I am." Every newspaper or magazine story written about the man has dutifully, sometimes incredulously, noted he does not drink, smoke, or curse.

It does not help that he looks a little like an Episcopal priest, erect and studious and measured. He appears, at sixty-six, fit as a man of thirty-five, managing to walk several miles daily without scuffing his white tennis shoes.

United Feature Syndicate loves the squeaky-clean image, of course, since many strip cartoonists are kept inside the bounds of Family Newspaper Decency only at metaphorical gunpoint. The syndicate, which feels a certain responsibility to traditional newspaper priggishness, never finds anything objectionable in *Peanuts.* No sexual innuendo. No cheap visual shots. No doggie humor.

It's for sure Schulz has never been a syndicate problem child. As he rigorously edits his own life, so he polices his comic strip. His standards also limit all licensing products to articles of unquestionable propriety. Same goes for the animated shows, as he carefully deletes any twinge of offensive language or behavior and outlaws alcohol or tobacco sponsors. Unseemly associations are studiously avoided, from greeting cards with messages that might be construed as double entendre to breakfast cereals with too much sugar.

Vulgar is simply not in his vocabulary. You're a good man, Charlie Brown, and a conscientious staff, obsessed with quality control, is dedicated to keeping you that way.

He steadfastly sticks to his G-rated formula despite the changing mores on the comic pages. The younger comic strip revolutionaries may put editors on the spot with four-letter words, but Schulz never will. He would rather strive to draw a funny baseball glove than reap the shock value of a toilet bowl. He is proud that, in drawing strips about a dog for forty years, he has never connected him with a fire hydrant. Earthiness is simply not one of the ingredients of the Schulz humor.

Art copies life. When Snoopy quaffs a root beer instead of the real stuff, it is no accident. Schulz is a lifelong teetotaler. Once, at a party, a well-meaning woman cornered him to say how she once had the privilege to meet his drinking buddy, a man who claimed he "helped" Schulz home after a memorable bout with the bottle. The incident never happened, but celebrities get used to finding "friends" in the strangest places, and faces.

To his real friends who knew Sparky Schulz B.P. (Before *Peanuts*), his abstinence was a fact of life. Charlie Brown, his friend from Art Instruction Schools, the person for whom the comic strip character was named, noted years later that he and other buddies would share a secret laugh when they visited Sparky's second-floor apartment in St. Paul. They were well aware of their friend's predilections, and they couldn't escape the irony of the flashing neon whiskey bottle outside his window, a sign for a liquor store on the street below.

"Sparky was as temperate as a man could be," wrote Charlie Brown. "I often wondered how he could sleep with the huge neon liquor bottle nightly flashing on and off; it might have sent me to the nearest bar."

Even now, Schulz sometimes queries new friends about their drinking habits and explains to them why he abstains.

"I can't see doing something that's going to make you feel bad later," and "You can get into habits very easily. You can, for instance, acquire the habit of having an English muffin at the same time every morning. We are creatures of habit. I never wanted to be in the habit of having to have a drink." In this area, too, he is guided by fear. His compulsive personality, he reasons, might lend itself to destructive drinking habits.

Schulz is proud his own children do not drink or smoke, though he swears the choice was entirely theirs.

"It's true," says daughter Amy. "He never told us not to drink or smoke, but none of us do. I really don't know why. We all have our reasons. I guess it was the example."

Likewise, Schulz never badgered his offspring about attending Sunday school or church; they made their own choices. "I never pushed them toward anything like that," he says. He was not the disciplinarian, anyway; their mother was. Whatever happened, Amy says, you got his support. His advice "you had to beg for."

Sparky did not inherit his rigid code that prohibits drinking. His parents indulged in an occasional beer and had no hard-and-fast rules about alcohol. They did not attend church regularly, either, "because my father liked to fish on Sunday morning."

When the *Peanuts* characters discuss scripture, the thought balloons are not filled with verses Schulz has randomly plucked while browsing through some stiff Bible in search of his next cartoon gag. He has led Bible classes through the Book four times, word by word. And his Bible is filled with underlining, some of which, he admits, seems to have no earth-shattering significance upon rereading. He actually thinks about these sorts of things; ponders them in his heart, as the Good Book might say.

"How did Jesus know all the things he did? That's what fascinates me, that he was so young. How did he come up with those amazing little stories, those parables?"

This bright Santa Rosa morning Schulz is humming "Blessed Assurance" as he stalks his office looking for a mailing tube. His mental needle is stuck on the old hymn because he has been remembering a scene from *The Trip to Bountiful,* his favorite movie from the last decade. One of his children gave Schulz a video copy of it for Christmas.

In that poignant film, the actress Geraldine Page joyfully begins an odyssey to her home, Bountiful, Texas, running away from a harping, dingbat daughter-in-law who will not permit the old woman to sing hymns around the house and who routinely duns the poor creature of her Social Security check. As Page's character sits in a Greyhound bus station, free at last, she punches out the words to "Blessed Assurance" like a battle anthem. Sung that way it is, indeed, a hymn of personal redemption.

Schulz sings the hymn with gusto. A less sincere man would seem silly, in his pastel golf sweater, cruising a modern office with jangling telephones, singing the old songs of an Indiana camp meeting. It fits, somehow.

"That scene got to me. 'Blessed Assurance.' I sat there in the theater, and emotion came over me. I started trembling. It was everything I could do to keep from breaking down. But all those old hymns do that to me.

"One of the great memories of my life is standing next to my friend Harold Ramsberger in camp meeting singing 'Blessed Assurance.' He died of cancer at about the age of forty-seven or so. I miss him so much. I always think of Harold with 'Blessed Assurance.' "

Schulz tends to spontaneous, heartfelt little soliloquies, often at the oddest moments, sometimes on subjects not being discussed. "Aren't you astounded by the creativity of dreams?" he will say. A verbal essay—and beautifully coherent—about the creativity of dreams follows.

But of all the aspects of the Schulz personality, none is more compelling than his spiritual side. He is religious but never pious. Faith is private. He is reticent about discussing religion for publication. Too often he is misquoted, misunderstood. The necessary qualifiers always get lost in translation.

"Sometimes I feel almost like the Jews, where God became so holy you couldn't speak His name."

Yet he has managed to let his cartoon characters quote the scriptures extensively and debate theology, all within the bounds of four panels and good taste, never demeaning any denomination or, equally important, suggesting one. Among the many firsts to his cartooning credit, his meaningful yet playful employment of religion would have to be near the top of the list. He has found a way to make religion funny without mocking it, exploring and reflecting Christian values with a serene unobtrusiveness.

"I'm proud of the fact that I always treat such things with dignity. I would never cheapen the scriptures for a laugh."

So prevalent are religious references in the strip that, in 1964, an ambitious Methodist seminary student, Robert L. Short, wrote a slim book called *The Gospel According to Peanuts,* illustrating it with what he deemed appropriate strips, pointing out the possibility that, as he put it, Charlie Brown "might just be a twentieth-century Everyman wearing a T-shirt of thorns, Lucy a crabby symbol of Original Sin, Schroeder a victim of Idolatry, and Snoopy a little Christ who afflicts the comfortable and comforts the afflicted."

The book actually evolved from slide shows Short used while working his way through Perkins School of Theology in Dallas, Texas. He was, at the time, thirty-one years old, charmed by both *Peanuts* and *Pogo* and the ethical verities of both strips. His professors frequently used the strips in class, and Short began reading them "religiously."

"I sent the manuscript for my slide presentation to several publishers, but the form was all wrong. It didn't read like a book," says Short.

Then Short published an article about theology in *Peanuts* for *Motive* magazine, the organ of the Methodist student movement. John Knox Press then bought book rights, based on the article and the slide presentations, and *Gospel* immediately took off.

The book was number one on the nonfiction bestseller list for 1965, not really surprising Short, who was all the while confident "I had the first of its kind."

The author is now living in Wilmette, Illinois, and studying to become a Presbyterian minister. Over the years he has published four other books, including *The Parables of Peanuts* in 1968, none of which was the commercial success of *Gospel,* for which he still regularly receives royalties.

Schulz credits the book with spreading the word, if not about religion, certainly about the comic strip. He considers its publication among the top four events that over the forty years of the strip's life did the most to bolster *Peanuts* sales. The other three were a *Time* magazine cover in 1965, the musical play *You're a Good Man, Charlie Brown* opening off-Broadway in 1967, and Snoopy and Charlie Brown going to the moon in 1969.

"Sparky used his strip, when it first began, to illustrate major themes of Christian teaching but in a subtle way," says Short. "It's much more apparent and direct now. He can say it up front. Early on, the subtlety was necessary. The syndicate was hesitant, nervous, about having a comic strip quote scripture.

"So he was forced to approach it in a symbolic way."

Schulz, however, disagrees with his friend Bob Short about that point, at least. "I think I'm a lot more subtle now than I was at first. For instance, there was an early cartoon of Linus building an elaborate sand castle. Then the rain comes, slowly at first, gradually more and more, and finally Linus's castle is washed away and he says 'There's a lesson to be learned here somewhere. But I don't know what it is.'

"I would never draw that strip now. It's a little too obvious or sweet or something."

Indeed, *Gospel* was not a collaboration. Schulz allowed use of the comic strip but kept his distance from the book's theology. The policy came in handy as the book inevitably drew fire. It was once described by another author as "a bilious homily on sin" that undid the fine job the strip had done in making the scripture palatable. Schulz joked that he wanted to be able to shirk the criticism and bask in the praise, something he apparently accomplished.

Dena and Carl Schulz, 1920

Young Sparky

Sophia Halverson. Sparky's maternal grandmother...and first goalie

Sparky and Spike, a pointer not a beagle, but an inspiration nonetheless

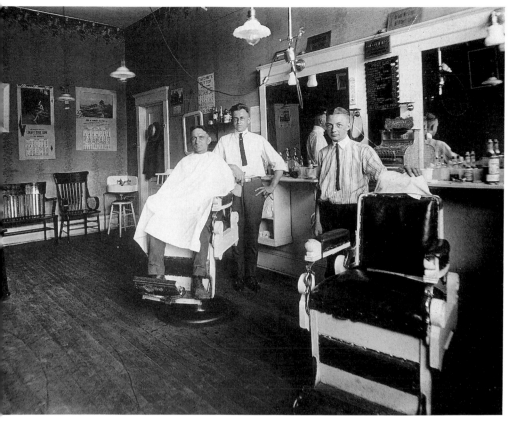

Carl (in white shirt) in his barbershop. Monroe Halverson stands behind the second chair

The apartment over the barbershop—Sparky's bedroom window is at the top right

The Schulz family—Sparky, Dena, and Carl

Sparky and his little red-haired girl, Donna Johnson (April, 1950)

Feeding Spike

*Army buddies Elmer Hagemeyer, Jim
Calvin (a friend from another company),
and Schulz*

The Bureaucats—Art Instruction's women's softball team; Charles Schulz, coach. Donna Johnson is in the front row, third from left

The Art Insruction School before the day's rendition of Aida's Grand March

An early publicity still

St. Paul's Walk of Fame

Sparky and his friend, Charlie Brown

Three generations—Sparky, Monte, and Carl

Sports are central to Schulz's life

Outside the studio at One Snoopy Place

The Redwood Empire Ice Arena

Jeannie Schulz

A hockey game at the arena

Skating with cartoonist Cathy Guisewite (creator, Cathy)

In the studio

"His name is Andy and I can't remember ever having a dog I was so fond of. I'm afraid, however, that he only likes me because I give him cookies."—CMS

"I tell Bob the only theology is no theology."

Whatever their differences, the two men genuinely liked one another from the very beginning. Today they are close friends.

The first day they met face to face, they appeared on a San Francisco television show together to "debate" the author's observations. Short "explained" five cartoons in the presence of the man who had conceived them.

"When I got to the fifth strip, Sparky disagreed with my conclusions. I was obviously reading into that one strip what he did not intend. But, then, I think I made some points he had not considered before, too."

Were all Short's observations valid?

"No," Schulz says, shaking his head and laughing. But the book kept people talking about *Peanuts* and exploring theological ideas. The effort certainly was valid. And the book sold 150,000 copies the first year.

"At first some people were scandalized by the whole idea of my book," says Short. "They felt it was nothing short of blasphemous, even the title. But one of the things I wanted to do was break down the compartmentalized approach we have to things sacred. So I put the gospel cheek to jowl with the newspaper, with the comic pages yet. I blended Christianity and real life."

At the time it was a true and radical departure for the comic strip medium, where *Blondie* creator Chic Young used to advise young artists to avoid liquor, cigarettes, divorce, infirmities of the body, racial subjects, snakes, and—of course—religion.

Other cartoonists have, since Schulz shattered the taboo, delved into the forbidden realm. The somewhat fusty *Family Circus* takes a now-I-lay-me-down-to-sleep approach to things sacred. Dead grandparents routinely take the stage in the form of ghosts, Disney-like holograms that watch over the kneeling children and bring the concept of Heaven heavy-handedly to the comic pages.

Largely with the rebel priest Scott Sloan, *Doonesbury* has tackled religion with its customary irreverence, once using one of Schulz's favorite vehicles—the Christmas pageant, where "the part of baby Jesus is played by a sixty-watt bulb."

Schulz walks the fence between pap and put-down. He gets

away with a beagle quoting the Bible or Linus sharing copies of the Dead Sea Scrolls at "Show and Tell." Religion simply exists in the lives of the characters, not an icon to be walked around or a delusion to be punctured. No syrup, no sacrilege.

When Peppermint Patty thinks she is a prophet because a butterfly lands on her nose and then flys away—an angel, according to Marcie—we are treated to a lesson about miracles and our own unwillingness to accept them in a jaded world. Or is it a lesson about self-deception and phony prophecy? We never really know until someone like Robert Short comes along and explains it to us.

We just thought it was a funny story. That's what Charles Schulz thought, too.

And when querulous Lucy ignores Linus's plodding, determined theology—"The Bible contains 3,566,480 letters and 773,893 words"—we laugh, because we all know someone who substitutes biblical trivia for deep, religious faith without realizing the difference.

Yet Schulz hates a "preachy" strip and resists firmly, sometimes irritably, when, for instance, well-meaning promoters want Peppermint Patty to stop falling asleep and concentrate in school.

"I'm fed up with the people who want to take what you have and then use it to educate others," Schulz says. "They are always wanting to take my strip and use it for something else. 'Couldn't Peppermint Patty be put to better use,' they say, 'by having her study hard and make good grades? And then that would inspire other children.' That's so dumb! What's funny about that? The idea of a comic strip is to be funny and to sell newspapers. They always want to educate, to tell others something. I'm not interested in telling them things. I'm interested in being funny. This business of trying to sway other people over to your way of thinking doesn't interest me at all."

The comic strip, he insists, is not a message medium.

He has serious doubts that causes—hunger, homelessness, and so on—should ever be the assigned subject of a cartoonist. Recently, other cartoonists have coordinated well-meaning projects, where all comic strip artists were invited to address a specific problem on a specific day. The first and most notable of these efforts was Garry

Trudeau's 1985 invitation to other cartoonists to use their space on Thanksgiving Day to address the epidemic of world hunger. Most did, and the effort received much publicity. Trudeau even invited Schulz and Milton Caniff to join him as chairmen of the effort, and both men accepted. But Schulz thinks it was a terrible idea.

Besides experiencing a certain creative resentment of another cartoonist telling him how to fill his panels on a given day, Schulz believes the comics exist to be funny. Cartoonists participating in the hunger project were instructed to be funny, but it was not their primary function that day. When a cartoonist starts to subjugate his humor, he has lost sight of his goal and is in danger of failing. Schulz feels so strongly about this that he doesn't consider it permissible once in a while, not even for a good cause.

Besides, he thinks it is a bad precedent, for there are many good causes out there. And some bad ones. What does the cartoonist tell the next organizer? Since the first hunger project there has been a second day of hunger cartoons, a day devoted to the homeless, and an appeal for cartoonists to help drum up support for the renovation of the Statue of Liberty.

If Schulz avoids high dudgeon when dealing with comic strip religion, it is because he cannot abide dogmatism in real life.

"I hear you're writing a book on theology," Charlie Brown says to Snoopy, who is sitting atop his doghouse pounding his typewriter.

"I have the perfect title," muses Snoopy. *"Has It Ever Occurred to You That You Might Be Wrong?"*

Schulz is put off by piety and autocratic theology in its many forms. And, he says, "I don't believe in religions that preach 'This is the end of the world.' I feel strongly about 'last days' preaching."

He is now proud—"relieved" might be the better word—that he turned down an invitation to appear on Pat Robertson's 700 Club. Beyond the "last days" preaching, he deplores the persistent solicitation methods of the televangelists.

"I saw Jerry Falwell advertising a Bible one night, saying, 'This Bible has my name, Jerry Falwell, right on the cover.' And I thought to myself: 'Wait. Why is Falwell's name on the cover? Is he the author?' "

If, in forty years of drawing *Peanuts,* Schulz has taken a stand on anything topical, it has been to attack the self-righteous, money-grubbing megaministries of fundamentalist media evangelists.

"This program needs your support," Linus is told in a 1985 strip as he sprawls in his beanbag, watching TV. "We need your donations. If we don't hear from you, we'll have to go off the air."

"So long!" answers Linus.

Sally faces the same situation in a 1988 strip:

"Send you money? I don't have any money! I'm just a little kid! Where would I get money? Tell you what I'll do . . . After I finish college and get a job, I'll try to send you a little, okay?" She listens to the television for one panel and finally implores: "STOP ASKING ME!!"

In an odd 1980 sequence, the *Peanuts* kids attend a fundamentalist religious camp, where, among other events, Linus causes an uproar by daring to attempt discussion of religion with a camp instructor.

The main plot, however, revolves around Peppermint Patty's alarm over an end-of-the-world sermon. The other players seem to absorb it with a grain of salt, but Peppermint Patty can't get it out of her head. It worries her. It scares her.

"He said it again," Peppermint Patty says to her bunkmate Marcie. "You heard him! He said we're in the last days! He stood right in front of all of us tonight and said the world is coming to an end! Aren't you scared, Marcie? Doesn't that bother you? Aren't you terrified?!" Marcie is asleep.

But Peppermint Patty can't sleep. She goes to the camp office to call her dad:

"Yes, ma'am, I'd like to use the telephone. My dad hasn't heard about the end of the world." In the office, Marcie draws her troubled friend's attention to something on the wall.

"Look at this, sir. It's a drawing of the new camp they're trying to raise money for. It should be beautiful. They're asking everyone to help raise eight million dollars." Peppermint Patty's hair flies up and the light of comprehension dawns in her ink-dot eyes.

"Forget the phone, ma'am! Maybe the world will end tomorrow, but I wasn't born yesterday!"

"I am very fearful," Schulz was quoted as saying in 1968, "of a church which equates itself with Americanism. This is a frightening trend: people who regard Christianity and Americanism as being virtually the same thing."

Despite the strip's compatibility with religion, Schulz does not parade his own. Once, absorbed in an ice hockey game, Schulz was approached by a man who asked his favorite Bible verse.

"I don't really know," Schulz said, taken aback. "I don't know that I have a favorite."

Then, not wanting to disappoint, he hastily quoted:

"Likewise the spirit helps us in our weakness; for we do not know how to pray as we ought, but the Spirit Himself intercedes for us with sighs too deep for words."

"Oh, yes," said the stranger. "Romans 8:26."

Good grief!

Born to casual members of the Lutheran Church, the largest Protestant denomination in the world and one with an old, established hierarchy, Sparky found appeal in the small, fervent, independent Church of God. He was introduced to it by a Church of God preacher who ministered to his dying mother and preached her funeral.

"That funeral service lacked the pomposity of the Lutheran church where I had grown up. I was impressed by it."

After returning from war, Schulz and his father began attending, occasionally, the Merriam Park Church of God.

"It wasn't until one Wednesday night, however, that I began a more active role. Due to a spell of loneliness, I decided to walk to the evening prayer meeting, and as I climbed the stairs to enter the church building, I noticed that the sign out in front was in need of repainting. After the prayer service was over, I told Brother Marvin Forbes that I thought I might be able to do something to improve the fading lettering. Thus began a friendship that has lasted over forty years. The mild but thoughtful preaching of Brother Forbes brought several of us into active participation in the nondenominational movement."

Later, in 1968, Schulz would describe his ideal church: "I tend to lean toward the primitive church, toward a basic church which is merely a gathering together of believers. I do not like a highly organized church. I think that as soon as the congregation reaches a level of one hundred people or so, it is time to build a new church. As soon as the congregation gets to the point where you are not on fairly intimate terms with every other person in that church, then you have become too big, you are no longer a gathering of believers, but have become a theater where people can attend services.

"I do not think you can attend a church service. *Service* is not something which is there to be viewed as if it were a play or movie. You should be part of this, because you are part of the people who have gathered together because you belong to God."

His memories of Church of God Bible studies and camp meetings in Anderson, Indiana, are vivid, some stained with the increasingly customary bouts of depression:

"I remember taking the train down once. I stayed with good friends and was having a wonderful time. Then, on the third day I felt terribly lonely."

Despite the memorable bout with homesickness and depression, he was dedicated to his new faith. He even preached on the sidewalks of St. Paul and at rescue missions for the down and out. Youth and new faith are a powerful mix, and the shy Schulz amazed his friends from high school who happened upon him giving curbside testimony.

"I only did that twice, really. I had the feeling we were all just playing a game, with no real understanding of the men at the missions and their tribulations. I think some of them might have been listening because that was the rule of the mission—you had to listen to the preaching to get something to eat.

"It always bothered me that here we youngsters were presuming to tell these craggy old guys the Secret of Life. Once, when my turn came to do this, I said, 'I'm not here to tell you anything. We're here simply to help you in any way we can. If you need money or anything else, tell us. We are not here to preach.'

"Of course, my buddies were shocked. Fortunately, nobody asked for money."

Years later Sally, embracing her newest discovery, religion, says: "I'm going to try to sign up for a course in theology. I want to learn all about religion. I want to learn about Moses, and St. Paul and Minneapolis."

"My role in the church was ill-defined," recalls Schulz, "and I had trouble combining my three lives: the friends at the correspondence school where I worked during the day, and sometimes saw socially at night; my church friends, and my oldest friends of all, the guys with whom I played golf on weekends, some dating back to the high school golf team and caddying and tournament competition. The after-work 'social life' consisted mainly of movies and games of Hearts played while listening to our growing collections of the new long-playing 33⅓ records. We did occasionally have parties, of course, but they were very harmless. We did lots of laughing and usually enjoyed ourselves immensely. Strangely enough, there was no drinking.

"I did try to balance these three groups and, at times, invited certain ones to mix with the others, but it never really worked. It was an impossible mix, and the first to go was the Sunday-morning golf, replaced by Sunday church."

Not long before he sold *Peanuts,* someone on the staff of *Gospel Trumpet,* the official Church of God weekly publication, expressed interest in Sparky's work.

"A meeting of ministers and church workers almost led me in another direction. One of the editorial staff was told about my *Li'l Folks* cartoons, and when I showed them to him, he seemed quite impressed. He was puzzled, however, because he couldn't figure out where just such a strange talent would fit. His name was Steele Smith, and if he had offered me a job with their publications, I would have moved to Anderson, Indiana, home of the Church of God headquarters and college. To me, it would have been like a pilgrimage.

"Cartoons were not accepted in church publications at that time, however, and conservatives had not been enlightened to the fact that spiritual truths can be conveyed with cartoon humor just as well as from the pulpit. It wasn't until after I had begun to draw the *Peanuts* strip that I was asked by Kenneth Hall, editor of the youth magazine, if I would consider contributing a cartoon every other week. In a way, I had now found my niche, for I never really felt comfortable in my previous roles of church work.

"I was a disaster at visitation and never liked telling people things as a Sunday school teacher, although guiding discussions had a certain appeal. I actually 'guided' adult classes for a period of about ten years, both in the Minneapolis church and, eventually, in our Methodist church in Sebastopol."

Schulz's Church of God cartoons were one-panel gag cartoons featuring teenagers who looked like tall *Peanuts* characters. There was a central character who was a dead ringer for a seventeen-year-old Charlie Brown.

"It was a bold move on Kenneth Hall's part, and I drew what could very well have been the first cartoons to appear in a church publication. I really am not sure. I do know, however, that mine were the first to contain black youngsters and Catholic nuns. With the tolerance of Kenny Hall and his fine editorial insight, I was able to poke fun at all kinds of otherwise untouchable subjects. Some of the ideas I got from the old-timers' prejudice against movies, which caused them difficulty in the dawning television age, and some from personal experience in Bible classes and shoveling the snow-covered sidewalks in front of the church, or mowing the lawn, but all with a love for the message of the Church of God movement.

"We always denied that we were a denomination. The doctrine insisted that we were a movement within the 'church universal.'

"In the meantime, of course, I was growing older. *Peanuts* was taking up most of my time, and I had begun to forget what it was like to be young and be part of a youth group. A cartoonist can exist for a long time on memories, but if the subject is narrow, those memories need to be replaced by new experiences.

"After seven years, I had to tell Kenny it was time I stopped. He understood and, much to my satisfaction, found a replacement in his own son, to whom I had actually given a few tips years before. He now is drawing his own syndicated feature, *Simple Beasts.*"

From 1958 to 1964 Schulz drew the youth-oriented cartoons, consolidated by the Church of God's Warner Press into a series of four books of reprints: *What Was Bugging Ol' Pharaoh?*, *"Teenager" Is Not a Disease, Young Pillars,* and *Two-by-Fours.*

People still quote the religion in *Peanuts,* chapter and verse.

Short, who has continued to follow the Schulz theology through *Peanuts* and his friendship with the cartoonist, likens its point of view today with that of Leo Tolstoy.

"Tolstoy eventually gave up writing as an artist and became a religious essayist. He believed in a churchless Christianity, and I think that Sparky is headed in that direction, if he's not already there.

"Tolstoy believed love is what it was all about, that people were capable of this, that the spirit of love was inherent in people. Culture causes people to be mean and short-sighted. So Tolstoy wanted to withdraw from culture, live very simply, working with his own hands. I think Sparky's religious orientation is typified by Tolstoy."

The Schulz theology has evolved, if not in the direction of Tolstoy, certainly to the point the cartoonist feels uncomfortable in any one church, though he retains "a certain fondness" for the Church of God.

"I do not go to church anymore, because I could not be an active part of things. I guess you might say I've come around to secular humanism, an obligation I believe all humans have to others and the world we live in."

During the 1988 fracas over the movie *The Last Temptation of Christ*, Schulz was amazed at the pettifogging critics, most of whom had not seen the movie. He was anxious to see the movie version of a book he had enjoyed immensely some years ago at the recommendation of Bob Short.

"They [the movie's critics] are the same ones who write me angry letters whenever I quote the scriptures in the strip. That is so dumb. They have no imagination."

The *Peanuts* gang capitalizes on mankind's innate quest for spiritual explanations of the absurdity of life. They seemingly realize, in the confines of their thought balloons, one of the most divine gifts is a sense of humor.

Sally to Charlie Brown: "I have to do a paper for school on Ken and Abel. I've been looking all through the Old Testament, and I've found Abel, but I can't find Ken. Do you think maybe I'm using the wrong translation?"

12

Snoopy Groupies

When Freddi Margolin was mugged on a New York City subway a few years ago, the gold Cartier Snoopy yanked from a chain around her neck fell between the legs of the man sitting obliviously beside her.

Bleeding and scared, Freddi waited until her attackers fled and then turned to her seatmate. He sat absolutely still and said nothing. Freddi was convinced he planned to keep her treasure, so she pinched his leg and retrieved the Snoopy when the startled stranger jumped.

Like all of us, Freddi Margolin has priorities. To her, Snoopy is certainly worth a daring rescue.

She is an attractive, slim, and silver-haired Long Island housewife, a former teacher who tools about town in a white Volkswagen Rabbit with a bumper sticker that says I REFUSE TO GROW UP. Her personalized license tag reads SNOOPY-HI. People call her The Snoopy Lady, a salutation that thrills her no end.

138

The basement of her attractive Bay Shore home is a museum, where visitors are encouraged to tread barefoot lest they disturb one of the 10,000 *Peanuts* licensing products she has collected from all over the world.

After leaving shoes at the top of the stairs, you tiptoe down into a different world that Freddi calls her "realm of sanity." The basement has bright green carpet and *Peanuts* wallpaper and glass showcases filled with more shimmering bric-a-brac than Tiffany's. *Peanuts* Christmas ornaments hang on a clothesline affair that stretches across the room.

The museum is so crowded with *Peanuts* memorabilia that Freddi's husband Bob, who owns a formal-wear store, says in a resigned and weary voice: "I hope I die first."

The collector's virus hit Freddi hard after a fire in 1978 destroyed a third of her home. The few Snoopy music boxes and toys she had casually acquired were destroyed.

"I lost every Snoopy. People kept telling me how lucky I was that my family was safe, that I was safe, which is certainly true. But you can feel something from the loss of an inanimate object, too. I was devastated."

She kept a large stuffed Snoopy that had half its head burned off; even today it is in a place of honor on her bed, wearing a hat to disguise the injury.

When fire gutted Freddi Margolin's house, the Snoopy Lady rose from the ashes.

A stiff wind rolls through the town from the Great South Bay. It brings rain and impenetrable grayness to this community most recently noted for its municipal contributions to the infamous Islip garbage barge that could find no port. Inside the Margolin house, however, there is light and warmth. Freddi sits at her table in a friendly kitchen telling the story of how a *Peanuts* collection became, well, the most important thing in her life.

A slender wrist encircled with a Snoopy watch stirs cream from a Snoopy cream pitcher into coffee in a Snoopy mug. Snoopy sunglasses are pushed back into her wavy hair. A Snoopy clock strikes the hour.

It was about the time of the fire, Freddi says, that she quit her teaching job because of a hearing loss.

"There was a void in me. Snoopy helped fill it."

Laugh if you will—some people do—but Freddi Margolin's therapy was a beagle. It seems to have worked. At least there aren't many voids in the Margolin house anymore.

At first Freddi treated her treasures as contraband, sneaking Snoopy into the house behind her back, worried about Bob's reaction to a grown woman obsessed with "toys."

"He's a good man, but there was nothing from his childhood that prepared him for this."

Nobody could be prepared for this. Looking at photographs of the collection, Sparky Schulz said "Gee!"

It soon became impossible to hide the hundreds, eventually thousands, of items that so captivated her imagination and drained her pocketbook. Her mainline habit was out of the closet, spilling into every room of the house.

The basement houses the bulk of the items, but evidence of Freddi's fixation is everywhere. The attic is filled with overflow, mostly Snoopy lunchboxes that she considers less important than other types of items in the collection. Entire closets are stuffed with aprons and wall hangings. Snoopy and company are above the kitchen sink, on the bathroom floor, on the beds, the wallpaper, the dog bowl.

Freddi's dog is named Sparky, after Schulz. Her telephone answering machine says "Good grief! You've missed us again. . . ."

She has made Snoopy-hunting expeditions to Italy, France, Japan, Switzerland, and Hong Kong. On one trip to Japan, for instance, she mailed four thousand dollars' worth of *Peanuts* paraphernalia back to the States.

She once persuaded an English bobby checking passports at Gibraltar to use his off-duty time to purchase a certain ceramic Flying Ace bank from a store that was closed when her tour group had passed. The bobby met her later at a designated time and place with the bank. She is a comely, winning woman and uses her wiles if it becomes necessary in the quest for Snoopy.

Freddi, believe it or not, is not alone. She estimates serious *Peanuts* collectors now number in the thousands in the United States; they have a chatty newsletter and meet occasionally to compare notes and acquisitions. Some specialize, concentrating on a particular kind of item—all ceramic replicas, for instance, or all stuffed toys.

Not Freddi. Anything with the registered trademark she wants. She has baby beds, books, banks, bangles, buttons, bowls, bumper stickers, and balloons. And that simply covers one letter of the alphabet. She has Snoopy, Charlie Brown, and the rest of the gang in crystal, ceramic, gold, silver, plastic, fiberglass, cardboard, and rubber.

She speaks with disdain about all other comic characters. "None of the others have the depth of Snoopy." Here is a woman for whom *Peanuts* collecting has become a holy mission, an endless hunt for one more item.

She once owned and ran a retail outlet for *Peanuts* products called Freddi's Friends; it was housed in a corner of her husband's formal-wear store, but she abandoned it and retreated to her private collection when manufacturers dared to approach her with Smurf products.

"Smurfs were dumb. They were ugly. I wouldn't do it." She says this without a hint of a smile. You might as well convince Ted Kennedy to vote Republican.

There is no estimated value of such a collection, and Freddi's not saying what she has spent, total. "Money is no problem now. The challenge is finding the stuff. At one time I didn't have the financial resources to indulge in this; now I do." So she does.

And, as final proof of her allegiance, Freddi gives a journalist a Polaroid snapshot of her high right thigh and its Snoopy tattoo, reminding us that *fan* is short for *fanatic.*

Such is the devotion of one brand of Snoopy groupies, those who buy and collect their way into Charlie Brown's world. But fans come in every age and size and exhibit their loyalty in myriad ways. Some write letters. Some send Schulz gifts. Some ask for money.

Schulz likes to tell the story of the man who wrote and asked for a million dollars. It was God's will that he comply, the letter matter-of-factly informed the cartoonist. Schulz ignored the request.

About a year later Schulz got a second letter from the same man. God had changed his mind; Schulz need not send the million dollars after all. There had been a mistake.

"Boy, I was relieved," Schulz says, chuckling.

There was the woman, too, who wrote intensely personal letters to Schulz, believing everything happening in the strip was directed only to her.

"I called her husband and expressed my concern. He thanked me and said she had had a nervous breakdown."

On the one hand, Schulz seems perpetually concerned his phenomenal popularity might someday inexplicably fade, might be overcome by his nearest licensing rival *Garfield* or a hipper strip like *Bloom County.* He is extremely competitive, amazingly wary for a man at the top of the heap.

"I worry sometimes that I may never think of another broad theme, that I may never come up with another Snoopy versus the Red Baron. It's something you cannot force. I don't know where those witty little statements the kids say to one another come from. I take that blank piece of paper and go at it cold-blooded, day after day."

On the other hand, he has ended his gung-ho days of traipsing the country giving chalk talks to every men's church group that issues an invitation. "For one thing, I'll never again speak to a Baptist men's group. They never heard of Beethoven."

He can be firm, even curt, about such requests. He puts a time limit on autograph sessions after speeches and sometimes refuses to sign things at all, saving his hand for the drawing of the strip itself. Autograph sessions tend to drag on longer than the speeches beforehand, he complains, and people want you to sign everything from T-shirts to stuffed animals.

"The trouble with speeches is they expect you to be an entertainer as well as a cartoonist. It's like being an actor. You have to work yourself into a pitch for performing."

Once, addressing students at Berkeley, Schulz quizzed his young audience, which was supposed to be made up of aspiring cartoonists: "How many of you here know the work of Charles Payne? How about Roy Crane?"

The students sat silent and with blank faces.

"I don't even want to talk to you," Schulz said. Then he did anyway.

Nancy Nicolelis and Jill Decker of the United Feature Syndicate promotion department are constantly surprised by his public relations decisions, which (to put it mildly) are unpredictable.

"He will turn down an interview request for *People* magazine and then give one the same day to some little newspaper in Arkansas," says Decker.

That decision made perfect sense to Schulz. He sees newspapers as the lifeblood of his profession and of his success. He almost never denies a newspaper reporter an interview if he can help it.

In 1988, when *People* canvassed cartoonists on the sixtieth birthday of Mickey Mouse, Schulz contributed. "He'll do it for Mickey on his sixtieth birthday and probably not for Snoopy on his fortieth," Nicolelis predicts. "He definitely makes our lives interesting." In that interview, Schulz coyly pointed out that Snoopy was older than Mickey—in dog years.

When the national Horatio Alger Society wanted to present Schulz with one of its prestigious awards for 1989, the only condition was a guarantee Schulz would be in attendance for the presentation ceremony. Organizers, at the time Schulz was approached, did not know exactly where that ceremony would be. This, to Schulz, presented a problem.

"Sparky said we'd better not promise," says Nicolelis. "So we didn't."

The syndicate often uses a person wearing a Snoopy suit to pinch-hit for the diffident Schulz. "Snoopy is a nice alternative," the public relations people say. All manner of bigwigs have had to settle for shaking a paw instead of a hand.

Sparky handpicked the first-chair Snoopy, the one who, if possible, makes all the major appearances, at the White House, Carnegie Hall, television shows, ice shows, and the Macy's Thanksgiving Day Parade.

The licensed Snoopy Lady is Judy Sladky, and she has been Snoopy for eleven years, a job she approaches with the same quirky devotion as Freddi Margolin. Judy is so serious about her task that she took child development and psychology courses to learn how best to approach children in the costume. So serious that she believes there is not much need for a costume, really.

"I am Snoopy, personalitywise," she says. "There was some type-casting involved. He's such a happy beagle, so full of energy. I'm that way, too. Our birthdays are even close, only a few weeks apart. I'll be turning forty November 14, 1990, after Snoopy turns forty in October."

Five times the United States ice-dancing champion, Judy Sladky skated in the ice show that opened the Redwood Empire Ice Arena and impressed the cartoonist with her performance. She got a call not long after that, from Sparky, who deadpanned, "We wanted to get the best person possible to play Snoopy. She couldn't do it, so we want you."

Thus began her career as Snoopy. For eleven years children have been wrapping themselves in her black ears, talking to her, trusting her, recognizing her. "You get hugs you would otherwise not get. You get to meet people you wouldn't otherwise meet."

Backstage at Carnegie Hall before a benefit for children with AIDS, conductor Leonard Bernstein noticed Snoopy waiting in the wings. He took the beagle's nose in both hands and said, "You're a genius."

"He was talking to Snoopy, not to me. But I was so elated to have him say anything I went out on stage walking on air."

Snoopy has directed the Mormon Tabernacle Choir, rolled Easter eggs at the White House, and teamed with Nancy Reagan for anti-drug appearances. And, while there are other people who play Snoopy, Judy Sladky doesn't like to think—much less talk—about them.

"The Florida lottery got up to about fifty-four million dollars once, and my husband and I were taking a few days off, staying in the woods. We bought a couple of the lottery tickets and were talking about what we'd do if we won. 'I'd never give up Snoopy,' I told him. And I wouldn't. It upsets me to think I might have to quit for some reason."

She keeps the secrets of her unique profession to herself. "One of the most important parts of my job is maintaining the mystique," she says; when asked if it's true, does she see out of the costume's nose? "I don't like to talk about a costume, because that's not how I think about it. When Snoopy appears, Judy Sladky does not exist at all. The best part is, Snoopy never speaks, so I can't really say anything wrong." Judy Sladky, a fan for the fans.

Schulz can be genuinely touched by the attentions of his admirers. One of Woodstock's feathered friends is named Harriet for Harriet Crossland, the Santa Rosa woman who makes him angel-food cakes with his favorite seven-minute icing. "She is embarrassingly proud of me."

In fact, many of the characters are named for Santa Rosa friends. Molly Volley, Snoopy's tennis partner, has a namesake in Molly Ackley, Schulz's real-life tennis companion. Dr. Ward Wick, ophthalmologist and golfing buddy, shows up as a name on the comic strip golf course every now and then. Other golfers who appear on the course are Shirley Nelson and Betty Bartley; Shirley is the wife of Schulz business manager Ron Nelson. Betty is married to Charles Bartley, a close Schulz friend. Linus's teacher, Miss Othmar, was named after Sparky's good friend, Othmar Jarisch, who ran the local humane society and died in 1988. When Miss Othmar got married she became Mrs. Hagemeyer, after the real Margaret Hagemeyer of St. Louis, the wife of Sparky's Army buddy Elmer Hagemeyer. Mrs. Hagemeyer also gives organ lessons to Marcie. Marcie, in fact, took her name from a family friend, Marcie Carlin. Van Pelt is the family name of friends from Colorado Springs. Besides Charlie Brown, Sparky borrowed the names of other Art Instruction Schools co-workers: Linus came from Linus Maurer and Frieda from Frieda Rich, both employees of the correspondence school.

Famous fans, or at least their names, also make cameo appearances in the strip. Snoopy, foiled again at his tennis game, shrugs off all detractors. "Billie Jean King still loves me," he consoles himself.

"That's Sparky's way of letting me know he's thinking about me," says Billie Jean King.

"We have a kinship. We both grew up believing in the work ethic, and we both still do. I grew up the daughter of a fireman in Long Beach, California. He was the son of a barber."

Singer Joni James, popular in the 1970s, was plucked from the esoteric blue and mentioned in the strip one day by Schulz. Snoopy, it seems, has a collection of her records inside his doghouse. James called Schulz, thrilled to be remembered.

Cartoonist Bill Mauldin is mentioned in the strip each Veterans Day as Snoopy makes a trip to drink root beer with the creator of World War II's most famous enlisted men, Willie and Joe.

"I asked Schulz once, 'Why are you doing this?' " says Mauldin. " 'You're keeping me alive,' I said. 'I'm the forgotten cartoonist, except for this.' "

Schulz told Mauldin he had been a machine-gunner in France during World War II.

"That was all the explanation I needed," says Mauldin.

Even with all his fans, famous and anonymous, Schulz has managed to keep a fairly low profile, hiding behind his characters. Bobby Miller, once his editor at United Feature Syndicate, remembers a rare and wonderful moment in Central Park with Schulz:

"We had been at Tavern on the Green, and we all had balloons from the restaurant. We got into one of the horse-drawn carriages and drove through the park. Sparky was hanging out of the carriage, trailing his balloons.

"Finally, one person recognized him. But that was all. I think it's a lovely kind of fame to have."

Robert Roy Metz, president and chief executive officer of United Media, United Feature's parent company, says Schulz handles fame extremely well.

"He does not play the celebrity. Yet he's not unduly modest or humble or even retiring. His behavior is appropriate. I've never seen anyone more generous with his time."

Perhaps most amazing among the Snoopy groupies are some of the employees of United Feature Syndicate, who seem genuinely starstruck though the comic feature is part of their daily work.

Liz Dunn is the first hurdle potential licensees must pass when submitting product ideas. She is disarmingly bright and direct, even-handedly receiving proposals from giants like General Electric or one-man operations who want to put Snoopy on a ceiling fan. She believes in the beagle and gets almost downright belligerent when her counterpart for the Garfield line bests her in any way.

"I would quit my job if they assigned me to another strip."

Helyn Rippert, the young woman who was on the United Feature Syndicate switchboard in 1950 the day Schulz walked in for the first time, became perhaps his biggest fan there. Thirty-three years after their first meeting she retired from the syndicate. To honor her and to repay an early kindness, Schulz entertained Mrs. Rippert and her husband in Santa Rosa. Actually, an evening with Sparky had been her one request upon leaving.

"I was so nervous I don't remember much, except that he showed us a wonderful time. He took us to the ice arena and the gift shop and museum and out to eat. I had to keep pinching myself to believe it was true. . . And on the cartoon he drew for me there was Snoopy with a bouquet of flowers. And he spelled my name right. With a *y.* That was the best thing of all."

After welcoming Schulz to United Feature Syndicate, Helyn Rippert became, on her own initiative, a walking, talking encyclopedia of *Peanuts.* Because of her fanaticism she would come to be regarded as United Feature Syndicate's resident expert on the strip. Anyone calling with a question about *Peanuts* automatically was routed to her.

Numerous queries came from television quiz shows, curious fans, and "people who simply had a bet going." She knew the answers. You could mention a punch line from a strip and Helyn Rippert usually could come up with the year it ran. Or come close.

Even today, in retirement, she keeps at her fingertips the file of questions and answers that grew fatter over the years as she cataloged *Peanuts* trivia.

"How old is Charlie Brown?" some caller once asked Helyn Rippert.

Her quick reply: "On April 3, 1971, Charlie Brown was eight years old, because in a strip that day he said he would be twenty-one in 1983."

Typical question: Is Woodstock a girl or a boy?

Answer: A boy. (She checked this one out with Schulz.)

Mrs. Rippert even went so far as to record the changing rates at Lucy's psychiatry booth, which first appeared on March 27, 1959, without its sign on top. In 1959 Lucy charged five cents for her expert advice; one winter's day in 1967, without warning, the famous fussbudget raised her rates to seven cents; in 1972, it was ten cents; in 1973, back down to five; in 1976, back up to ten cents; in 1979, inflation hit: Lucy charged a quarter. Now she's back down to five cents.

Sarah Gillespie, Schulz's current editor at United Feature Syndicate, used to stand up to talk to the cartoonist on the telephone when she first came on board. "My secretary could always tell when Sparky was on the other end because I'd hop up and stand there during the entire conversation."

She almost fell down one day in 1988, when she mistakenly thought she heard the cartoonist say he was about to quit. He had, instead, told her "I'm going to quit drawing the strip in four panels." It was a big decision in itself, but Sarah was conducting a distracting meeting in her office at the time, and all she heard was "I'm going to quit drawing the strip." She chased the visitors out of her office like so many cats, closed her door, and returned to the phone shaken, thinking, "This is it."

It is Gillespie's job to ride herd on the syndicate's stable of cartoonists. Grammar, spelling, taste all fall within her purview. Nominally she is Schulz's immediate superior within the structure, but for her, editing Schulz is like eating soup with a fork. Everything goes through. Fortunately, as mentioned, he doesn't require a lot of supervision.

"The only thing I remember is once he misspelled 'sandal,' " says Sarah. "I called and asked his permission to change it."

Such respect isn't entirely born of love, however. Schulz can be very protective of his creation in the presence of editors. If some blockhead changes something, she'd better have a good reason!

Perhaps the biggest *Peanuts* fan in the world is Brad Bushell. Bushell is in charge of selling United Media comics in the United States, and he can be expected to glow when he speaks of the man whose strip runs in over 2000 newspapers.

"I met with some of the salesmen out in California once, and we asked to meet briefly with Sparky. He agreed. I'll never forget what he told us:

" 'I get a little nervous when a syndicate salesperson asks to see me. I'm afraid you aren't proud to be showing my stuff anymore.' " Bushell laughs. And laughs.

For all the pleasure his fans give him, Schulz is a prisoner of his fame as well.

He worries some about the lunatics who sometimes stalk celebrity. "Sometimes I'll be walking across the parking lot of the shopping mall and I'll think how easy it would be for somebody to get at me. Or I'll think about a white van with men with machine guns jumping out the back. For some reason, it's always a white van."

13

The Syndicate Game

*F*ish tales. All syndicates have them. Sad stories about the ones that got away.

In the newspaper business, *syndicate* is the name for a mass producer and seller of comics, written columns, crossword puzzles, and other popular features that newspapers want and cannot realistically produce locally. Individual newspapers, in effect, pay the syndicate to locate, groom, package, and deliver a talent to their newsroom doorsteps weekly or daily.

The written word has been syndicated to American newspapers since the eighteenth century, but the comic strip end of the business—and the modern syndicating operation—grew out of the fierce circulation wars of William Randolph Hearst and Joseph Pulitzer at the turn of the twentieth century. Newspapers were state-of-the-art mass entertainment at that time, and publishers jockeyed constantly for readers' devotion. Pulitzer, Hearst, and others worked to develop (or steal) artists who could help them take sensational advantage of the rapidly improving printing technology. It was only a small leap when someone realized this expensive proposition could be underwritten by selling reprint rights to poor relations in the boonies.

The syndicate trade, with the newspapers it served, enjoyed a brief golden age but quickly came up against deadly competition from radio and then television. Like many businesses, major syndicates today—syndicates that serve the general needs of mainstream newspapers—are decreasing in overall number and growing in size and scope.

There are less than half a dozen major syndicates remaining that feature a sizable menu of comic strips: United Feature Syndicate, King Features Syndicate, Tribune Media Services, North America Syndicate, Universal Press Syndicate, and Newspaper Enterprise Association. Still, there are hundreds of others that specialize, distributing everything from news and television logs to stories exclusively about chess.

Traditionally there have been brave, brazen syndicates, and then there have been hidebound syndicates staffed by fogies who still think in hot type. Some syndicates pride themselves on up-to-date offerings; others pound on the theme of tradition. Most often, their attitudes reflect the philosophy and style of their most lucrative property.

The relationship between syndicate and artist is akin to that of a mother and child, really. The syndicate gives a feature its very life, nurtures it a short while, slaps its hand when it threatens to get out of line, parades it around the neighborhood proudly. There is sometimes friction, sometimes rebellion, and ofttimes resentment. But the artist and syndicate need each other.

Thousands of submissions cross the desks of syndicate editors annually. It is definitely a buyer's market.

King Features Syndicate gets 3500 submissions from cartoonists a year. It releases only six to eight new features a year.

The secret for the syndicate is to pick the right features from the impossibly crowded field of contenders. Every editor has banged his head against the wall after turning down a comic strip or column that immediately became the hot new property across the street. That's part of the game. For every artistic gamble that's paid off, dozens have been losing bets, too.

A syndicate makes its money from what a newspaper will pay for a particular artist or writer. Usually the syndicate and the artist split the profits after production costs down the middle. The rates are based on the newspaper's circulation. For any syndicate, a feature like *Peanuts,* which has been sold to virtually every newspaper in America, is a franchise player.

Particularly in the old days, what a large metropolitan newspaper in a competitive market could be made to pay each week for a popular feature could run into four figures. Medium-size dailies usually pay less than a hundred, and the many small dailies can have leading features for less than ten dollars a week in most cases.

"The syndicate business is like owning a candy store," explains Sid Goldberg of United Feature Syndicate. "It's thirteen cents for this and twenty-eight cents for that. You're dealing mostly with small sums from unknown newspapers. This job is over when you can't get excited about selling a feature to a small newspaper for three and a half dollars a week."

Things were getting tight by 1950, but it wasn't quite as brutal as now when Sparky Schulz pounded the Chicago sidewalks, carrying his cartoon portfolio. There were more syndicates, for one thing, and more newspapers and, paradoxically, fewer aspiring cartoonists. Yet it was still no mean feat to interest a busy syndicate executive with an unproved comic strip, and considerable shoe leather was about the best investment a cartoonist could make. Schulz invested. Despite his shyness and on his modest Art Instruction salary, he bought train tickets to Chicago, and once there he dutifully made the rounds.

In his book *North Toward Home,* Mississippi author Willie Morris describes the agonizing process of peddling one's creative wares to the people who are in charge. After a five-day bus trip to Manhattan, Morris met with the editor of a large publishing firm. The editor took telephone calls, glanced repeatedly at his watch, and

made it clear through language, body and verbal, he hadn't much
use for Willie Morris:

> A slow Mississippi boil was rising north from my guts, a
> physical presence that had always warned me to go easy, to be
> aware of my heritage and bloodshed and spur-of-the-moment
> mayhem. Confederate colonels on horseback flashed in my
> mind and Jeb Stuart and his men and the siege of Vicksburg; I
> would not have wished to have begun my new life in the city
> by throwing this little man out of a second story window into a
> courtyard.
> At this point, however, the editor had to terminate the
> conversation. We shook hands again, and he expressed a faint
> good-luck. I walked down the marble stairs to the entrance
> and out again onto the street. The whole session had lasted five
> minutes. I would see the editor several times in the course of
> the following year, professionally and otherwise. I would still
> think of him as one of the important editors in the whole of
> the Cave. But I resolved to myself that day, a little naively, and
> sententiously perhaps, that if I were ever in a similar posi-
> tion and someone came in fresh off the Greyhound, I would
> not make him feel the pluperfect hick.

Sparky Schulz remembers, too, those who made him feel like a
"pluperfect hick," the ones who could spare no time, the ones who
were abrupt. He remembers the way they handled his precious cartoons. The smirks. The lifted eyebrows. He remembers names. It is
to his credit he not only remembers those who treated him badly,
but those who were of help as well. He is in the enviable position of
having been proved, indisputably, right.

John Dille, Jr., at his National Newspaper Syndicate, was invariably kind to the young man from Minnesota who knocked on
his door and forthrightly asked for time and advice.

Recalls Schulz: "*Buck Rogers* was John Dille's biggest strip at
the time, and we'd sit and have these really pleasant conversations
about *Buck Rogers* and comic strips in general, and we would share

ideas. He was patient to listen to me, but I never really took anything definite to show him. One day he finally said, 'I can't really make any judgment until I see what you are doing.' But he never stopped being nice to me. A few years ago he stopped by to see me in Santa Rosa, and I was able to take him out and thank him in a small way for his kindness."

Publishers Syndicate of Chicago, in the person of Harold Anderson, treated the cartoonist rudely, as Sparky remembers it.

"Not professional enough" was Anderson's abrupt assessment of Schulz's work. Schulz resents that terse trio of words even today, after time has proved him plenty professional enough.

"He had no right to say what he did. He didn't even separate my cartoons and look at them carefully. He made no attempt at conversation, no 'How was your trip?' or anything. It was the total brush-off."

At the Chicago Tribune Syndicate Schulz didn't get past the receptionist's desk.

Walt Ditzen, comics editor for The Chicago Sun-Times Syndicate at the time, was enthusiastic about what he saw Schulz spread before him. "I certainly can't say no to this," Ditzen told an elated Schulz. Then Ditzen took Schulz and his work in to see the boss, Harry Baker, who barely looked at the cartoon before saying "No."

"That made Ditzen furious," says Schulz.

King Features Syndicate sent Schulz a polite rejection letter that happened to arrive in the mail the same day as another letter from Newspaper Enterprise Association, called NEA, then located in Cleveland.

"I opened the letter from King first. They had just started another kids' feature, it said, and I thought 'Oh, well. That's the way it goes. Another rejection!' "

He opened the second letter, prepared for another disappointment. Only NEA was not rejecting his submission, but accepting it.

"They said they were quite taken with my work." NEA invited Schulz to Cleveland to sign a contract for a Sunday feature. Sparky took his first airplane ride ever to get there, marveling at the patches of green that were the heartland below him, landing in Cleveland on a Sunday. Because it was Sunday, Schulz went to services at a Church of God he found in the phone book, where the pastor caused him a brief moment of agony by asking "our visiting brother from Minnesota" to pray. Aloud.

But it was a happy, confident Schulz who the next day signed his first syndicate contract and on the spot delivered to NEA six Sunday cartoons. He returned to Art Instruction a "real" cartoonist.

"When I got back from Cleveland and walked into the school, they all applauded me."

The glory was short-lived. Newspaper Enterprise Association broke the contract without receiving any further work from Schulz, giving the cartoonist a hundred-dollar severance check for his troubles.

"I don't know what happened; just that they didn't use them, and I was forced to start all over again." NEA did return the six unpublished cartoons. "I took the six Sunday pages to *The St. Paul Pioneer Press,* and I didn't have to draw anything more for them for six weeks."

Ironically, NEA later merged with its sister company, United Feature Syndicate, and is now operated under the same umbrella company, United Media, with the same offices and staff. Undoubtedly the income from *Peanuts* was an important nutrient that helped put United Feature Syndicate in the big-fish position. NEA was swallowed up by one it had thrown back.

14

Surpassing the Mouse

Sparky made his first dollar at the age of eight, modeling knickers at the Emporium department store in St. Paul at the behest of a neighbor. He immediately went out and spent twenty cents of the largess on a beautiful ceramic frog for his mother, saving the rest for dime sodas.

He has made a little money since. But the modeling dollar may well be the last one he understood.

"None of us know the meaning of a dollar anymore," he complains. "My father knew. He knew exactly how many haircuts he had to finish to have a dollar. Now, it's all so confusing."

Schulz is no businessman. Without Ronald Nelson, vice president of Creative Associates, who handles all money matters for him, Schulz would be too busy to draw. He would be overwhelmed by financial matters that interest him not in the least. He admits it. His friends and associates know it. He carries little cash and never writes a check.

156

In essence, a billion-dollar business is being headed by a man with no head for business.

When daughter Amy was a child, she approached her father with a fantastic idea: "Wouldn't it be interesting, Dad, if you lost your job drawing the cartoon and all of us children had to go out and make the money?"

Maybe she had seen one too many old Shirley Temple movies. At any rate Schulz, intrigued by the guileless question, quizzed his daughter in return. "How would you earn money, Amy?"

"I could make my bed." Maybe it runs in the family.

One thing he does understand. The comic strip must come first—before the stuffed dolls and greeting cards, lunch pails, and Bill Ditfort designer sweaters. Before the animated specials, ceiling fans, and even the endless paperback collections of reprints. Before Plush Snoopy. The strip is the blood of the operation, and Schulz never forgets.

The syndicate once forgot, back in the 1970s when *Peanuts* went overseas big-time and licensing burgeoned and became harder and harder to monitor. Before, *Peanuts* had made big money but had not been big business, at least not a complicated business. Schulz drew seven strips weekly and got a check from the syndicate for his share. Simple as that.

Then came licensing. And, in the 1970s, products began showing up on the market that Schulz had not even seen, much less endorsed. It seemed United Feature Syndicate's New York-based *Peanuts* operation had forsaken its Santa Rosa roots, or at best was ignoring them. The resulting discord was based less on what happened than the fear of what could.

The relationship between Schulz and the syndicate, by all accounts, cooled considerably during that period.

Then, eleven years ago, Schulz and United Feature Syndicate agreed to a new contract, leaving a fifty-fifty royalty split intact but allowing the cartoonist to have final say over every single licensing product sold. He did not at that time, nor has he ever, sought a bigger percentage, although he could get it.

Robert Metz, the United Media president who had just come

on board when the negotiations were tackled, seemed to understand Schulz instinctively, unlike the two presidents before, who had ignored the cartoonist's vague but persistent dissatisfaction.

"I first met him in 1977 at one of those typical lunches at the Warm Puppy," says Metz. "There were about six people at the table, but Sparky and I immediately got into a direct and personal conversation. I knew what he wanted."

What Schulz wanted was simple. He wanted to control the use of his own creation. "Some thought I was going to go off and do wild things with licensing myself. That wasn't it. It was just the opposite; I was afraid they were the ones planning wild things. Now I simply say 'Do it my way, or I quit.' "

Peanuts was, believe it or not, surprisingly slow to adapt to licensing, with the first plastic doll appearing in 1958, when the strip already was eight years old. No successful strip hobbles to eight years old these days without accessorizing itself with money-making licensing products. *Peanuts* did. Even those strips whose creators publicly deplore "commercialization" have T-shirts and reprint books before their strips reach a third birthday.

Like the child slow to talk who suddenly erupts into an indefatigable conversationalist, *Peanuts* seemed tailor-made for licensing. For one thing, there was a large cast of characters, each with a well-defined, distinctive personality. "Nobody knows the personality of Mickey Mouse," Nelson argues, rightly or wrongly. From Snoopy's Joe Cool to repressible Charlie Brown, *Peanuts* had something for everybody.

Schulz tried to see everything done even before he had contractual rights to do so. "I wanted to make sure everything we did was right, that the products, the language, were all in character with the comic strip, although my old contract really spelled out no rights in that regard. I probably was the first cartoonist who watched over licensing, who insisted that he see everything."

The forerunner of Schulz's fanaticism about keeping quality control over commercial spinoffs might have been the discriminating eye of Beatrix Potter, creator of Peter Rabbit. She sewed the first Peter Rabbit doll herself, filling it with lead shot and worrying that the rabbit's upholstery was sturdy enough. She certainly did not turn up her nose at merchandising per se. Hardly. But she did insist that the products stay true to the original artwork and characters and that her books stay small for little hands to hold.

Unfortunately, such control, "seeing everything," entails meetings that Nelson presides over and Schulz endures.

It would seem, at first, like any old business conference, with grown men seated around a table talking in no-nonsense voices about trends and trademarks, some armed with astute observations rehearsed for weeks: "This shopping mall will be the ultimate fusion of retail and entertainment, since the two are headed for each other on a collision course."

If you visit long enough, however, this corporate meeting sounds like no other:

"Snoopy should eventually surpass The Mouse."

"I did not know exactly where Snoopy was in Japan or how tied up he was there."

"Pound per pound, Snoopy is bigger in Japan than in America. In Japan, Snoopy is God."

It's a funny business and sounds that way.

Terry E. Van Gorder is a robust, white-haired man who wears a red sweater emblazoned with a Joe Cool insignia. Van Gorder is the congenial chief executive officer of Knott's Berry Farm, which in 1983 added a theme park, Camp Snoopy, at its Buena Park, California, headquarters. A proposed second Camp Snoopy, this one in a futuristic, seven-acre shopping mall about to be built in Minnesota, is, Van Gorder announces, "The first thing on the agenda today."

"I always worry about people who have an agenda," says Schulz wistfully, and everyone laughs politely. The money men proceed quickly with talk about the shopping mall amusement park, which could generate millions. Then sample jars of a new line of Knott's Berry Farm products tentatively called Peanuts Butter and Jam Company appear on the conference table, complete with mock labels featuring the *Peanuts* gang.

"Children are beginning to make the jam decision," says an earnest Van Gorder lieutenant.

"It seems like I remember not liking your grape jelly," interjects Schulz, heretofore silent, and all conversation stops. Then someone laughs.

And so the meetings go; from cupcakes to insurance campaigns, people pitch their ideas and vie for the privilege of permanently affixing a beagle's mug and a loser's personality to their products. Those who come with an idea are warned that even the popularity of Snoopy cannot carry an inferior product.

The licensees—those who are granted permission to market products using the characters—pay a royalty, usually between 5 and 10 percent of the wholesale price of the item. Then that money is split equally between syndicate and cartoonist. Retail sales run in the neighborhood of a billion dollars annually. Business is split in almost perfect thirds among the United States, Japan, and the rest of the world, where there are wide-open markets still to conquer.

In Sweden, for instance, the comic strip runs in forty-five different newspapers. "And you can't even name that many cities in Sweden," says Sid Goldberg, in charge of international syndication sales for United Feature Syndicate. And in Japan, well, "MacArthur did have to ask Snoopy to step down from his divinity," says Goldberg.

Translation of the strip into other languages poses a challenge, of course. How do you make the proper name Zamboni clear in Thailand, "where they don't have ice skating?"

Peanuts, Goldberg says, poses "no special problem" like some strips that deal heavily in puns. "How is the author ever going to know a good translation, anyway? He has to take the word of someone else. It ends up being an act of faith." Foreign translation may be Schulz's only act of faith when it comes to *Peanuts* products.

Licensees run the free-enterprise gamut from major leaguers like Metropolitan Life to clothes designer Ditfort, who each year makes only a limited number of his expensive, upscale sweaters using *Peanuts* themes, including the distinctive pattern of Charlie Brown's trademark zigzag shirt.

Most of the drawings of the characters on licensed merchandise are photographic reproductions of the comic strip. Schulz himself makes some special drawings; he produced original artwork for the Metropolitan Life Insurance Company's printed advertising campaign in conjunction with the 1988 Summer Olympics.

"We prefer companies with solid reputations, of course," says Nelson, who can afford to be picky. Licensees almost always approach Creative Associates or the syndicate and not the other way around. "People keep banging on our door."

Schulz puts a lot of faith in Nelson, who bridges a gap between businessmen and the artist. Nelson understands Schulz's bottom line, which is drastically different from that of other financial empires:

"Whether Sparky makes some more money or not doesn't make any difference to him. It will not change his lifestyle."

Or, as Metz said: "One more coffee cup just doesn't interest Sparky that much."

Yet Nelson estimates that 80 percent of the *Peanuts*-related revenue comes from merchandising and only 20 percent from the books and newspaper syndication royalties.

There are onionlike layers of quality control. Liz Dunn often fields the first proposal from a manufacturer, which usually comes by telephone or mail. Liz, at twenty-five, is tougher than she might appear. Would-be licensees who fail to take her seriously because of her age or sex usually find that letters and phone calls directed over her head fall right back to her doorstep.

"We don't have to license willy-nilly, and we don't," she says. Liz even impounds the prototypes of some "tacky" products that might embarrass the strip, answering demands she return them with a shrug. "You won't be selling it; why do you need it back?"

Liz flew in a bucking ten-seater over the hills of West Virginia to attend a trial after a group of Hare Krishnas was charged with violating the copyright with a warehouse full of bootleg *Peanuts* stickers and hats. When someone wants to put a Uzi machine gun into the hands of Plush Snoopy she nixes the idea without consulting anyone. She knows better. "That's probably the most horrendous idea I've been approached with."

Thermal jugs for holding beer—no. Cheap paper airplanes—

no. Every phone call is an adventure, a potential General Electric or Metropolitan Life.

"Every person is just as important as the next, though. Those small operations that might only produce a thousand dollars a year in revenue are given the same amount of attention and care. If the product is a quality one, if we're not already doing something in that area, I consider it. But that's what makes this job so much fun."

Those whose products are welcomed into the fold are indoctrinated with the UFS and Creative Associates philosophy about the characters. They receive a sheaf of materials, including a personality sketch of the players. Snoopy, for instance, is "an extrovert Beagle with a Walter Mitty complex. He is a virtuoso at every endeavor—at least in his daydreams atop his doghouse. He regards his master, Charlie Brown, as 'that round-headed kid' who brings him his supper dish. . . ."

With the approved personalities in mind, the licensee is free to develop a bifold door with the "extrovert Beagle" in glass on the top half, "with attractive ponderosa pine underneath." Or a ceiling fan featuring "a different *Peanuts* sports theme in color on each of the four blades, including Charlie Brown at home on the pitcher's mound, or in another attempt to kick the football with Lucy as holder." Gooseneck desk lamps, toddler sleepwear, children's leotards, jelly jars, and a remote-control Snoopy toy—all new products that have passed muster.

The hardest part of her job, Dunn says, is informing the honest people who write for permission to use the copyrighted figures for nonprofit causes that they cannot.

"You get a teacher writing in, representing five-year-olds who want to use Snoopy in some form or fashion, and you have to say 'No.' Because next week you get the Gay and Lesbian Society from the University of Chicago who want to put Charlie Brown on a sign that says 'Straight person for Gay Rights.' "

There are those, of course, who ignore the proper channels and use the characters without permission and without paying. From a San Diego home-cleaning service to a neo-Nazi group in Michigan, people have stolen the famous mugs and warped (or changed, at

least) the personalities of the *Peanuts* gang. Policing the unautho-
rized use of Snoopy and the other characters costs about a million
dollars a year.

There are the innocent offenders, who mean their copies only
as a salute to Schulz and his accomplishments. No profit is realized
or intended. For instance, a real brouhaha erupted when a farmer
near Cooperstown, New York, was asked by syndicate lawyers to re-
move from his barn roof a copyright-violating Snoopy and Woodstock mural that had, over the years, become a popular rural land-
mark. The barn art had been brought to the syndicate's attention by
a neighbor of the farmer's, a veterinarian, who wanted to use the
characters on a business sign himself. When the veterinarian was refused, he angrily reported his farmer neighbor, an action that, of
course, forced the syndicate to move.

New York newspaper readers apprised of the situation almost
unanimously supported the farmer against the faceless syndicate.
The farmer, quite naturally, did not want to paint over his handi-
work. Some *Peanuts* fans felt hurt and deceived and called Schulz everything from greedy to downright despotic in angry letters to the
editor. Why should this multimillionaire cartoonist care that a retired farmer and passing motorists were getting a little additional
mileage from the warm feelings Snoopy and Woodstock generate?

Schulz knew nothing of the copyright ruckus until the farmer
made a direct appeal to him. Like everyone else, Schulz was at the
mercy of the legal system. For the law sees no distinction between
barn murals and full-fledged rip-off production lines like the one a
group of Moonies ran for profit in San Francisco.

A copyright infringement must be diligently protested, the law
states, or the copyright, for all practical purposes, eventually may be
lost. If any known violation of the copyright is tolerated, the syndicate then would be guilty of *laches*, a legal term that simply means
"silence," the failure to do something which should be done to en-
force a right at a proper time.

So, when someone spots a "Snoopy Is a Transvestite" button,
as someone did, and reports it to Creative Associates, veteran Schulz
aide George Pipal fires off a report to United Feature Syndicate's Cin-

cinnati lawyers and the offender gets a letter. It is a letter similar to
the one Liz Dunn mails the kindergarten teacher—polite but firm,
asking the person/company/school/cult in question to stop stealing
what belongs to another.

Pipal recalls one newspaper photograph of a Snoopy doll collection mailed to him that included about seventy-five dolls, almost every one of them fraudulent products, Snoopys bearing no copyright.
(Ripoff Snoopys have been used for both commercial and political
purposes. Snoopy impersonators have been pro-union, anti-union,
pro-abortion, anti-abortion, and exploited in a thousand ways and a
dozen languages.) It is especially hard to monitor licensing abroad, a
market that has mushroomed in the last ten years.

Even those with permission to use the *Peanuts* characters must
do so carefully or risk losing that privilege.

All licensees must submit proposed drawings to Evelyn Ellison,
Creative Associates' assistant vice president. She decides if the drawing is complete and makes sure it is reproduced photographically,
and not traced, as required.

"The important thing is, Sparky's will now prevails," says Nelson. If the cartoonist or his staff is uncomfortable with a product or
business relationship for any reason, the deal is off.

The comic strip is the core, and money is a happy by-product
not allowed to pollute or muddy the waters.

"I would be drawing the comic strip if I only made fifty dollars
a week," says Sparky.

His daughter Amy, the same one who wanted to make her bed
to support the family, says her father sometimes wrestles quietly
with guilt about all the money. "He has said to me, 'If I were a man
digging ditches, and I dug more ditches, I'd get more money. I'm still
doing the same thing, the same amount of work, and look how
much more money I'm making.' "

Schulz made $90 the first month of cartooning. The second
month he made $500; the third, $1000. At the end of the first year
he had earned about $10,000 ("more money than my father ever
made in a year in his life"), and in the strip's second year he made
$18,000. By the time *Time* chronicled the up-and-coming cartoonist

in 1965 he was making $300,000 a year from the strip, not count-
ing money from a smattering of licensing products and rich royalties
from an advertising campaign for the Ford Falcon.

Even in 1965, with the licensing lion only awakening, some
devout *Peanuts* readers were beginning to grouse about "commercialization" and oversaturation of their favorite strip. The *Time* writer differed and concluded "if anything, the strip has improved over
the years; both its drawing and satire have sharpened."

Whether an artistic endeavor truly improves is often up to the
individual, but Schulz works as hard today to improve and maintain
the comic strip as he did originally and when the generous *Time*
writer drew his conclusions more than twenty years ago. The criti-
cisms remain, too. The Metropolitan Life Insurance campaign of the
eighties brought complaints from readers who resent all insurance
companies.

Schulz is sensitive to criticism, especially from other cartoonists, that his strip has grown "too commercial."

"The strip is a commercial product to begin with. How can you
go commercial with something that's already there? Comic strips sell
newspapers. That's what they are there for.

"I tell the critics, 'I have seven children to support,' " says
Schulz, counting his five children and his second wife's two. The
seven children each get 1 percent of his monthly income.

Peanuts isn't a bonanza for the Schulz family alone. Schulz actually gets only a small fraction of every dollar generated by his characters. Scripps Howard stockholders, his employees, syndicate employees, countless entrepreneurs and their employees, and a zillion
other middlemen and women also come in for a tiny cut. And
Snoopy is certainly doing more to restore the foreign-trade balance
than any other dog in America.

Which dollar is hard-earned and which dollar is gratuitous is
really a pointless discussion. Maybe someone else would have cut it
off by now for vague artistic reasons. One thing is certain. Many
more would have exploited the situation more greedily, killing the
Easter beagle for one more golden egg. And another thing is certain:

It beats modeling knickers.

15

"You're a Blockhead, Charlie Brown!"

You're a good man, Charlie Brown,
You're the kind of reminder we need.
You have humility, nobility and a sense of honor
that is very rare indeed.
You're a good man, Charlie Brown,
And we know you will go very far.
Yes, it's hard to believe,
almost frightening to conceive,
what a good man you are!

I'm not very handsome or clever or lucid,
I've always been stupid at spelling and numbers.
I've never been much playing football or baseball,
or stickball or checkers, or marbles, or ping pong. . .
I'm usually awful at parties or dances,
I stand like a stick or I cough,

or I laugh,
Or I don't bring a present
or I spill the ice cream,
or I get so depressed that I
stand and I scream:
"Oh, how can there possibly be,
one small person as thoroughly, totally, utterly
'Blah' as me?"
— from *You're A Good Man, Charlie Brown*

Peanuts is not a roman à clef starring Charlie Brown as Charles M. Schulz. The flesh-and-blood cartoonist almost never finds himself hanging upside down from a tree, tangled in kite string and waiting to be rescued by two sparrows with a crosscut saw. Beyond that, however, the two characters have a lot in common.

While the two are not one and the same, Schulz freely admits that he and Charlie Brown are fellow travelers and that the round-headed kid is his personal emissary to the court of *Peanuts.* Schulz's creation is one of the most highly individual and personal comic strips ever, which is an important element of its success. Almost everything in it contains something of the artist, but nothing in *Peanuts* is a more direct, intentional reflection of Schulz's idea of life and himself than Charlie Brown.

In addition to being a wide-open conduit for the emotions and experiences of Schulz, Charlie Brown serves another, equally important purpose. He is the host of the *Peanuts* anthology, the master of ceremonies who, if only by his presence, coordinates a frenetic milieu where he is the common denominator. The very common denominator.

Charlie Brown wasn't conceived as an alter ego for Schulz; their similarities surfaced over time. The character who would become known as Charlie Brown appeared in Schulz's *Saturday Evening Post* gag cartoons and in his *St. Paul Pioneer Press* feature *Li'l Folks,* where he was called by name for the first time. The first *Peanuts* strip ever published served to introduce him personally, mentioning his name three times, and he was tacitly given top billing over the strip's other original cast members—Shermy, Patty, and Snoopy. In fact, Schulz seriously lobbied in 1950 to name his new comic strip *Good Ol' Charlie Brown,* when United Feature Syndicate decided it could not use the name *Li'l Folks.*

The first *Peanuts* reprint book that did not include the name of the strip itself in the title (the fourth book) was called *Good Ol' Charlie Brown.* (The next one was entitled *Snoopy.*) Charlie Brown's name has always been virtually a subtitle for *Peanuts.*

The character Charlie Brown was named for a friend and fellow worker of Schulz at Art Instruction Schools. The christening had no significance beyond being the sort of compliment creative friends pay one another, and none at the time suspected the immortality thus bestowed. In fact, the sensitive Schulz would later chafe to hear his old friend Brown referred to as "the real Charlie Brown"; to him it impugned the originality of his creation.

"As the years went by, I sometimes felt guilty over what I did to my friend Charlie Brown when I borrowed his name. Of course, I did ask his permission when it all started, but neither of us ever dreamed of the little troubles it sometimes caused him. As someone who knew us both once said, however, 'But look at all the fun and attention he also got from it.' One thing is for certain, too, and that is that I *never* used him as a model for any of the ideas. After his death there were articles calling him the real Charlie Brown, but it was the name only that I used. I regarded Charlie as too good a friend ever to play upon him in any other way, and I still grieve over the physical sufferings he had to endure."

Brown died of cancer in 1983, and his death received national mention because of his round-headed namesake.

Charles Frances Brown of Minneapolis did have a time of it. In a little book published posthumously—a volume Brown envisioned as one third of an autobiographical trilogy—he writes of bouts with emotional stress, hard drinking, and cancer, all of them wrapped around a lifelong search for some answers about life and himself through religion.

He was, at times, an art instructor, a social worker, an editor of a young people's journal. He rode motorcycles and wrote, off and on for seven years, about himself.

When Charles Schulz "borrowed" his friend's name for his cartoon creation, Schulz simply liked the sound of it, the same way he would later prefer the sound of Beethoven to Brahms, Sopwith Camel to de Havilland, ophthalmologist to optometrist. Ian Fleming did the same sort of thing when he created his 007 fantasy spy, James Bond. With permission, Fleming used the name of a renowned ornithologist. The nonfiction version of James Bond was not a martini-drinking spy but an author and expert on birds in the Caribbean. As Fleming explained in a letter: "This brief, unromantic, Anglo-Saxon and yet very masculine name was just what I needed."

Charlie Brown, the person, was willing to let others think his personality, as well as his name, was the basis for the famous strip, which was not true, according to Schulz. Brown told a newspaper interviewer "For legal reasons, Charlie [Schulz] has to take the position that the thoughts and acts of his characters aren't related to live people. That doesn't bother me. How could it?"

He complained in his book that his name sometimes made others think "I'm a gag, a con man, or just mental." He told of being stopped for jaywalking in downtown Minneapolis. When asked his name, he replied "Charlie Brown." According to Brown, the police thought he was joking. "Listen, wise guy, you can't afford to kid us." Brown produced his driver's license, to which an officer said "Look, with that name I guess you got troubles enough."

More often, though, his comic strip namesake brought him favorable attention, long newspaper write-ups, and even an expenses-paid trip to New York to appear on a television game show, *To Tell the Truth,* where the celebrity panel failed to pick out "the Real Charlie Brown." The self-professed dreamer never used Chuck, or Charles F., or any other name deviation that could have ended any confusion. Possibly, the notoriety brought him more pleasure than almost anything in his unsettled life. Or possibly he forfeited a personal cohesion in subconscious emulation of the hapless cartoon character. The whole subject is a little troubling to Schulz today.

From the start of *Peanuts,* Shermy displayed a distressing lack of star quality. He fell naturally into a supporting role for Charlie Brown, and, soon, Patty and the new girl Violet likewise were serving as foils for Charlie Brown. In the first couple of years of *Peanuts*

only Snoopy challenged Charlie Brown for the best gags, pointing
out early a major direction of the future. Lucy and Linus soon came
along and quickly accomplished what Shermy and Patty and Violet
could not. They worked well in harness and eventually brought a
parity to the ensemble cast that would become the norm. Charlie
Brown's role would grow in importance and scope, but he would
never again be called upon singly to carry as much of *Peanuts* as he
did the first five years or so.

Charles Schulz didn't start out America's premier cartoonist,
and Charlie Brown didn't start out as the most complex of
characters.

"This is my favorite picture," he tells Patty in a strip circa
1951. "It was taken by a sidewalk photographer."

"But what is it?" asks Patty.

"A sidewalk, of course!"

In the beginning, part of Charlie Brown was a feisty, wisecrack-
ing little ladies' man. "Hello there, handsome," Patty says to him.
"You're wonderful, Charlie Brown," says Violet.

"This is my hope chest," says Patty to Violet.

"What's a hope chest for?" she responds.

"You save things in it that you'll need when you get married!"

"What do you have in yours?" Patty opens the lid, and up pops
a gasping Charlie Brown in a strip that probably wouldn't be permitted today lest someone infer the syndicate advocates asphyxiating
children. While certain cartoonists succeed in rolling back frontiers
of taste and frankness in the modern comics, syndicates at the same
time are finding themselves increasingly under the guns of serious,
literal-minded advocacy groups who exist to police the media's treatment of their particular issue in our litigious society. The list of
things that can be taken lightly grows shorter.

While part of the embryonic Charlie Brown was a winner, the
part we know today has been evident all along, too.

"Somebody's at the door," says Shermy to Patty.

"Oh, it's you, Charlie Brown," says Patty when she answers
the knock and finds her round-headed neighbor. "I thought it was
somebody important." Significantly, such deprecating humor in the

early strips did not fall on Charlie Brown exclusively. Had their roles been reversed, with Charlie Brown afflicting Patty, it wouldn't have appeared uncharacteristic at all. Charlie Brown gratuitously insulted Patty quite often.

In a 1951 strip particularly illustrative of the battle for Charlie Brown's soul, he is walking down the street, musing to himself: "I'd like to be president, or a five-star general or a big-time operator. . ."

"Hello, there, Charlie Brown," hail Patty and Violet as they walk past. "That Charlie Brown's a good guy, isn't he?" says Patty to Violet, who replies, "He sure is! Good Ol' Charlie Brown!" Dejected, Charlie Brown continues to muse:

"But that's all I'll ever be . . . Just Good Ol' Charlie Brown. . ."

Soon after, Charlie Brown lost the battle for his soul, and the world came to share his humble opinion of himself. In fact, the muscling in of Lucy and Linus about this time wasn't just a coincidence. Their development closely paralleled Charlie Brown's complete submersion into Blahdom, for they provided Schulz an entirely new point of reference from which to redefine his increasingly wishy-washy protagonist. From the primordial goo of the Van Pelt infants arose the *Peanuts* today's readers recognize.

Not until he shed his leading-man inclinations and unreservedly embraced the goat did Charlie Brown achieve his Charlie Brownness. The fact was not lost on Schulz.

By 1956, Violet had changed her tune:

"I can't really like you, because you're not perfect. I'm sorry, Charlie Brown, but that's just the way I feel."

"But I'm pretty perfect," laments Charlie Brown.

A year later, things were not getting any better:

"You know what bothers me the most," Charlie Brown confides in Schroeder after another baseball disaster. "I feel that I've let down you players, who had faith in me as a manager."

"Oh, well, if that's what's bothering you, just forget it," Schroeder replies. "We never really had any faith in you." As usual, Lucy is more direct:

" 'Manager'. . .HA!"

Life on earth is futile. Ultimate defeat is inevitable. Fame is ephemeral, but blahness goes on forever. Nobility is not in winning but in trying, though losing is certain. This rather bleak message, embodied by the tribulations of Charlie Brown, became the underlying theme of the entire comic strip. People read it and laughed. They applied words like "charming" and "cute" and "adorable" to *Peanuts*, but their increasing devotion indicated that, subconsciously at least, they empathized with its hopelessness. When *Peanuts* first became well known, when editors began snapping it up and newspaper readers were asking each other "Have you ever read Charlie Brown?," it was the downtrodden condition of the round-headed kid that defined the feature.

Charles Schulz put a lot into Charlie Brown, and the public has taken even more out. "Favorite" characters can be debated all day, but Charlie Brown unquestionably is the most analyzed. Some readers can't seem to resist sifting through the shards of Charlie Brown's broken heart to decipher the *real* meaning of *Peanuts.*

"When Charlie Brown is referred to as that 'round-headed boy,' we are confronted with the incongruity of characters in the strip calling attention to the predilections of the artist. It is as though the characters in a novel began to question the motives of the author. This incongruity is appropriate, however, because the figure we have come to know as Charlie Brown *is* exceptionally round-headed" [from an essay by Elliott Oring in *The Graphic Art of Charles Schulz*].

"In its center is Charlie Brown: ingenuous, stubborn, always awkward and doomed to failure. Requiring, to a critical degree, communication and popularity, and repaid by the matriarchal, know-it-all girls of his group with scorn, references to his round head, accusations of stupidity, all the little digs that strike home, Charlie Brown, undaunted, seeks tenderness and fulfillment on every side: in baseball, in building kites, in his relationship with his dog, Snoopy, in play with the girls. He always fails. His solitude becomes an abyss, his inferiority complex is pervasive—tinged by the constant suspicion (which the reader also comes to share) that Charlie Brown does not have an inferiority complex, but really is inferior. The tragedy is that Charlie Brown is not inferior. Worse: he is absolutely normal. He is like everybody else. This is why he proceeds always on the brink of suicide or at least of nervous breakdown; because he seeks salvation through the routine formulas suggested to him by the society in which he lives (the art of making friends, culture in four easy lessons, the pursuit of happiness, how to make out with girls. . .he has been ruined, obviously, by Dr. Kinsey, Dale Carnegie, Erich Fromm and Lin Yutang)" [from *The World of Charlie Brown* by Umberto Eco, translated from Italian by William Weaver].

"You're a blockhead, Charlie Brown!!" [Lucy Van Pelt]

The source of humor is a historically daunting topic. It is tricky to not overlook the obvious: it's supposed to be *funny.* Sometimes English teachers and literary critics imply that truth is cleverly hidden within entertainment, which amuses the artists who know it's the other way around.

Actually, Charlie Brown says more about the cartoonist than about his strip or its meaning. Charles Schulz didn't originally intend to make Charlie Brown the daily Everyman, but Schulz wouldn't know how to begin to separate his life and his art. His anxieties, his misgivings, his insecurities—the underlying forces of his uneasy persona—soon were reflected in the round-headed kid.

Schulz is everywhere in *Peanuts,* really. His wit is apparent in Snoopy; his crabby side lives in Lucy; his love of books and knowledge falls to Linus, and his reverence for music to Schroeder. It's Charlie Brown who gets the good stuff, though. He inherits Schulz's storehouse of anxiety, the negotiable currency of the human realm.

But maybe there's something to the consoling old myth that losing builds character. He still can't fly a kite, the little red-haired girl still doesn't know he's alive, and he'll never win a baseball game. Yet Charlie Brown's losing has become shtick. From the void on the face of the planet that was Charlie Brown has grown a wise, understanding young man. Seldom persecuted directly and far less hysterical than in his younger days, the modern Charlie Brown has become almost a father figure for the cast. The others look to him for guidance and hold for him something distantly, vaguely, kind-of-if-you-squint-real-hard resembling esteem. He's as powerless as ever to influence a situation much, but everyone, for some unfathomable reason, looks increasingly to him.

Much of this was brought about by the influence of the outsiders, Peppermint Patty and Marcie, who rescued "Chuck" from the neurotic pull of the Van Pelts and by a general drift of the strip toward a more subtle examination of the human condition.

Charlie Brown's patrician status atop the large cast of today sometimes tempts readers to forget just how integral he has been to *Peanuts,* especially during the heady rise to initial fame. The only de facto survivors of the original cast, Charlie Brown and his dog Snoopy are the nucleus around which it all formed. Charles Schulz never forgets.

"He's still the backbone of the strip," says Schulz. "No matter what happens, I still like to have it all come back around to him somehow."

16

Neighborhoods

Where does Good Ol' Charlie Brown live, anyway? Over forty years, Charles Schulz has dropped a lot of clues without saying exactly where *Peanuts* is set. There are specific places we know the *Peanuts* kids do not live.

They don't live in Petaluma. That's the town in California where Snoopy traveled for the wrist-wrestling championships. They do not live in Kansas City. Snoopy's sister Belle lives there, so we can surmise Snoopy does not. Likewise, his brother Spike lives in Needles, in the southeastern California desert. Whenever he visits Snoopy, it is a long and painful (he travels with a cactus) journey, so Snoopy and friends don't live in the Mojave Desert.

Peppermint Patty's star baseball player, Jose Peterson, immigrated to the neighborhood via New Mexico and North Dakota, so they don't live in either of those places. Charlie Brown apparently doesn't live in Alaska; he considered entering a cereal company's contest to win a trip there.

175

Many, many more places can be eliminated on the basis of weather. It snows in *Peanuts.* A lot. So the children don't live in Miami, or Los Angeles, or New Orleans, or Atlanta, or Houston, to name only a few nonpossibilities.

There is a lot of emphasis on skating and hockey but little on downhill sports, so they probably don't live in the mountains. The birds, however, do maintain a chair lift to the summit of Snoopy's nose.

We do know it's a city. Charlie Brown attends baseball games in a large stadium that obviously is home to a major-league franchise. The children have the benefits of Tiny Tots concerts and a specialized medical community with ophthalmologists and sleep-disorder clinics.

It would be more correct to assume Charlie Brown and his friends live *near* a city, for they certainly live in the suburbs. Although in an early strip Charlie Brown revealed that his grandmother lived "in the apartment upstairs," his family obviously escaped soon afterward to a single-family dwelling of their own in a predominantly white, upper-middle-class neighborhood. We know it's a new subdivision, because there aren't many trees to bang your head against. Snoopy openly complains about living in the suburbs, because he has to take the bus downtown to chase cars.

Pumpkins are grown there, but the children most assuredly do not live on a farm; no way. You might see polar bears and bald eagles and cougars in *Peanuts,* but you never, ever will see a cow or a horse.

The characters routinely go to the beach in the summer, apparently on a day trip, so they would live within an easy drive of an ocean. Or maybe the Great Lakes. Linus notes "Some people think there may even be sunken ships from the War of 1812 right around here." Obviously a reference to the Battle of Lake Erie. Or maybe just to Woodstock's theory of a relic at the bottom of Snoopy's water dish.

We know between the homes of Charlie Brown and Linus lies Fort Zinderneuf. We know there is a species of kite-eating tree. We know the birds hike to Point Lobos. We know it is a strange and exotic place that owes much to Schulz's boyhood home of Minnesota and his current home in northern California. But we know, really, that the neighborhood exists only in the cartoonist's mind. It can be visited only at his invitation.

Actually, there are three distinct neighborhoods, or theaters, within *Peanuts.* There is the classic neighborhood, the original, suburban streets of Charlie Brown and Lucy and Linus and Schroeder; there is Snoopy's neighborhood, a fantastic world of imagination; and there is the other neighborhood, the parallel existence of Marcie and Peppermint Patty.

Charlie Brown's environment is the original setting of the comic strip, of course, and is the only real physical stage for *Peanuts*—the point of reference for everything. As such, it is the most tangibly defined of the three major arenas. Early on, Schulz detailed it as a pleasant community of postwar ranch homes and green, spacious lawns. This was understandable. *Peanuts* was a new strip, and it was necessary consciously to devise a setting for the benefit of readers who had never heard of Charlie Brown or Snoopy. It was 1950 in America. Where else could kids possibly live but in the suburbs?

Peanuts has always been an economically drawn strip, but in the beginning the artwork could be downright intricate compared to that which would follow. Freely included in the earliest strips were literal drawings of houses, trees, telephone poles, and garbage cans. Some interior sequences were equally elaborate, with furniture, drapery, and woodwork often in the background.

Schulz was primarily a gag cartoonist before launching the strip. He was accustomed to relying on props and sets, which were often necessary to stage a one-shot joke. Also, he was a burgeoning artist. As a good artist matures, he naturally develops an efficiency of effort, an instinct for eliminating the superfluous.

The young artist was finding his way, and it wasn't long before his imagination and sensitivity took over for him. The humor and the characters achieved such a distinctiveness that it quickly became moot whether *Peanuts* was set in Connecticut or Katmandu.

Yet the old neighborhood exists still, and we are intimately familiar with it, although for years now it has been depicted subliminally—a chair, a stone wall, a sidewalk, a window.

Although Snoopy was coming on like gangbusters, the classic

neighborhood was the only theater of *Peanuts* for the first decade. It was where the children grew up. Literally, they did start out as children, some of them as infants, and their activities were very childish. They pulled wagons, played with dolls, resisted bathing, and ate ice cream, but they evolved rapidly. Within five years *Peanuts* more closely resembled the strip of today than the strip of 1950.

Schulz ran through many major players in the formative years: Shermy, Patty, Violet, Pig-Pen, Frieda. Eventually the human cast settled down to Charlie Brown, Sally Brown, Lucy, Linus, and Schroeder. All but Charlie Brown were babies when introduced. Soon they were assigned very rigid personalities and idiosyncrasies that interlocked superbly to form the backbone of the strip.

Lucy still took her meals from a high chair when she was introduced into *Peanuts* in 1952, and she's been looking down on the world ever since. Egotistical, devious, selfish, and materialistic, she was thirty years ahead of her time. Her pushy personality quickly shoved Patty and Violet out of the strip's female lead, and for the next fifteen years or so nobody had a meatier role than Lucy.

The one thing Lucy was always willing to share was her enormous dearth of knowledge.

"Some stars are big, and some stars are little," she tells Linus one Eisenhower night.

"You sure know a lot about stars, Lucy."

"Well, I've done quite a bit of studying. One of my best subjects in school was agriculture."

Over time she has become a hardworking character actor who has surrendered her star status with surprising grace.

Lucy's second banana Linus also was introduced in 1952 and, despite his exposure to his sister's disinformation, he eventually became the most intellectual character of all. Which is not to say his driveway goes all the way to the street. Despite his IQ, Linus is the quintessential follower; his sister never gives him any choice. With little internal ballast, all that sail aloft just makes him the victim of any wind that blows. One can say for Linus that he has the courage of his convictions. It's his convictions that are suspect.

Led by Lucy, Linus participated in the overthrow of Shermy,

Patty, and Violet as leading players. They were the only siblings in *Peanuts* during the salad days and, with Charlie Brown and Snoopy, became cornerstones upon which fame was built.

Essentially a straight man, Schroeder has survived and quietly thrived for almost the entire forty years of *Peanuts'* history. His claim to fame, of course, has always been his music, but beyond that he is a dependable, level-headed kid whose chief function is to say "What are you going to do now, Charlie Brown?" His longevity is partially attributable to his role on the baseball team. Every pitcher needs a catcher.

Charlie Brown is widely regarded as Charles Schulz's alter ego, but Schulz also has a lot in common with his blond musician. Music is Schroeder's life. It's what he does. Beyond it, he contributes little more than a physical presence, albeit a benign, well-informed presence.

Schroeder is hit on the hand by a foul tip. "Is it going to be all right? Are you going to be able to play?" asks Charlie Brown. Schroeder runs home and bangs out a few bars of classical music and runs back to inform Charlie Brown, "It's all right. I can play."

"That isn't exactly what I meant," sighs Charlie Brown.

Schroeder's obsession with music closely parallels Schulz's dedication to *Peanuts* itself. Life for Schulz breaks down into two categories: the comic strip and things that interfere with the comic strip. Schroeder slumped over his piano even recalls Schulz hunkered over his drawing board.

In 1954 Schulz introduced Good Ol' Charlotte Braun, a female counterpart to Charlie Brown whose gimmick was a loud mouth. She didn't work out and quickly disappeared. In 1959 Schulz landed a keeper in Sally Brown, Charlie Brown's little sister. Sally went on to become perhaps the most underrated character in the strip. Not only did she team effectively with Charlie Brown, humbling him into a role as her straight man, she matured into a distinctive personality in her own right. Yet when readers envision *Peanuts,* Sally somehow manages to fall through the cracks.

Perhaps this is because Sally was born into the old neighborhood crowd after it was firmly established and grew up just in time to see more and more emphasis placed on Snoopy and new players from outside. Like most of us, Sally was born a baby. It was well into the sixties before she was awarded peer status. Crabby and self-centered like Lucy, Sally's concerns were more worldly than her forebears'. Demanding and shallow of intellect, she was something of a transitional character who foreshadowed Peppermint Patty. She would flourish in the coming environment.

Many faithful readers regard this cast with fond nostalgia, loyally taking them to heart as the "real" characters of *Peanuts.* Such is human nature to resist change in the things we love, but Charles Schulz could no more return to an earlier phase of *Peanuts* than he could roll back the years. He has been creating *Peanuts* for four decades, not just drawing it, and to turn back would be the end.

It irritates and depresses Schulz when a devotee of any particular period wastes breath asking "Why don't you do cartoons like that anymore?" Despite his efforts to be inoffensive, despite his care to respond to fans' requests and comments, Schulz has never pandered to the tastes of others. The only way he can draw a strip, he believes, is to draw it the way he sees fit. If he is right, the fans will follow. So far, his approach has been borne out.

By 1960, *Peanuts* was regarded as sophisticated, but in that time the cast never quite lost its innocence or its childish perspective. When he began, Schulz was a young man. The introspective cartoonist could draw upon what must have seemed an inexhaustible repertoire of his own childhood experiences. Soon he had a houseful of children of his own. Although he has rarely capitalized on their exploits directly (as Bil Keane does in *The Family Circus*), Schulz's throbbing family surely infected him and his work with vigor and even optimism, at least the optimism that believes if everything is a mess today, someday it will work out all right. The fears, problems, and disappointments of little children growing up were always central to *Peanuts* in the first ten or fifteen years.

In a 1957 daily strip, Lucy is briefing Linus on the rigors of kindergarten: "You have to know a lot of things before you can go to kindergarten, Linus. You have to be able to use a handkerchief, get a drink of water alone, put on your own coat, and cut with scissors."

"Wow!" says Linus. "I never realized the requirements were so rigid!"

After ten years, the humor in *Peanuts* had become very verbal, with conversations and witticisms among the players the primary Schulz gimmick. Early in its life, *Peanuts* earned the reputation of a thoughtful, deliberate comic strip of great depth, an image that persists today as the readers' overriding impression of the ever-changing feature. The kids, though, were still kids, toting blankets and wearing cowboy hats, and if their conversation was increasingly focused on life at large, it still reflected an inexperienced ignorance.

Lucy, circa 1961, tells Linus: "Charlie Brown says that we're put here on earth to make others happy."

"Is that why we're here?" reacts Linus. "I guess I'd better start doing a better job. I'd hate to be shipped back."

They were all young, but they weren't all children. There was a dog. Snoopy was part of the original cast. He was a cute, four-legged puppy who started off mooching snacks and defying the children's attempts to teach him tricks. Within two or three years, he was thinking to himself. After about five years he was discovered to be a talented impressionist. He danced on two feet. In 1958, he started sleeping on top of his doghouse. That was the same year Snoopy was copyrighted a second time, because his character had changed so much in appearance. About that time Charlie Brown wrote to his pencilpal: "I thought you might be interested in hearing about my family. My dad is a barber. My mother is a housewife. Oh, yes, I also have a dog named Snoopy. He's kind of crazy."

Charlie Brown was right. Charles Schulz was about to go crazy with Snoopy.

Peanuts was in a verbose period in the early sixties, and Snoopy had become a relief valve for the sometimes complicated repartee of the humans. In fact, Schulz was beginning to chafe a bit under all those weighty accolades being heaped upon him: sophisticated, intellectual, philosophical. He wanted to try something different, to have a little fun, and Snoopy was in the right place at the right time.

Snoopy had come a long way in the first ten years of *Peanuts,* and it occurred to Schulz that from there the beagle could go any- place! He gave Snoopy his head, and the rest is hysteria.

Comic strips usually evolve or die. They rarely remain the same unique, hilarious, relevant features the salesmen at the outset claim they are. A cartoonist usually conceives a new strip, but it isn't taken on by a syndicate unless the strip happens to be what the syndicate thinks will sell at the moment. Then syndicates will usually make suggestions to the creator of the new comic strip, which thereby be- comes something of a collaboration. It will either fail rather quickly or become established and begin to evolve in the direction the cre- ator would have it go—with close syndicate supervision. In rare cases, a strip will become a runaway success, bringing in so much dough that the 900-pound-gorilla principle takes effect and the cre- ator can go anywhere he wants.

This was the enviable position of Schulz by the mid-sixties, and what he did basically was create a new comic strip within a comic strip.

When Schulz was a little boy dreaming of being a cartoonist, he didn't dream of drawing a funny strip like *Peanuts.* The rage on the comic pages was the adventure strip like *Terry and the Pirates, Steve Canyon, Captain Easy*, and *Prince Valiant.* Artists like Milt Caniff, Roy Crane, Hal Foster, and Alex Raymond were Schulz's heroes. He wanted to draw an adventure strip. Today he lives that dream through Snoopy. When the beagle leads a patrol out of Fort Zinder- neuf or when he buzzes off to seek the Red Baron, it is Schulz's way of paying homage to the adventure serials that dominated the com- ics industry when he was a boy.

Even a dispassionate reader can tell Schulz has fun with Snoopy. He admits to having great good feeling for the beagle and his sidekick Woodstock. As Lucy notes, man is born to suffer, and in *Peanuts,* that includes dogs. Snoopy has his share of anxiety and set- backs, but he is by far the most irrepressible spirit in the cast. He is a perfect antidote for all that black humor which, without him, might be overwhelming.

Snoopy's neighborhood is surreal, of course. His doghouse is firmly planted in the Brown soil, but it is a portal to the universe. Snoopy has been to France, to the Sahara, to the Student Union, and to the Moon. Snoopy has been a writer, a surveyor, a world-famous surgeon, a scout leader, an attorney, a vulture, even a rotary-wing aircraft.

Birds can go anywhere, so what better minions to share Snoopy's vast neighborhood than his fine feathered friends? They unquestioningly follow the lead of their black-and-white Beau Jest, a dog without a single redeeming virtue save humor.

Providing the elements of conflict and danger is World War II, the off-camera cat next door. World War II is described by his owners as a kitten; by Snoopy's estimate the feline weighs anywhere up to 200 pounds.

Snoopy's neighborhood also encompasses an extended family as unconventional as Snoopy himself. There are his sister Belle and her teenage son, his smart brother Marbles, who wears jogging shoes, and his ugly brother Olaf, who (like Schulz and most of the cast) hates coconut. These are all walk-on characters without any long-term importance except to *Peanuts* trivia freaks. Then there is Snoopy's wormy brother Spike. Spike maintains a wacky little sub-world of his own, where he plays opposite a stoic stand of saguaro cacti that never move or speak. Spike's insanity and Schulz's wit combine to cast the inert succulents in a zany comedy of seemingly endless visual gags.

Spike plays a supporting role to Snoopy. They visit, but Schulz consciously works to keep Spike distant and subordinate. He is the strip within a strip within a strip.

Somehow the children are vaguely and uncomfortably aware of what goes on in Snoopy's head, and they take it all with a grain of salt. They wander by his doghouse and offer criticism—constructive and otherwise—of his latest manuscript. They've always laid down sardonic flak for his flights of fancy. Snoopy has served the humans as coach, attorney, and skating partner, among other things, but they've never expected too much of him, and he's never failed to meet their expectations.

Peppermint Patty retains Snoopy to sue the school board because the roof leaks above her desk, but he abruptly recuses himself when the principal quotes Henry VI: "The first thing we do, is kill all the lawyers."

Clients and critics notwithstanding, not everyone easily enters Snoopy's realm of the ridiculous. Woodstock can, of course. Among the humans, the empathetic soul Marcie seems to display a peculiar ability to share Snoopy's delirium. Kind, placating Marcie. She even loves Charlie Brown. If Snoopy thinks he is a World War I Flying Ace, Marcie accepts it. Although she occasionally haunts French bistros with the Flying Ace, Marcie is a denizen of the other neighborhood.

In 1966, at the height of *Peanuts'* cult popularity, Schulz introduced a gregarious little girl from outside the old neighborhood and named her Peppermint Patty, after a brand of candy. At first she seemed to be all the *Peanuts* kids were not: brash, confident, insensitive, athletic, a real take-charge type. At first Peppermint Patty functioned primarily to give the strip something else it had never had besides bonhomie: flesh-and-blood opposition on the baseball diamond. Peppermint Patty was the manager of her own baseball team, a team as proficient as Chuck's was hapless. The archetypical nickname sort, she hung "Chuck" on good ol' Charlie Brown, who, if it bothered him, was much too wishy-washy to protest. She was a perfect foil, but you've got to develop some neuroses if you want to become a major player in *Peanuts.* She did, and she has.

Obviously, her neighborhood was shaping up to be something quite different from what readers were used to. We have never been shown Marcie and Peppermint Patty's neighborhood in any visual detail, but we can assume it is similar to Charlie Brown's. Schulz does use a few devices to accentuate their physical apartness: They communicate with the original cast by telephone a lot. They attend different schools. Although they do mingle, the casts of the two neighborhoods function separately, and often when they are together there is a reason, such as a baseball game or camp or a dance class. Chuck shares an intimate friendship with Marcie and Peppermint Patty, but discreet tribal barriers are in place for most of the other players.

For the first few years, Peppermint Patty served as a walk-on, a guest star who breezed in from afar. In 1971, her companion Marcie was introduced, and the other neighborhood began to coalesce as a true third ring.

As mentioned, the new kids were different. Externally, they were tougher. Peppermint Patty and her baseball team were boys and girls of action; they didn't tend to brood so much. They could be prone to a brand of violence more real than Lucy's clamorous posturing. It was the new players who wandered in and introduced themselves. They were adventurous and outgoing. No one had known them as infants. The *Peanuts* kids were forced to assimilate the unfamiliar, a very real process of maturing. It was never really stated, but the new kids seemed older. Their influence was broadening, and it served to age and advance the original cast as well without contriving to do so.

While not necessarily planned, all of this didn't just happen, either. Schulz's household of real-life moppets was quickly becoming a household of adolescents. Eventually, there would be grandchildren even. Not baby-boomers but products of the seventies and eighties. Schulz needed an updated vehicle for all the new baggage accumulating in his sensibilities.

The other neighborhood—more hip, more with-it—proved to be that vehicle. The teacher grades essays with "Grody to the Max." Peppermint Patty "corn-rows" her hair and gets her ears pierced. Their world is not so insular; Charlie Brown's neighborhood is a cultural contemporary of *The Donna Reed Show* and *Father Knows Best.* Schulz works carefully to make the humor timeless, so its vintage isn't readily apparent or even important, yet this timelessness works against *Peanuts* as well, preventing it from taking root. Peppermint Patty and Marcie live in a sacrificial neighborhood, if you will. Through it, Schulz can venture out into the real world without weakening the original personality of the strip, which after all is the soul of *Peanuts.*

Peppermint Patty is not as tough as she first appeared. In fact, she develops into a rare, multifaceted gem. As she and Marcie begin to function on their own, readers become aware of an entirely new set of problems in *Peanuts.*

Peppermint Patty has problems with authority. She runs afoul of the dress code at school. She is the worst scholar of the entire *Peanuts* crew. She falls asleep in class. She's cheeky. Many of her troubles are externalized.

But not all her troubles. Like her buddy Charlie Brown, she's insecure. Yet her insecurity stems from a girl-like dissatisfaction with her appearance more than from a baseless self-loathing that approaches a personality disorder. Her nose is too big. Her hair is stringy. She isn't beautiful. The boys won't like her.

"Do you think I'm beautiful, Chuck?" she asks.

"Of course," he answers. "You have what is sometimes called a 'quiet beauty.' "

"You may be right, Chuck. I just wish it would speak up now and then."

In short, here is a kid showing all the early symptoms of a raging case of puberty. Yes, in the other neighborhood, sexuality is budding.

On her birthday, Peppermint Patty gets a dozen roses from her father:

"He said that I'm growing up fast, and soon I'll be a beautiful young lady, and all the boys will be calling me up, so he just wanted to be the first one in my life to give me a dozen roses." She concludes: "Suddenly, I feel very feminine!" Schulz actually did this for his daughter Amy.

Charlie Brown's love for the little red-haired girl is unrequited, but it is a fallacy that Charlie Brown is unloved. Both Peppermint Patty and Marcie carry a smoldering flame for the boy from the old neighborhood. Their gentle competition for his favor and their almost matronly indulgence of him and his inadequacies ring truer than most of the strip's other established crushes, such as Lucy's attraction to Schroeder.

Poor Marcie. Smart as a whip and sweet as an angel, she quite openly professes her love for Charlie Brown. She is convinced, however, that he could never love someone who wears glasses. And she's right! Charlie Brown would rather moon over the cute little red-haired girl, who doesn't know he's alive. Very human stuff.

Amid all this youth flowering in the other neighborhood is the shriveled stalk of fatalism. As with most parents, all the regeneration around him reminds Schulz that he is growing old. A deep, continuing dialogue has sprung up between Charlie Brown and Peppermint Patty that centers on a restless anxiety about the meaning of life. Echoed in the ponderings of adolescents on the threshold of the unknown can be heard the ruminations of a man at the other end, desperately asking the same questions as time grows shorter.

"Life is like a bracelet, Chuck. . . It has little jewels around it which are like the little bright moments that come along in our lives every now and then. Do you feel that this has been one of those bright moments, Chuck? Do you feel that this hour we have had together has been like a diamond set in a bracelet?"

During the seventies, when the team of Peppermint Patty and Marcie was developing, Schulz was pushing back other boundaries with increasingly outlandish use of visual gags and absurd situations. Much of it was visited upon the kids in the new neighborhood, but they still managed to come across a little differently. With their tendency to get involved in long story lines and plausible conflicts, they acquired a depth all their own. They were human in a humble way. The two little girls from the outside brought to *Peanuts* a dimension the illustrious strip had never really had before: relative to their predecessors, the new kids were true-to-life children.

From the classic neighborhood, from the roots of *Peanuts,* Schulz went two opposite directions. With Snoopy he explores unlimited fantasy, and with Peppermint Patty and Marcie he dabbles in unexaggerated human drama and pathos.

However, this is all a general vision. All the theaters of *Peanuts* share many generic characteristics, and none exists entirely independent of the others. Not even Snoopy's bizarre realm. Clever overlapping of the various elements strengthens the whole.

When Woodstock's snowmen melt, he disconsolately stacks their hats on his head and trudges off. From a window Marcie sees this and observes "A tiny bird just walked by with five hats on his head, and I think he was crying." To which Peppermint Patty can only reply, "You're weird, Marcie."

In fact, roughly beginning with the eighties, another theater that might be described as "the World of *Peanuts*" began to solidify. What has emerged is an unabashed blending of the various elements into a more homogenous amalgam. This fourth area is formed by a drastic breach of the already porous boundaries between the various neighborhoods and is characterized by the elevation of whimsy to a new and exalted status. Charlie Brown and the classic cast have become less childlike and more resilient while Peppermint Patty and Marcie have become more flighty and buffoonish. And Snoopy continues on his merry way, but his anything-goes version of reality has finally permeated the entire cast.

In 1982, Charlie Brown discovers that he can no longer field his baseball team on the vacant lot, because the owner has been advised that he might be liable for any mishap. It is, of course, devastating news to Charlie Brown, whose friends fear for his mental well-being. To encourage and console him, Marcie puts her pride on the line and tells "Charles" how much she likes him, and she kisses him. That doesn't do much for Charlie Brown's mental well-being, as it turns out, but the entire matter is resolved when Snoopy's brother Spike arranges the sale of the lot to coyotes in Needles, who can't be expected to care who plays baseball there.

Another time Snoopy and his feathered legionnaires fire a cannon in an effort to retake Fort Zinderneuf, which turns out not to be a fort at all but the doghouse. The cannonball destroys the doghouse roof, goes on to demolish Lucy's psychiatry booth, and comes to rest on top of Schroeder's flattened piano.

In a 1986 Sunday strip Marcie pointedly visits the old neighborhood "To watch Charles fly a kite. It's something I've always wanted to see." In the end, she winds up hanging upside down with Charlie Brown in a classic *Peanuts* situation. "It was an experience," she reports.

Marcie catches the flu from the World War I Flying Ace in the great influenza epidemic of 1918.

Schroeder books passage to music camp through Lucy the travel agent. Linus the baggage handler throws his piano into the hold of the doghouse as Woodstock the mechanic makes some last-minute repairs. Marcie the stewardess serves him a banana and assures him that Snoopy the pilot is OK ("He faints after every landing"). After all this, Schroeder expresses genuine dismay and outrage when he discovers he hasn't arrived at music camp at all.

The interplay among the traditionally distinct elements and the level of absurdity within these and many other *Peanuts* episodes over the past ten years or so denote not a departure but a progression. After forty years, it is still coming together.

Peanuts is not, after all, simply a comic strip about children growing up in the suburbs; it is not about a pet dog with an active imagination. It is a highly mobile literary vehicle with a vast and increasing range, maintained by a dynamic cast whose only directive is to keep it moving without losing track of where it's been. And keep it funny.

17

"My Citizen Kane"

Craig Schulz, the quiet son, skillfully taxis the sleek Citation I into its spot at the Burbank Airport, an airport unremarkable except in its utter grayness. Nothing but its proximity to Hollywood suggests this is the spot where the silver screen's most historic good-bye was filmed.

Once upon a time an actor and an actress stood on this very apron, the fog machines and cameras rolling, acting out an ending, finally, for a love story that had just about painted itself into a screenwriter's corner.

"You're going to get on that plane. If you don't, you'll regret it. Maybe not today. Maybe not tomorrow, but soon and for the rest of your life." Rick and Ilsa were actually in Burbank, not Casablanca. No wonder the letters of transit were so valuable.

During the short flight from Santa Rosa to Hollywood, Schulz, who does not like to fly, had commented with noticeable pride on son Craig's calm and therefore comforting demeanor. "He really

190

knows what he is doing," Schulz would say from time to time, reassuring himself as well as all the others aboard the eight-seater.

"Craig has always been incredibly mechanical," his brother Monte attests. "When we were kids he made his own Flintstones car."

A few years back, Schulz apologetically asked his business manager about purchasing the jet, an idea directly inspired by Craig's consuming interest in flying. He was assured he could afford it. Since Schulz honestly has no idea how much money he has, or how much things cost, or how many cartoons he must draw to fuel a jet, the question was typical.

At any rate, the purchase has made the frequent shuttle between Number One Snoopy Place in Santa Rosa and the animation studio in Hollywood infinitely more convenient and bearable for the anxious homebody Schulz.

It is a bright spring day. Sparky Schulz and his entourage stretch their legs and rent a car. The sights through the rental-car windows are typical Hollywood—Bogie's Liquor, sheepskin seat covers cheap-cheap-cheap, Eleanor's Body Shop, the Brown Derby, New York Pizza Express—a montage of old and new. Vintage cinematic landmarks float by, as unreal and detached through the car window as on a late-night television screen. So, too, pass the freaks, the heads, the grime-varnished sidewalks, street stuff as unappealing and lacking in glamour as yesterday's garbage.

"I like Hollywood," says Schulz, undaunted. "I like driving around on a warm evening in Hollywood."

The destination is Larchmont Boulevard, near the corner of Rosewood Avenue, where two gleaming white houses of California stucco provide a home for Lee Mendelson—Bill Melendez Productions, an animation studio. Mendelson produces; Melendez animates.

The studio itself seems animated, with its happy clutter, shop shorthand that everyone seems to understand, and urgent, endless hunts for lost film. The secretaries all wear tight denim, which emphasizes their anatomically impossible movements among the storyboards and Movieolas. They are Olive Oyls all, stretching and reaching, as if in momentary suspension over the ubiquitous cartoon rail-road track. Melendez, with his handlebar mustache and mischie-vous grin, needs only a top hat and cloak to portray the cartoon villain.

It is real work unfolding, however, not make-believe. Earnest men and women bend over viewing projectors, perfecting the thou-sands of individual cartoons that somehow eventually come together in one fluid and continuous motion. Between twelve and twenty-four sketches are needed for just one second of animation.

Since 1965, when Mendelson first approached Schulz about possible animation of the *Peanuts* gang, the unlikely marriage of illu-sory Hollywood and purist Charles Schulz has prospered.

Sparky was naturally wary of "Hollywood types," as he called them, but he had seen and been impressed by Mendelson's indepen-dently produced documentary film on Willie Mays in 1963. He agreed to cooperate on an hour-long documentary about the comic strip and its creator that would feature only a few moments of animation.

The sponsors and networks were not interested when it was first offered. Mendelson, of course, was disappointed he could not sell his documentary, but *Peanuts* was becoming a pop phenomenon without the networks' blessing. In April 1965, *Peanuts* made the cover of *Time* magazine, piquing the interest of readers and, indi-rectly, potential sponsors. Coca-Cola was shown the Mendelson film and particularly liked the animated portion. They asked for an all-an-imated *Peanuts* Christmas show.

The result, *A Charlie Brown Christmas,* won raves right out of the gate, copping the George Foster Peabody Award for "distin-guished and meritorious public service" in programming and an Emmy. More important, letters from viewers poured into the Schulz studio. The animated *Peanuts* had begun.

Network experts had worried aloud that the show might be too slow, too religious, too subtle for the world of commercial television. With its airing, they were effectively silenced.

In retrospect, it was daring.

Here they were, smack in the year of spies and espionage with

Early drawings

Inspired by the little red-haired girl

Perspective lesson

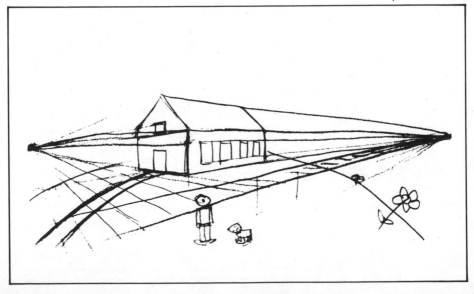

APR. 11, 1950
TUESDAY

101 - TUES., APR. 11, 1950 - 264

From Donna Johnson's desk diary at Art Instruction

APR. 22, 1950
SATURDAY

Church of God - 3:pm

112 - SAT., APR. 22, 1950 - 253

"Last night just before I went to sleep, I prayed that if I asked you for a date, you'd accept...sort of puts you on the spot, doesn't it?"

"I'm creating a very special protrait of John the Baptist...no matter where you stand, the eyes follow you and make you feel real
guilty."

From Schulz's army sketchbook

Oct. 4, 1944

Elmer Hagemeyer's letters home — illustrated by Charles Schulz

Li'l Folks *drawn for* The St. Paul Pioneer Press

From The Saturday Evening Post, *Schulz's first sale to a major market*

TWELVE DEVICES

The kite-eating tree

Schroeder's music

Linus's blanket

Lucy's psychiatry booth

Snoopy's doghouse

Snoopy

The Red Baron

Woodstock

The Great Pumpkin

The little red-haired girl

The baseball games

The football episodes

Some recent strips, favorites of Charles Schulz

The Man from U.N.C.L.E, I Spy, and *Secret Agent* the rages on commercial television, introducing to viewers the quiet charm of an animated *Peanuts* as subtle as its comic strip counterpart.

Even television's sitcoms that year were outrageous and exotic: *Gilligan's Island, I Dream of Jeannie,* and *The Beverly Hillbillies.* (Point of trivia: it was the fabulously successful, half-hour *Hillbillies* that was preempted the first time *A Charlie Brown Christmas* was shown.)

Onto that action-packed stage stepped Linus—who, of all things, simply stood still and read the Christmas story from Luke. It was an unprecedented and, yes, startling departure for an animated character.

The jazz of Vince Guaraldi audibly marked the feature as adult fare, whereas cartoon specials in the past had targeted children exclusively. The traditional laughter soundtrack was left out, at Schulz's insistence.

Important, too, was the "voice" of the film. Charles Schulz was not and is not the voice of Charlie Brown. People often ask.

Children did all the talking, not adults speaking as children. Because of that, every couple of years or so, as the members of the cast mature and the timbre of voices changes, a new Charlie Brown, Linus, Lucy, and so on, must be found. Children between the ages of nine and eleven are auditioned, and each new cast is chosen to best match the voices of the original group in *A Charlie Brown Christmas.*

Sometimes the right children are living right under the noses of the shows' creators. Mendelson, for instance, found a key player at the home of his business partner, Walt DeFaria. DeFaria's daughter Gai came into the room, spoke, and Mendelson immediately recognized the voice of Peppermint Patty. Often a younger sibling will take up the role when the older child "graduates."

Schulz has never been completely satisfied with the Charlie Brown voice, he complains. Just as Charlie Brown is the hardest to draw because of his round head, he also is the hardest to match with a believable voice. One Charlie Brown was a girl.

On the other hand, Schulz has liked all the Linuses, especially the first one. Animator Melendez makes the Snoopy and Woodstock noises, the grunts and howls and inhuman harpings. He gets to keep his job, year after year, since puberty is comfortably behind him. Using children is not all joy: "Those stupid kids keep forgetting their lines," Schulz grouses.

"We downplay Lucy in the animated specials," he says. "She was always too shrill, shrieking and screaming in the specials. What worked with her in the cartoon strip didn't necessarily work on television."

In the quarter-century since Mendelson quickly whipped up a Christmas show for Coca-Cola and got a 45 share, *Peanuts* animation projects have garnered twenty-four Emmy nominations and won five.

More important, perhaps, some of the shows have become cultural landmarks, traditional viewing on certain holidays, not unlike Truman Capote's *A Christmas Memory,* Jimmy Stewart in *It's a Wonderful Life,* or the timeless *Miracle on 34th Street.* Families gather around the television screen to celebrate a holiday, a season, with Charlie Brown. And now the video market has made it possible to own Good Ol' Charlie Brown.

For every season there is a show: *It's the Great Pumpkin, Charlie Brown, You're in Love, Charlie Brown, It Was a Great Summer, Charlie Brown,* and, of course, *A Charlie Brown Thanksgiving* and *A Charlie Brown Christmas.*

Schulz writes the story and dialogue and decides himself how the action should look. Melendez produces a story board, rough drawings that Schulz must approve, with over 800 sketches just to outline a thirty-minute film. Using the pictures as a framework, a soundtrack is recorded. Mendelson sells the show, usually giving preference to the same half-dozen sponsors who have bought all the animated specials.

The finished animation used is called "limited" in the trade, a cheaper variety originally made necessary because of the insatiable appetite of television. It is stiffer, not as "human," as the cartoons produced by the big studios for the big screen in the golden days of animation and Hollywood.

As its name suggests, limited animation contains less movement than older cartoons, and the most casual observer will note the
staccato movement of modern television characters when compared
to the frenetic activity of a Tom and Jerry. Simply, it involves less
movement, therefore less drawing, saving money.

This is decried by purist critics but is an inevitable fact of studio
life. Hours of weekly animation required by children's programming
could not be produced by the old "masterpiece" approach to animation. It's the way things are, the reason gingerbread architecture is
not found in tract homes.

Inevitable or not, Schulz is always sensitive to the charge he's
not doing things right. He defends, effectively, Melendez's use of
limited animation.

"We're not working with human characters," Schulz says. "If
that were the case, why would we need cartoons? You don't want it
to flow that smoothly; you want it to look like a cartoon."

"Limited animation" is something literally in between the old-
fashioned printed cartoon and the kinetic carnivals of the pioneering
animators, it is well suited for the adaptation of *Peanuts,* which is after all a comic strip, and a rather passive one at that. There is no reason to believe a thousand animators working around the clock could
bring *Peanuts* to the screen with more fealty to the original product
than Mendelson and Melendez, Schulz contends.

Certainly, Schulz and his animators have demonstrated that
limited animation can be quality animation.

From time to time well-meaning critics allow that Schulz might
become "the next Walt Disney," a comparison that mildly infuriates
Schulz (foremost among the rare individuals who can be mildly infuriated). "I don't want to be Walt Disney. He was a producer, not a
cartoonist! I am a cartoonist."

From the start, Disney basically dreamed up Mickey Mouse
and his other characters, leaving it to others to "design" them and
put them to work.

Schulz is in Hollywood this particular day to view his latest
movie effort, *The Girl in the Red Truck.* Four years and millions of
dollars have been invested in the film, in which Schulz had placed

high hopes. Every time somebody suggests an addition or change, Schulz jokes: "What will that cost me, another four hundred thousand?"

It is a departure, a risk. For starters, it is a story about Snoopy's brother Spike. Schulz was slightly offended when others involved with the project insisted that Spike needed an introduction as Snoopy's brother; Schulz felt *Peanuts* fans know Spike. Not only is Spike the only *Peanuts* character with an important role in the show, he is—after the brief introduction featuring Charlie Brown and Snoopy—the only animation. He will interact with a live cast on real sets. A number of Schulz's friends and associates have been brought in on the project, including his daughter Jill as the female lead. The theme is close to his heart—unrequited love. And as it nears completion, outsiders who have seen it aren't moved. There are a number of reasons Schulz wants to see *The Girl in the Red Truck* do well.

Plus, he wants a masterpiece.

"I wanted this to be my *Citizen Kane,* but it's not," he says.

Schulz is a serious movie buff, traveling once a week or so from Santa Rosa to Petaluma to a cinema that offers numerous foreign and art films. He sits near the back of the theater, on the end of the row, his long legs overflowing into the dark aisle, critically watching the likes of *Le Grand Chemin* or *Bagdad Cafe.* Occasionally he naps.

He keeps current on films and film-making techniques and has strong negative opinions about gratuitous sex and violence. "Why don't some of those famous actresses say 'No, I won't say these words, and I won't act this way'? Why don't some of the ones with clout take a stand?" Graphic language interferes with the pure pleasure movies have given him since he was eighteen years old and saw *Lost Horizon.* "I came out of that one in a trance." Making a personal masterpiece is his dream.

There are several problems with *Red Truck.*

Because of countless delays for Schulz's people, *Who Framed Roger Rabbit* will hit theaters shortly before the CBS airing of *Red Truck* in 1988. Great things already are being forecast for *Roger,* and Schulz is worried viewers will assume he copied the actor/animation format, although neither recent effort is the first such hybrid *(Song of the South* and *Mary Poppins).*

A concerned Schulz, who likes to do things first and best, emphasizes to daughter Jill she should mention *Red Truck*'s conception date whenever possible in her publicity tours.

Red Truck is a beauty-and-beast kind of tale, with Spike co-starring. It is unlike anything Schulz has ever done, a casting call of friends and neighbors and family. Besides Jill as the girl in the red truck, son Monte helped with the writing.

And Mollie Boice, whom Schulz first saw perform in a Santa Rosa Little Theater production of *The Oldest Living Graduate,* has a bit part. She has a young Patricia Neal quality that is so good it is almost distracting.

The music is done by Paul Rodriguez, a friendly bear of a fellow who works on Redwood Empire's annual ice shows.

Director Walter Miller, known for Hollywood extravaganzas like the Academy Awards show, found *Red Truck* a different kind of challenge, shooting all of it without one of his stars. Spike, of course, had to be drawn in later.

"I never shot so much plain brown dirt in my life."

Miller first met Schulz in Oakland, where Miller directed a televised ice show for the cartoonist. "Someone on the crew told me that his nickname was Sparky but that he wasn't known to everyone by that name. 'It's up to you,' the person said. 'If you think you have established a rapport with him, you might want to use it.' " Miller approached Schulz and, in a flush of well-meaning familiarity, said, "Hi, Spooky!" Every now and then, Sparky reminds him.

For *Red Truck* Schulz and company even bought fake saguaro cacti at a thousand dollars a pop, since the live ones were not always in convenient spots for filming. The truck itself cost three hundred bucks and looks it.

There were perspective problems the veteran crew of animated Snoopy shows had never before experienced. Spike hit Jill right about midcalf, an awkward disadvantage for a love affair. Spike, every bit as silent as Snoopy, had to have a way of expressing himself. So Spike used his French lesson tapes to communicate with the elusive girl in the red truck. The actors found themselves talking to rocks, dirt, cacti, and blue sky during the filming.

These, however, were the kinds of creative challenges Schulz

covets. The finessing was expensive, but what if, despite all the res-
ervations, this show proves to be The One?

It didn't. Reviewers roasted *Red Truck*. As Schulz had feared,
they compared it unfavorably with *Roger Rabbit*. Some had disparaging things to say about Jill's performance, suggesting Schulz should
look outside his own family for talent.

But Schulz has not given up on making a *Citizen Kane*. A quiet
story about children with cancer may be the sleeper.

Four years ago a nurse approached Schulz about creating a five-
minute film for children hospitalized with cancer. He explained to
her the time and expense involved with such a project; she came
back to him a few months later with financing. Schulz donated his
own time, as did Melendez, and the result is a touching story about a
classmate of Linus and Charlie Brown's who discovers she has cancer. The five-minute format has been expanded to a full-length animated program for CBS.

Instead of directing the show solely to children hospitalized
with cancer, it targets all their friends, the ones left behind at school
and on the playground, grappling with concepts they cannot even
pronounce—mortality, insensitivity, chemotherapy. It is educational, teaching children that cancer is not contagious, for one thing.

It is aptly named *Why, Charlie Brown, Why?* and Linus
emerges the sensitive hero, gallantly shielding his friend when her
hair falls out or when she must spend Christmas in the hospital.

Another educational venture released in 1988 was *This Is
America, Charlie Brown,* the first animated miniseries in the history
of television. Somehow, Charlie Brown and company find themselves conveniently in historic hotspots—aboard the *Mayflower*; in
Kitty Hawk, North Carolina, with the Wright brothers; and high
above earth in a space station.

Perhaps the most poignant of the celebrated specials thus far
has been *What Have We Learned, Charlie Brown?*, in which Schulz
sends the gang to France. Linus leads the troops to Omaha Beach, recalling June 6, 1944, D-Day.

Melendez traced actual World War II combat footage onto animation paper, giving Linus's mental reenactment a surreal and dra-

matic quality. Eisenhower's words of hope and humanity are heard.

Schulz made this special after a trip to France during which he revisited the chateau where he had bivouacked as a young soldier. It was a trip he almost did not make.

As is his habit, Schulz made plans for the journey months ahead, but the closer the departure date came the less appealing the idea seemed. The rest of his party went on without him. Finally, his son Monte made the ten-hour transoceanic flight with him, then turned right around and flew back. "It was the only reason I went," recalls Monte.

What Have We Learned? won Schulz his second Peabody Award and gave Linus some of the most powerful philosophizing of his career. Schulz has a photograph of the lonely chateau hanging on a wall behind his drawing board.

The industry that had shunned Mendelson and Schulz in the early sixties grew to love them. CBS wanted a regular *Peanuts* show on Saturday morning. In 1983, Schulz succumbed to their requests and *Peanuts* went, for the first time, to Saturday-morning television. He had avoided it before, fearing it would "cheapen the product." In his prime-time spots he had been writing primarily for intelligent people—not necessarily children or adults—just as his strip is written. The Saturday-morning shows would be different, targeting children exclusively, competing in that fast-paced land of monsters, mayhem, and magic.

After much hoopla at an announcement party in New York, the show premiered. Called *The Charlie Brown and Snoopy Show,* it lasted only one season. "It was just too much work," Schulz says. "All those episodes, something like eighteen of them, instead of the two or so shows we were used to doing a year. There just wasn't the time to do it right."

The animated projects will never replace the strip as his number-one interest, but Schulz does enjoy the visual extensions possible through animation. "It's fun to think of things when you know you're not going to have to draw them."

18

Other Palettes

*C*harles M. Schulz, playwright. Has a nice ring.

Schulz keeps a cloth-bound notebook with blank pages in a waist-high drawer of his desk these days. Every now and then he jots a note to himself on one of the clean pages. Not some cartoon idea against a future barren day but a memory beckoned from his stint as an instructor, after the war, at Art Instruction Schools.

He was one of fifteen such employees situated in a big room at the correspondence school and charged with correcting the lessons of students who answered the famous "Draw Me" ads and received their fundamental art training through the U.S. Mail.

Schulz never got to work in a newspaper office, as he once dreamed of doing as a cartoonist, but Art Instruction Schools was an ambient first cousin, he believes.

Art Instruction, with its rare collection of sophisticated wits and creative minds, would make a terrific setting for a play, he insists today. The instructors had eclectic and highbrow tastes and, to

200

a person, moonlighted as cartoonists and illustrators. They knew music and literature and actually discussed symphonies and books. They understood the value of harvesting humor from the uninspired lessons that daily fell through the mail slot at Art Instruction. Otherwise the repetitiveness of the job would have quickly disillusioned and bored the whole ambitious lot of them, professionals who wanted more from life than correcting yet one more lesson in basic perspective.

All Schulz lacks for his proposed play is a plot. The players could easily be taken from the people who sat at the desks all around him. There was Walter J. Wilwerding, a famous magazine illustrator of the period, who headed the department.

It was Wilwerding, incidentally, who designed the running greyhound that was adopted as the logo of Greyhound Bus Lines, a lovely bit of trivia Sparky managed to incorporate into *The Girl in the Red Truck.*

There was, too, Frank Wing, the instructor who once gave student Sparky Schulz a low grade in part of the Art Instruction course called "Drawing of Children." Ironically, it was also Wing who first complimented Schulz on his little folks; in his words, they were "pretty good," and Wing suggested Schulz do more.

Wing was a capable artist himself, drawing a beautifully rendered newspaper feature in the 1930s called *Yesterdays.* Wing was adamant that his students "draw from life" and not just from their imaginations.

Art Instruction, after all, was a practical school, its end goal employment for all graduates. It stressed lettering, which enabled graduates to paint signs or letter tombstones, if it came to it, for that most ennobling of all artistic achievements—a job.

Every afternoon at four Sparky began whistling "Grand March" from the opera *Aida,* and Wing picked it up in midstanza like a musical relay baton. Every day the same routine got a laugh. Perhaps it was then Schulz learned the value of repetitiveness in humor. It was certainly where he learned to whistle "Grand March."

Not a day passed that some hapless student did not unintentionally entertain the Art Instruction troops by misinterpreting an assignment. In the rudimentary package of art supplies sent to each new subscriber, for instance, a bottle of India ink was carefully packaged in sawdust, meant to soak up any leak.

One student wrote he understood what to do with the ink, the paper, and the brush. "But what is the sawdust for?"

Routine instructions included the suggestion students draw on a drawing board. So, a literal-minded subscriber mailed in his lesson, painted (you guessed it) directly on a large drawing board. The board remained in the office, a shrine, of sorts, to student naivety.

When students were told to moisten their brushes with saliva, one wrote back asking where to buy a bottle.

And, when asked to draw thumbnail sketches, inevitably at least one aspiring artist from a new crop of students would furnish a drawing of his own opposing digit.

Because of the volume of student lessons, instructors used what was called the "paragraph system" to grade them. They were not form letters as such, but enough of the novice artists shared the same problems to make it convenient to assign a number to paragraphs enlightening the students on certain points. Paragraph 12B, for example, might deal with perspective. The instructor would judge the student's work, mark down the appropriate paragraphs for a reply and then give the outlined letter to a typist.

"Sometimes the letters ended up reading enough alike that occasionally we'd have students who lived near one another who compared letters and then complained the instruction was a sham. It wasn't."

The love interest for the hypothetical play was there, in the person of Donna Johnson, of course. A little red-haired girl in a violet dress, traipsing across the classroom set with her daily apple for a certain aspiring cartoonist.

There is the topic of creative camaraderie to explore. The employees of Art Instruction reveled in one another's outside sales and successes.

Wilwerding wrote this about his single-minded instructor Sparky Schulz in 1948, before *Peanuts:*

One day we saw him lay aside his adventure cartoons and

turn out some sketches of children. He was just fooling
around with these to begin with, having fun making sketches
of a tough miss whom he labeled "Judy" after one of our
young lady instructors. We all enjoyed following the adventures of Judy as the days passed and her life unfolded under
Sparky's pencil and brush. We encouraged him to follow this
type of cartooning in place of adventure cartoons. He had
the knack; his kid characters were alive. We would like to take
credit for pushing him into success, but we know he needed
no pushing. Sparky's mind was made up, even when he was a
boy, to someday be a cartoonist, and nothing could stop
him.

There is dramatic and comic material from those days beyond
what he has gleaned for the strip, Schulz contends. Someday, maybe, he will use it. He similarly has ideas for a book and several magazine articles. The book he has in mind would explore the motivations of preachers, especially those who spread the word for no
apparent earthly reward. The Minnesota Church of God minister
who inspired the young Sparky and lured him from the Lutherans, a
man for whom Schulz bought a retirement house, is the sort of honest, driven preacher such a book would profile.

Percolating intermittently in his active mind is an article on
golfing holes in one, a subject about which Schulz jokingly admits he
has no firsthand knowledge.

The work of Charles Schulz already has infiltrated other media.
A musician named Clark Gesner sent Schulz a test record and asked
his opinion about some songs he had written with lyrics that dealt
with the foibles of the *Peanuts* characters. "They were very good
songs," recalls Schulz, "and we said at the time, 'You know this
would make a wonderful Broadway show.' "

On March 7, 1967, *You're a Good Man, Charlie Brown* began
its off-Broadway run at Theatre 80, St. Marks, in New York City.
Produced by Arthur Whitelaw and Gene Persson, the show starred
Gary Burghoff as Charlie Brown. Burghoff later went on to fame in
the role of Radar in *M*A*S*H*. The play ran for four years in New
York, and there were nine touring companies. It was an undisputed

hit and since has become the most performed musical in the history of the American theater. Says Schulz: "I have seen photographs of the cast who performed in a Copenhagen production; they were amusing because the fellow who played Linus was over six feet tall, an enormous man. I've seen the play performed with girls playing Snoopy and even Charlie Brown, but no matter how they do the play, it survives."

You're a Good Man, Charlie Brown was not the first musical adaptation of the *Peanuts* theme, however. Before that, nightclub entertainer Kaye Ballard had used *Peanuts* banter and references in her singing act. Schulz was flattered: "She had this wonderful act, full of Fannie Brice numbers, and she'd turn to her piano player and say, 'Charlie Brown, what about this or that?,' and then she'd use one of my little jokes from the strip. Well, I heard she was in San Francisco, and I called her up, and we met for dinner and then later I saw her show. She was a wonderful lady. Later we gave her permission to do a long-playing record for Columbia Records, but as these things usually go, Columbia fouled it up somewhere along the way, and it never really sold well or was in any stores."

As much as the idea of writing his own play intrigues him, it both flatters and troubles him if someone else suggests he dabble in another medium.

"I do a comic strip seven days a week. Isn't that enough? Why would I want to write a book?"

He thinks about it, nonetheless, and takes pride in a collection of short essays he wrote as the accompanying text for a thirty-fifth-anniversary cartoon collection, *You Don't Look 35, Charlie Brown.*

"His own writing is very synthesized," says son Monte Schulz. "He definitely is not long-winded.

"His writing is very much like his drawing—clear and traditional. He is a forties and fifties kind of writer who uses timeless references and a classic style. He's not in the least gimmick-oriented."

Monte, thirty-seven, is a writer himself, struggling to put the finishing touches on his first novel, a thriller. It was his father who directed a teenage Monte to the works of certain writers—Carl Sandburg and Joan Didion, Flannery O'Connor, Carson McCullers and Thomas Wolfe—for the lyrical quality of their work.

Of all his rewards and awards—the Emmys, the Reubens, the Hall of Fame inductions, honorary degrees, and the Boy Scout Silver Buffalo—Schulz may be most pleased with the A he got a few years ago on a paper he wrote for a community college night course about Katherine Anne Porter's *Pale Horse, Pale Rider.*

One of his favorite compliments of *Peanuts* was hearing it compared to Lewis Carroll's *Alice in Wonderland.*

Only rarely does Schulz drop his famous name and certainly never wastes it to meet a politician or movie star. He saves his sway.

He will, however, occasionally use his considerable clout to meet a writer, for Schulz, above all else, loves books and words and writers. He loves their ideas, their personalities, their company. He will telephone them, arrange luncheon meetings with them, congratulate them on new books. While he can be harsh, downright cruel, in private critiques of fellow cartoonists, Schulz stands in absolute awe of famous writers. He likes to mingle and talk with the literati. Toward them he is solicitous.

Once he attended a gathering where author Eudora Welty spoke. After the lecture he plucked from his memory a detail from one of her short stories and used it to engage the Southern writer in conversation: "I remarked on how she described the curlicues, the little loops in a Coca-Cola sign. I thought that was a wonderful thing for her to notice and to write about."

He arranged a meeting with California writer Didion and once called Anne Tyler to say her newest novel was "wonderful." Lately he has been figuring a way to lunch with Sacramento's Pete Dexter, winner of the National Book Award for *Paris Trout.*

It is the grossest of misconceptions, of course, that cartoonists do not themselves write; they write daily and do the hardest kind of writing there is —short. There is much truth in the apology of French philosopher Pascal: "I have made this letter rather long only because I have not had time to make it shorter." Besides brevity, the good cartoonists master comic timing and dialogue. They tell a story in four panels or less, sometimes without using words at all. Only another writer could fully appreciate the skill that takes.

At any rate, Schulz has always regretted his lack of formal education and seems intent, even now, on paying educational penance by learning all he can about everything he can. Besides his voracious reading habits, he sometimes takes night courses at Santa Rosa's community college in subjects that generally involve literature.

There is a reason he prizes education. His parents both dropped out of school after the third grade, and son Sparky talks frankly of his abysmally poor record in high school. He did not attend college.

Carl Schulz, always well-respected and active in his profession, once served as recording secretary for the Master Barber's Association. He was ill suited for such a role. Poor Carl sat through the meetings, making sketchy notes the best way he knew how. Then later, at home, Sparky was drafted to decipher the notes and transfer them in legible handwriting into the official barbers' notebook.

"Being young and ungrateful, I usually grumbled. But I always did it."

Dena Schulz had neither the time nor inclination for reading until cancer began overtaking her slim body. As her fragile health waned, Sparky introduced her to the magazine *Omnibook,* which ran abridged versions of the current best-sellers. She might have become a reader, the son likes to believe, if only she had lived.

As a small child Sparky clipped newspaper coupons and redeemed them one by one at the neighborhood drugstore for volumes in a cheap set of encyclopedias.

"I was so proud of those encyclopedias, until the day I had to write an English report. I copied every word my encyclopedia had about the subject and turned in my paper. When I got a bad grade, I asked the teacher about it. 'I included everything my encyclopedia said,' I told her.

"'Well, you need a new set of encyclopedias, then,' she said. Teachers can be very cruel, you know."

Not until his army days did Schulz make any effort to read the classics—or to read much of anything, really, beyond his beloved comic magazines like *Famous Funnies* and *Big Little Books.*

When he did decide to improve his base of knowledge, he went at it with an inspired vengeance. If his time at Art Instruction Schools provided the impetus, the nigh-compulsive Schulz personality insisted he stick with it. Schulz began collecting classical records and attending community concerts. And he adopted a serious new habit: reading. It was a habit he never broke.

These days he keeps several books going at one time, grilling friends about what they may have read that he has not. By the next time they meet, he usually has read the book in question and is eager to discuss it.

He religiously reads all book reviews he finds and quietly complains that "his" newspaper, *The San Francisco Chronicle,* will not review cartoon collections.

His bookshelves are vast and varied: *The Agony and the Ecstasy, Clinical Cardiology, The* Citizen Kane *Book, Hans Brinker, Geoffrey Chaucer of England, Reuben/Reuben, The Call of the Wild.* He likes Southern writers, especially female southern writers who write about the human condition, but also can lose himself in the hard-boiled action of a George Higgins novel like *Rat on Fire* or a tedious biography of Nathaniel West.

Schulz made a recent contribution to *Favorite Recipes from Friends,* a celebrity cookbook assembled to raise money for a Connecticut school fund. The cartoonist gave his recipe for cold cereal:

Cold cereal can be enjoyed late at night when feeling lonely and recalling your high school days. It is also necessary to have something to read while eating. If books or magazines are not available, the printing on the cereal box itself may be read.

19

Peers and Politics

*B*y every right, they should be a nervous bunch, cartoonists. It is a highly competitive field, after all, with hundreds of working professionals and thousands of would-be-working amateurs vying to capture a shrinking hole on the shrinking comic pages of the nation's shrinking newspapers.

The comic strip itself has shriveled in a cycle of newsprint shortages. When the price of newsprint goes up the hungry syndicates, always looking for an angle, attempt to attract the editors with a space-saving comic. *Peanuts* itself was promoted for its smaller size as much as for its wit when it made its debut. This condition, which commenced virtually with the advent of comics themselves, has reached a critical state, long ago making extinct much of the virtuoso penwork that once characterized many, many features.

There are fewer comics overall today. Comic strips were conceived as circulation-builders, and surveys show they still work, but comic features receive harsh scrutiny in the corporate atmosphere of the modern newspaper. Newspapers have always been businesses, but with growing chain ownership and the rise of business "management" as deity, fewer and fewer editors are willing to put their careers on the line to fight the home office for six dollars a week to buy that marvelous new comic strip that everybody just loves. The result is fewer comic strips, although the readers actually want to see more. And always, always, when a new strip is added these days, one is dropped.

Then there are fewer newspapers as well. The real backbone of the newspaper syndication racket has always been the competition between large metropolitan dailies. At one time in America's recent past, every city of any size harbored at least two newspapers that went at it tooth and nail, to the delight and benefit of the readers. The bigger cities had three, four, even more newspapers, and the whole idea of the comic strip was to give such newspapers a competitive edge in cutthroat circulation wars. A number of demographic realities are taking a toll of the newspaper industry, however. Many once-prosperous journals are history, and large cities with only one newspaper are becoming common. Where more than one does exist, the second newspaper is often a weak sister in no position to challenge the dominant paper. The erosion of competition is an erosion in the basis of the comic strip's appeal to editors. In addition, of course, it means there simply are fewer places to sell comics today.

Yes, cartoonists have a right to be nervous. To be jealous. To worry. But mostly, comic strip artists are just as laymen expect them to be. They are nice people. Their satire may be biting, but personally they tend to be sweet and timid. A few may be famous, but they are generous with their time and patient with fans. The profession may face an uncertain future, but they feel specially blessed to be able to draw funny pictures for a living. There are literally thousands of young upstarts who want in on the diminishing action, but cartoonists are notoriously helpful to the uninitiated, willing to show the ropes to any self-professed cartoonist, remembering that someone did it for them.

Among themselves, they can be especially close-knit. Generally they have automatic respect for any fellow veteran who manages to

survive in the demanding field. Ask a cartoonist to recall a professional feud, and he invariably will mention an acrimonious and no-
torious set-to between a volatile Ham Fischer *(Joe Palooka)* and his
former assistant Al Capp *(Li'l Abner)*. That was during the Great Depression, and it was about the last one of any significance. There are
cliques and squabbles, but there mostly is a steadfast historic camaraderie among cartoonists, a standing credo that the meek shall inherit the goodwill of the powerful and established.

Perhaps it has something to do with the democratic and rudimentary procedure of the actual work: all cartoonists eventually
must sit down and face a blank piece of paper. The job stays the
same; only the paycheck changes. Whatever the reason, there are
few cartooning prima donnas. Lawsuits and loud words among the
brethren are rare.

At the annual black-tie National Cartoonists Society's awards
dinner, usually held in New York, they gather in one room for one
night, squirming beneath the restraints of tuxedos and company
manners, laughing for once at the same jokes. Yet there is no noticeable tension as the spotlights crisscross the room in search of a winner. Tonight they all win, for tonight they have someone else with
whom to talk cartooning. They speak in esoteric slang about dead-
lines, penpoints, paper weight, and strokes (both brush and golf).
They get a little bawdy. The master of ceremonies in 1988 was Bil
Keane, creator of the squeaky-clean *Family Circus*; on Reuben night,
Keane was downright risque.

The society gives a number of awards in different categories—
comic strips, editorial cartooning, animation, advertising, and so on
—and an overall award, the Reuben (named for NCS founder Rube
Goldberg), is given to one of the category winners.

When Schulz was first recognized by the society, winning its
Reuben in 1955, the honor shocked him. The membership itself se-
lects the winner. And he was definitely not a part of the clubby cartoonists' community that at that time still gravitated to New York
and its suburbs, where many cartoonists settled to be near the Manhattan magazine and syndicate offices. In those days, the New York
cartoonists got together regularly, peddling their drawings to poten-

tial customers and ending up later in some bar or restaurant for a martini and shop talk. Schulz was an outsider both because of geography and because of his temperament. He was simply not the type to savor "the hand-rolled cigar" without which the late George Kerr said no cartoonist could be. "Ladies don't look very good scooping low into a gutter to retrieve a butt," said Kerr, explaining why there are so few female cartoonists.

It certainly was not that Sparky Schulz did not have respect for his cartooning elders or some of his famous peers. On the contrary, there was not a more diligent, respectful student of the Old Masters than young Sparky. When he was a teenager, he wrote fan letters to both Roy Crane *(Captain Easy)* and Harold Foster *(Prince Valiant),* soliciting their opinions about ideas he had for comic strips. Roy Crane's wife promptly answered his letter, politely begging off for her husband, saying he got so many such letters she attempted to do what he could not possibly do—answer all of them.

Their paths crossed once. Crane was at one NCS meeting that Sparky attended early in his career, but Crane had a stomach virus and spent most of the time in his hotel room. Schulz left greatly disappointed.

Foster answered the young cartoonist himself. Sparky had suggested a golfing strip, which Foster dismissed as a comic premise with limited possibilities. The humor would quickly degenerate to locker-room chatter between the boys, Foster predicted. "I think now that he was right," says Schulz. As an adult, Schulz conceived and quickly abandoned a strip about sports, *It's Only a Game,* that he drew for one year (1957).

Now he is the premier cartoonist around, by almost any measure—money, number of newspapers, as of 1988 the one living member of the newly created Cartoonists Hall of Fame. Yet he still is not a hail-fellow-well-met. He rests uneasily at the top, keenly aware of any talent that might pose even a remote threat to his preeminence. If Schulz, renowned for his gentleness and clean living, has an unseemly side, it would have to do with his disdain for lesser lights in the trade, and there are many lesser lights than *Peanuts.* Usually the reason for his scorn is simple—and unfair: the other artist has less talent. Why it should matter to him that there are too many words in this strip, crude drawing in another is not readily apparent. Certainly, it has much to do with his insecurity. Sure, people loved him yesterday, but what about today? It is the stuff of many an unhappy success story in the entertainment business.

Perhaps the thing that gets under his skin the most is a certain type of strip. He absolutely, philosophically is opposed to comic strips with political overtones.

Probably not coincidentally, it was an overtly political strip, *Doonesbury,* that came along in 1970 and supplanted *Peanuts* as state-of-the-art in comic strips, attracting the media attention lavished on Charlie Brown et al. for their innovations in the sixties. The cover stories that once were Schulz's now belonged to someone else.

The Yellow Kid, considered the first true comic strip character, got in political licks, but the subject had been considered mostly taboo by the sensitive syndicate editors. Harold Gray was a founding father of the genre. In his *Little Orphan Annie,* he perhaps was the first strip artist routinely and willfully to break the established and cardinal rule about injecting one's own politics into the funny pages.

Gray was conservative and not the least subtle about it, lumping liberals and intellectuals and all their socialist inventions into one foul stew and gleefully stirring the political pot. He invented characters like Mrs. Bleeding Heart, hitting the densest reader over the head with a figurative two-by-four. And after Gray came Al Capp and Walt Kelly.

Schulz detests politics, of any stripe, on the comic pages. He does not indulge. He is never even tempted.

"Why do you want to offend fifty percent of your readers right off the bat? The targets are too easy, anyway. Anybody can criticize the president, and what does it mean, really?"

Political cartoons have no staying power, either, he says, and Schulz strives to have his gags make sense a hundred years from now.

Schulz has mixed feelings about editorial-page cartoons. He admires the drawing styles of Bill Mauldin, Pat Oliphant and Herblock. But many political cartoonists, he believes, are irresponsible, too quick to indict and make judgments based on inconclusive, preliminary news accounts. "If those cartoonists feel so strongly about things, why don't they run for their city councils or something?"

"I've decided to go into political cartooning," Lucy announces. "I'm going to ridicule everything!"

Charlie Brown: "I understand, Lucy . . . by the use of ridicule you hope to point up our faults in government, and thus improve our way of life."

"No. I just want to ridicule everything!"

In a follow-up strip, Lucy continues:

"I'm trying to draw a political cartoon that will solve all the world's problems. See? Here's Uncle Sam, and here's a dove of peace, and here's an elephant, and here's a donkey, and here's a figure I call 'The Grim Reaper.' Over here is a tiny figure I've labeled 'Taxpayer,' and down here is a snake saying 'Don't tread on me.'

"Don't you think this cartoon will solve all of the world's problems, Charlie Brown?"

"No, I think it will add a few more to it," he answers.

It also bothers Schulz that some young cartoonists are ignorant of the history and tradition behind newspaper comics and that one successful young cartoonist, Berke Breathed *(Bloom County),* publicly professes to being a non-fan of the comics, past and present. Schulz doesn't understand such ambivalence about the profession.

Schulz sees drawing a syndicated strip as a rare and anointed privilege, not something to be taken lightly or ignored for a year or so while working on other projects. He could no more take a professional sabbatical and drop Charlie Brown for a year than he could abandon his own children. To him, the whole idea of such professional nonchalance is repugnant.

"That's some way to repay the editors and the readers."

It truly does not seem to be a matter of Schulz disagreeing with the particular political slant of any cartoonist. He is not, for one thing, really a political animal. His personal politics might best be described as erratic, dependent more upon personalities than parties. He found Harold Stassen and Wendell Willkie fascinating, the latter because his radio voice was "so deep and throbbing, so great." He defends Ronald Reagan from critics "who cannot even manage to write a restaurant review without criticizing the man."

Yet "I could have voted for Mario Cuomo in 1988, had the Democrats nominated him. And I did vote for Lyndon Johnson, though later I was sorry I did. He was the first time I voted for a Democrat for president."

His ultimate political hero was—and is—Dwight D. Eisenhower.

"He was a great man. The GIs worshiped him. I worshiped him. Since then, it hasn't really mattered."

Carl Schulz was a staunchly conservative Republican, rightfully proud of his own resourcefulness and ability to build a small business and keep it going during the Depression. He was an employer, no thanks to the government, and viewed the world from that perspective. Sparky's Uncle Harris Halverson, on the other hand, worked at a cooperative creamery and was a dedicated member of Minnesota's Labor Party. He was an employee, and thus his views were opposite from Carl's. The in-laws never argued, but the unspoken debate did provide a smart youngster a vivid political contrast to contemplate.

The latest political issue that really mattered to Schulz, he insists, was the failed nomination of Judge Robert Bork to the U.S. Supreme Court.

"I sat there day after day with my leg in a cast [following a hockey accident], watching the hearings on television. I have never heard anybody who seemed to be so knowledgeable about the Constitution. Bork was wonderfully qualified. His detractors were just trying to get at Reagan."

Schulz has known a couple of presidents. He dined at home with Reagan when Reagan was California governor, a meeting that left him most impressed by the politician's cordiality ("Here I was, just an insignificant little cartoonist"). There was a lot of reciprocal fondness. In 1967 Reagan proclaimed a Charles Schulz Day; in 1969 Reagan honored the cartoonist with the state's Creative Citizenship Award. When President Reagan was shot in 1981, Schulz extended Snoopy's personal get-well wishes. Reagan drew a cartoon in return, the crude artwork posing no threat to Schulz's position as dean of American cartoonists, but appreciated just the same. Schulz has the presidential effort, a cartoon cowboy, framed and hanging in the *Peanuts* archives next to the ice arena.

Schulz met President Jimmy Carter while serving as national Easter Seals chairman. "We talked about teaching Sunday School." And he has declined more than a few invitations to dine at the White House. "There were always going to be a lot of other people there, a state dinner or something like that." He shrugs.

"Yeah, and one of those dinners was honoring the premier of China, for goodness sakes," says Nancy Nicolelis, United Feature Syndicate's director of public relations. Hers is a department often frustrated by the low-key approach of Schulz; turning down invitations to the White House simply does not compute in a public- relations-oriented mind. "It wasn't just any old gathering," she says.

His periodic petulance over politics expressed in comic strips is well known among his cartoonist colleagues. Cathy Guisewite, who considers Schulz her personal and professional hero, feared talking to her friend after a *Cathy* episode that in effect endorsed Democrat Michael Dukakis in the heat of the 1988 campaign.

"I'm dreading our next conversation," she said shortly after the election. "He'll think it was wrong, that I'm abusing my privilege of having a comic strip. I'm afraid he'll yell at me. Or, worse yet, he'll be disappointed in me."

"Actually, it's none of my business," says Sparky.

20

"A Perfect Sheet of Ice"

The lady was writing to thank Charles Schulz for the annual ice show he stages in Santa Rosa. It was absolutely perfect, she wrote, except . . .

The vocalist was off key. The show emphasized men's skating, giving all the athletic, powerful moves to the males, relegating the women skaters to cheesecake roles.

Oh, and there were no lights on the stairs that led to the bathrooms, almost precipitating a fall, which might have resulted in a sprained ankle.

And, while I have your attention, she persisted: about those television specials with Charlie Brown. They encourage young love, yes, early romance, which causes teenage pregnancies.

"Good grief!" says Schulz, returning the voluminous critique to the drawer where he has kept it for years. The two-million-dollar arena opened in 1969, and the Snoopy ice show, as it is informally known, has since become a popular northern California Christmas attraction, drawing spectators from surrounding communities, including what Santa Rosans invariably call The City, San Francisco. Schulz pulls the complaint-laden letter out every now and then and perversely savors it; it is, after all, tangible proof being a Good Guy gets you exactly nowhere.

The intended-for-profit rink where the shows are held loses nearly a million dollars a year, give or take a few thousand. It was conceived as a magnanimous gesture by Schulz and his former wife Joyce, who built the Redwood Empire Ice Arena for the citizens of Santa Rosa when the city's only ice rink went out of business. True, there was a selfish motive, but it wasn't profit. Growing up in frigid Minnesota, grinding over the hacked-up surface of puddles and ponds with dozens of other children, Schulz had dreamed of skating on "a perfect sheet of ice." Now he can.

The Redwood Empire's power bill alone averages about $10,000 monthly. In 1985, when insurance premiums jumped from $3000 a term to $125,000, the rink was forced to close for about a month, until more favorable rates could be drummed up.

There is not another skating rink exactly like it in the world. The ice has been covered and has become a concert hall featuring entertainers and artists, including Bob Newhart, Helen Reddy, and Bill Cosby. Poet and singer Rod McKuen, blinded by the spotlights, fell off the stage and ended up in traction after one memorable performance. The San Francisco Symphony once performed there, too. The shows ended when it was discovered the arena's outside booking agent was cheating.

"I always thought it was odd we lost about five thousand dollars on every show," Schulz said. "I couldn't understand why the agent continued to book acts. He kept reassuring us that this was a 'good house,' and he was acting with the future in mind." Schulz business manager Ron Nelson, then newly hired, discovered the scheme.

Despite its being something of a financial white elephant, the rink is an integral part of Schulz's daily existence, the physical seat of what is important to him beyond the comic strip.

"My whole life is filling in squares," he says dejectedly, in that sad, resigned way he has. Yet there are some mighty pleasant interludes, many of them enjoyed at the regulation-size rink. He takes at least one meal a day at the arena restaurant, The Warm Puppy, where the entire community is welcome. Except at his reserved seat by the window.

The rink is a sentimental fixture in the cartoonist's life. His sleeping children were hauled there at dawn for years, coaxed into their skates and action, a before-school ritual that ended with all of them becoming accomplished athletes. His second wife, Jeannie, was bringing a daughter to skating lessons at the rink when they met. In the early mornings he exercises in the arena's dance studio or has his first cup of coffee and reads the newspaper; in the evenings he learns to fox-trot and tango or referees hockey games. For a short time after the arena was opened and before the construction of his present studio, Schulz set up his drawing board in a tidy office upstairs, over the rink, but it quickly became obvious that the arrangement was going to be too distracting.

The arena doubles as community center for the town, and Schulz savors the pleasant milieu like a kid at the circus. Whenever he can kill time at the arena, contentment settles over him like a flannel blanket; he relishes talking and joking with his hockey friends, coming as close to being one of the boys as a sensitive, multi-millionaire celebrity who eschews bars and locker rooms ever gets.

The manager of the Redwood Empire Ice Arena is Craig Gates, who schedules the many activities, both public and private, that take place there and oversees the personnel and day-to-day business of the bustling facility. The staff is first-rate. One of the instructors is Skippy Baxter, who made *Ripley's Believe It or Not!* for a spectacular skating manuever—three complete turns in the air before landing on ice. Karen Kresge teaches classes and oversees the annual ice show; she was famous for her beauty and unparalleled showmanship during a long Ice Follies career.

Schulz watches as Karen oversees yet another rehearsal of the 1988 edition. She "allows" Schulz to choose a song or two for each of his own ice shows, and this year he has wangled a Hank Williams ballad sung by Joni James into the score. The number is "I Can't Help It If I'm Still in Love with You," the same sad ballad that one night, somehow, influenced the cartoonist to include his little red-haired girl in the *Peanuts* cast of characters. Most of the ice-show music, however, is more current and raucous.

"I never like any of the music," Sparky sighs, while a rock-videolike number full of gyrations and amazing athletics unfolds before him. Chorus skaters in punk costumes recline provocatively on scaffolding, a convincing takeoff of MTV.

"Too much?" asks Karen, skating toward him in her wild red wig and a black leather costume.

"No. Fine," he says.

He may not love every production number, but the weeks surrounding the show are great ones for Sparky. A hut near the arena fills with seamstresses perfecting costumes. There are dozens of minor emergencies: the show's Snoopy needs oral surgery; the skaters in the bowling sequence believe their white tights are too revealing; a motorcycle in a 1950s number keeps turning over on the ice, scarring it. The ice, that is.

One year Sparky was determined to have a skating, kite-eating tree. Judy Sladky, Schulz's favorite Snoopy, and her husband Jim Sladky, a frequent Charlie Brown, listened to Schulz's complaints that no one seemed able to produce an iceworthy kite-eating tree.

"I like to please him," says Judy. "Whatever he wants, I try to do. So I volunteered Jim." Jim Sladky bought materials and vowed to give it a shot. Judy came upon her husband and Sparky in the shop later that evening. "What are you guys doing?" she chirped.

"Shhhh!" warned Sparky. "I'm watching God."

"You're what?"

"Watching God. Only God can make a tree."

The ice shows bring out a combination Toby Tyler and Cecil B. deMille in Schulz. He attends countless rehearsals and offers opinions and detailed suggestions on everything from costumes to choreography. "I don't want lots of cold spots in this show," Sparky will instruct, and everyone takes heed. The hired skaters preen and practice, every so often casting a sideways glance toward their famous benefactor. He calls most of them by name and compliments them on particular performances. He plays a part.

Schulz has even been known to work backstage on opening night, moving props.

The show is his pet, his present to the community, and for weeks before the first performance Schulz is constantly jotting notes on a personal calendar, reserving tables for his local friends and out-of-town guests who might be persuaded to attend. A secretary might just as well handle it, but Schulz seems to enjoy immensely the business of scheduling his friends' trips to the ice show.

Over the years Schulz has also made several earnest efforts to keep an outdoor skating pond frozen; he remembers skating outdoors under the Minnesota moon and would like to furnish a similar thrill for the local youngsters. A refrigeration truck was hauled in, but it could not offset the temperate California climate. Despite the best efforts of science and technology, the 85-by-56-foot experimental pond turned to slush.

The Schulz affinity for sports is well known, of course, mostly through the cartoons. When Frank Zamboni died in 1987, newspapers everywhere noted his passing. Forty years earlier, Zamboni invented the ice-resurfacing machine used to restore rinks, and Snoopy, by constant references, has made the contraption familiar everywhere, from Miami to Honolulu and the many places in between that never see ice without cola over it.

Two things brought Frank Zamboni to the attention of the skating cartoonist: he made a major contribution to the sports Schulz loves most and he had a funny-sounding name.

"I don't think the coach likes me," says Snoopy. "He told me to stand in front of the Zamboni."

Schulz is a certified referee for amateur junior hockey and routinely plays the exertive game as well. In 1987, he was racing down the ice when he lost control and crashed into the backboard. He tore a ligament in his knee and required surgery and months of painful therapy. As soon as possible, still limping on land, he was back on the ice, wearing a knee brace for support.

The only other syndicated cartoon feature Schulz has ever

drawn besides *Peanuts* was the sports-oriented panel called *It's Only a Game,* which began in 1957 and lasted about a year. It was conceived by Schulz and the syndicate to fill a gap left by the death of H. T. Webster, an Eastern cartoonist famed for a lifetime of gag cartooning that often emphasized sport and games, particularly bridge. Sparky and Joyce were going through a bridge period themselves at the time. Schulz's heart was never in the second comic, although he loves sports as a cartoon subject.

"I've always liked drawing sports cartoons, but I don't need a separate outlet. My own strip has developed to the point I can handle any subject matter."

As a kid, Sparky was an average, if determined, athlete. Today, fame has gilded his playing fields. He has skated with Peggy Fleming, volleyed a few with Billie Jean King, and once paired with Alan Shephard, the astronaut golfer who hit the ball on the moon. He has two tennis courts next to One Snoopy Place, an indoor court and an outdoor court. Also, there is a baseball diamond that is the prettiest baseball diamond you ever saw, with the grass kept green and lush, maintained for community and private use. Schulz used to play ball more when he and his children were younger, but they're grown and gone, and "I'm too old to play much, now."

He tends to put great athletes on the same pedestal as writers, maybe one notch lower. Schulz came to know Billie Jean King, when the tennis star asked him to illustrate a book she was writing on children's tennis. They met for the first time in a San Francisco restaurant, the athlete and the artist, both initially nervous about exactly what to expect of the other. That day they managed to digest coffee and a lot of mutual admiration. They have been friends ever since.

"He's absolutely great," gushes King, who in 1980 appointed her friend to the Women's Sports Foundation board of directors. "I really love him, and I think if ever I needed someone he'd be there for me.

"Sparky is close to sports. He is so fair-minded, too, with a basic belief that girls and women should have the same opportunities in sports as the males. It probably helps that he had three daughters."

Schulz drew a cartoon especially for King, featuring Snoopy: "I'm only going to ask you one more time to play with me at Wimbledon." She has it framed on her wall at home.

For three years Schulz hosted a senior tennis tournament for women professionals, attracting such superstars as King, Rosie Casals, and Virginia Wade. The winner received, of course, the Snoopy Cup.

Sports are central to his life, but Schulz denies living a Snoopy-esque sports fantasy.

"I do think you have to know what you're writing about, and I do treat all these sports activities in the strip with great authenticity. I think that's very important, but I'm not living any fantasies by any means. Sports are funny. Once Linus said to Charlie Brown, 'Sports are a caricature of life.' Charlie Brown said, 'Oh, that's a relief. I was afraid it was life.' I feel sorry for people who get so involved in sports that it makes them unhappy. They get carried away with the winning and losing of their team. With all these professional games, somehow we've lost the joy of the individual game."

Two of Sparky's daughters are skilled and enthusiastic skaters. Schulz loves to remember one particular ice show when Amy rose slowly from a crouched position to skate to the graceful old hymns "In the Garden" and "Sweet Hour of Prayer." Columnist Carl Rowan watched that show and was moved to devote a piece of commentary to it. Amy gave up her skating for the Mormon church and later motherhood, but Jill Schulz continues to perform in her father's lavish productions. She turned professional at twenty-one, even touring South America with Holiday on Ice International. In amateur contests before, she had faced the normal, competitive challenges, plus occasional accusations that she fared well mainly because her last name is Schulz. "If anything, you might be judged a little harder and have to prove yourself more," counters Jill.

There are not too many sports Sparky has not tried at some time during his life. He and Jeannie, for a period, jogged two miles an evening together. A kayak, a recent acquisition, juts through the back window of his Jeep. Hockey paraphernalia is as much a part of the decor at the Schulz household as potted plants. And if a sport particularly interests him, like skating, he brings the best and bright-

est of the players to Santa Rosa. The ice shows have featured lumi-
naries like Fleming, Scott Hamilton, and Charles Tickner, affording
Schulz the rare opportunity to chat rinkside with the world's finest
skaters without ever leaving home.

In a touch of Hollywood, the skaters and other celebrities who
come by sign their names in wet cement outside. Among the visitors
who have left their signatures beneath the redwoods are Tenley Al-
bright, Richard Dwyer, Phyllis George, Lisa Marie Allen, Robin
Cousins, and Tim Wood.

Sports were not celebrity-studded and lavishly budgeted when
Sparky was a child. Hockey was played in the street. Baseball in vacant lots. Marbles were kept in cigar boxes. Balls fell through street
drains into sewers, and manhole covers were pried up so someone
could effect a rescue. There was no such thing in his neighborhood
as Little League; youngsters organized themselves and pooled their
ragtag equipment.

"None of the fathers had time to come out and get things organized for us. It was during the Depression, and most of them were
too busy doing other things, working late and all that, so all of our
sports were games we organized on our own. When spring came,
we played marbles and then baseball. With fall, the footballs came
out. Then winter. We didn't even have any good hills to slide on in
St. Paul. We'd have to take our sleds and run down the street as fast
as we could, belly-flop, and then coast along before a car came. We'd
play street hockey, or sometimes my dad made us a small rink in the
backyard."

His own athletic accomplishments were a mixed bag. He once
pitched a no-hit, no-run game, but his baseball team also lost one
game 40—0.

"The gym teachers in junior high and high school didn't pay
any attention to you unless you were a real hotshot, real big and husky. I was athletic, but not big and husky. I hated gym classes, anyway. They were all kind of dumb."

Baseball was an important spectator sport as well. He still has
his souvenir miniature Louisville Slugger bat sold at the park when
the triple-A St. Paul Saints played.

"We never cared about the Yankees, the Cubs, the Giants, or

any other big-league club. We lived in St. Paul and were much more interested in the St. Paul Saints and the Minneapolis Millers. Who cared about Joe DiMaggio? The Saints were our heroes."

When Sparky turned nine, golfing became his passion and Bobby Jones his hero. He was in his teens before he actually got the chance to play the game. He studied the golfing magazines religiously, forsaking the familiar fishing trips with his father to practice his strokes. At eighteen, his dedication paid off when he won the caddy championship of Highland Park Country Club. It was his last golfing championship.

Even cartooning took a backseat to golfing for a short while. A high school classmate, a fellow golf club member, wrote this in Sparky's senior yearbook:

> Leave the greens and roughs well cut, and make it so I won't four-putt/Allow the ball in the hole to pass, so my scores won't be in a two-number mass/And if I club into a bunker, don't tell me how I should have sunk'er.

Through sports Sparky could belong somewhere, could forget the buck-toothed, pimply image he saw staring back in puberty's harsh mirror. He could overcome his shyness on the ice, the links, the pitcher's mound. He could forget the girls who ignored him and the subjects he was systematically flunking, all the failures and fears, real and imagined. Not much has changed. Only now he skates on a perfect sheet of ice and owns all the marbles.

21

"The Strip Is His Life"

The hand shakes.

It is startling to see the coffee cup waggling wildly in the artist's unsteady right hand, the hand so many have come to depend upon for a daily fix of laughter.

It started trembling noticeably after his heart surgery in 1981 and has worsened with each succeeding month. Sometimes the tremble is worse than others. It especially gives him trouble with his lettering. And now, the arthritis in his right thumb is a companion pain.

Has he seen a doctor? "I see doctors all the time. Some of my best friends are doctors." That is Charles Schulz's stock, noncommittal answer to the question asked with annoying frequency.

Some days Schulz threatens he will retire to the peace of his ice rink and company of friends who play hockey and talk about long books over long lunches. Maybe he is retirement age anyway, he thinks on such days; after all, of the golfing foursome he played with two years ago, he is the only one still living.

225

But then he sits down behind the drawing board, only the second one he has owned in his forty-year cartooning career ("I've never been an equipment man") and steadies the palsied hand by propping it against the surface of the table. And he draws, not without difficulty, another installment, and it's a pretty good one, and on its heels comes another idea, and that's two ideas in one day and not half-bad ones.

Those who know him best say he will never retire.

"What would he do?" asks daughter Amy. "The strip is his life. His life is the strip."

In the unlikely event of Schulz's retirement, the production of *Peanuts* will cease forever. If death comes first, the same will be true. It's in writing. No one but Charles Monroe Schulz will ever draw *Peanuts*. His children took it upon themselves to call a meeting with the syndicate lawyers in 1979 and made it plain. They decided, first between themselves, then officially with the lawyers, the strip should never be drawn by another. Schulz, who took no active part in the discussions, was immensely pleased with their initiative.

The decision undoubtedly will cost everyone involved some money. While United Feature Syndicate did reserve the right to continue licensing *Peanuts* products and to recycle old strips, certainly the gold mine will begin to play out when Schulz is no longer producing a nugget a day.

"The last thing we need is more money," says Amy bluntly. Of course, they don't say such things at United Feature Syndicate.

The lawyers encouraged leaving a loophole, an "out," in case the family might want legal room to reconsider when faced with the actuality of ending *Peanuts*. They used the unfortunate analogy of a person on a life-support system who, at some earlier, healthier time, had asked to be cut off from sustaining machinery and now, in the face of death, suddenly changes his mind.

"I got angry then," says Monte Schulz, the oldest son. "That's why you make such decisions beforehand, when you're rational, when your mind is not clouded with drugs."

The family was firm.

A cartoonist and his family do not always have the luxury of dictating a feature's fate. In fact, it is the norm for syndicates to own a comic strip and its characters, lock, stock, and barrel—with the creator technically a hired hand. Until recently this was the situation almost exclusively, but syndicates increasingly allow creators, especially the powerful ones like Schulz, to own their features. It doesn't necessarily guarantee a lot more money, but it does permit the artist more control over production—even the ability to carry his property to another syndicate.

Cartoon historian Art Wood notes that only one other major cartoonist has purposely killed his own strip upon retirement. Fontaine Fox, who for forty-two years drew *The Toonerville Trolley That Meets All Trains* (usually called *Toonerville Trolley* for short), retired the rickety car in 1955. Several newspapers mistakenly ran Fox's obituary, thinking if the strip was dead, so must be the artist.

So, are Snoopy and Charlie Brown and the rest of the gang immortal? Will they have a life beyond the strip? Licensing experts at the syndicate, who tend to talk in terms of "properties," not comic strips, are predictably optimistic about the life of the characters after the death of the strip.

"My gut feeling is they will continue strong," says Peter Shore, UFS's vice president for marketing and licensing in the United States. "The characters are embedded in worldwide culture; they are part of your life. The strip's been there every morning, every time you open the newspaper, for forty years. Once a strip becomes a part of the culture like that, it is there. Basic. Classic. Very few properties have the ability to do that."

The success of Snoopy et al. in Japan would indicate Shore to be right. Although the strip itself runs in only a few Japanese newspapers, most of them English-language, product sales there account for one-third of all the licensing income. Some 40 percent of all new product ideas come from applicants in Japan.

United Feature Syndicate, faced with the inevitability of *Peanuts'* demise, might be expected to put a gracious public face on the eventual loss of its foremost comic property, and it does.

Says company president Bob Metz: "Sparky's talent has been responsible for millions of dollars of income. Nowhere is it written that something good for business is the right thing to do. . ."

Schulz has been asked to help select the strips that ultimately will be recycled, but the cartoonist understandably has little enthusiasm for the project. He keeps putting it off. He has noted, with a grim lack of surprise, the mediocre success of his own syndicate's efforts to resell old *L'il Abner* strips.

"It doesn't work. The strips are dated. That's why cartoon strips are not true art. Real art endures. Cartoon strips just don't hold up. Or, very few hold up. *Krazy Kat* maybe. The old *Popeye.*"

Every now and then he will make the flat statement, a disclaimer, really, that "I am not doing Great Art." Great Art, of course, often depends on the definition, whether you get paid for your irises before or after your death. And while it is fine to live an obsessed life creating Great Art, it is sometimes a tad depressing to believe, as Schulz seems to, that you are engulfed in the creation of something that has only fleeting appeal, something commercial, for goodness' sake. Something that will be cold before you are.

"There are so many other things it would be nice to do, and I don't have time to do them. Is it all worth it? Does it really matter that I sit here day after day, drawing this strip, not doing much else?"

Despite his disavowals of accomplishing enduring art he complains, somewhat paradoxically, about cartooning being treated as "the burlesque" of the art world. There is not even a specific Pulitzer Prize category for strip cartooning, something cartoonists Al Capp and Milt Caniff lobbied for when they were alive and eloquently championing their trade.

Regardless of the respect or lack of respect the work gets, or its durability, or even its raison d'être, the final assessment is that he has no choice. "I do it because I have to. These people who claim to be creating for unselfish reasons, for humanity, are not honest. They do it for themselves, because they have to. Because they are driven to."

Schulz is scared, perhaps, of putting his own creation to the most unforgiving of tests—time. Books are full of cartoons that once were the rage. So he keeps drawing. Keeps current. Keeps the strip alive. He quite possibly has more faith in Snoopy as ultimate icon than in the strip's timelessness. He is blessed, at least, to believe a five-year-old child fifty years from now will see a Snoopy balloon in Macy's Thanksgiving Day Parade and call it by name.

But all this talk about immortality and retirement and death probably is premature. It would seem so, at least, watching Schulz whisk about the ice, playing a wild game of hockey. At sixty-six, he is in remarkably good health, especially for a man who eight years ago stood in the parking lot of the Santa Rosa Community Hospital with his worried wife and debated whether or not to correct dangerously blocked arteries with dangerous open-heart surgery.

He had entered the hospital with mild chest pains, pains he might well have ignored if his good friend Raul Diez had not gone to the hospital three days earlier with blood clots that traveled to his lungs. Tests on Schulz showed one artery was completely closed and others 50 to 90 percent blocked. The man who had never drunk so much as a bottle of beer or puffed at a single weed was to pay the sin tax, anyway. He was in danger. Surgery was recommended.

"Every night I would think to myself, 'Is this it? Am I going to be able to play golf and tennis?' "

The decision to go ahead with the heart surgery did not come easily. Daughters Jill and Amy both were scheduled to leave the country about the time Schulz learned of his medical problems. Jill was headed to South America with Holiday on Ice International, Amy to Utah for an orientation period that would prepare her for a year-long stint in England as a Mormon missionary. "We all made a pledge not to worry about one another," says Schulz.

They worried anyway. "It was so hard for Dad to see us go," says Amy. "Dad cried so hard. I've never seen him do that, and I felt so guilty leaving. I went on to Utah and said extra prayers for him."

Schulz spoke at his daughter's "mission farewell," the traditional Mormon send-off for its new missionaries. "I know that was hard for him," says Amy. "I told him he didn't have to do it. But he was supportive."

The cartoonist made his final decision to have surgery after talking to the surgeon, Dr. Ted Folkerth, who had made two tours of Vietnam. Schulz decided he could trust his heart to a man like that. In typically conscientious fashion, he prepared for his own surgery and convalescence the only way he knew how: by drawing. And drawing some more. For the first time in his professional life, he became virtually inaccessible, warding off all visitors and telephone calls, declining interviews and concentrating only on the strip. He managed to draw an extra three months' worth of strips, giving himself even more lead time than usual, and, more importantly, the time to be ill.

But at the request of the hospital staff, Sparky even drew in the hospital, putting a series of cartoons featuring Snoopy on a blank wall before his release. Today, an orderly will proudly point the way for visitors to see the original art in the telemetry waiting room, work meant to cheer other patients who find themselves in the same cardiological boat as Charles Schulz. Snoopy is drawn five times, struggling with an inhalator, a device designed to clear the lungs. The wing of the hospital where Schulz was a model patient was remodeled, and the cartoonist was asked to return and redraw the Snoopy mural months after his release. He did.

In the comic strips roughly corresponding with Schulz's hospital stay, Charlie Brown endures an illness and also is hospitalized. His friends fret. Snoopy makes an appearance as the World Famous Surgeon. All ends well with another disastrous attempt by Charlie Brown to kick the football.

In sickness and health, Schulz is married to his medium. Until death do them part.

22

"Do You Like Me?"

"*I*'m not all that modest," says Sparky when complimented for the umpteenth time on his humility. "Let someone else
say it. That's the secret." They say it. From young cartoonists held
spellbound with his casual bits of advice doled out in a cool Minnesota accent to established comic veterans like Bill Mauldin, most cartoonists refuse to find any fault with the master. For one thing, those
who do the same thing for a living admire *anyone* who can produce
anything daily for forty years. Producing something of quality that
long is even more astounding.

Cathy Guisewite, creator of the successful strip *Cathy,* is a pe-
tite, frail beauty, nothing like her chubby, diet-weary comic counterpart. Cathy's features are so striking and photogenic, as a matter of
fact, that she has lent her face to Neutrogena soap ads that run in
glamour and beauty-advice magazines. The real-life Cathy resembles
her cartoon heroine only in possessing an inexplicable lack of confidence. Like Sparky, she needs constant reassurance.

231

"Sparky has been a big rooter for me from the beginning. I had to speak to a group in San Francisco, California, and he came down to hear my talk. I was astounded. I looked out, and there he was, My Total Hero, in attendance. He is still my hero. And my friend as well. For him to pay attention to me is a source of constant moral support."

Sparky Schulz arranged a house-sitting job in Santa Rosa for Cathy when she wanted to make the move from Detroit, her hometown, to California. Once she arrived he even gave her some impromptu drawing lessons, showing her how to make the loosely sketched *Cathy* characters walk and move a little more realistically. It still bothers him that Cathy (the comic strip character) has no nose. Cathy eventually moved on to Studio City, her own sphere of influence, and a six-figure income, but the good will between them is intact. The subject matter of *Peanuts,* she says, is not so different from that of *Cathy.*

"His work totally paved the way for a strip like mine. He broke the new ground. Before *Peanuts* nobody knew it was all right to talk about human insecurities or awkward moments that we all experience. Without the example of *Peanuts,* I never would have thought it was okay to laugh about such moments with a girlfriend, much less to write about them and exploit them publicly. He made it fine to laugh about those things.

"The most remarkable quality about Sparky is that he has maintained the integrity of the strip for all these years. He could coast or do anything he wanted to do. He never has. He's a great standard for all of us."

The two cartoonists share certain personality quirks, lonely moments that seem to go beyond mere artistic temperament.

"The better writers are the ones who have endured a lot. I certainly believe that. I find him real easy to talk to, because there's a bit of common ground as far as sensibilities go. We are both torn between needing to be alone and needing people around. And then, we don't want too many people, ever."

It is cartoonist custom to make goodwill tours en masse during every National Cartoonist Society convention. In 1988, when the meeting was held in San Francisco, Cathy Guisewite and Sparky Schulz were in the group that visited a soup kitchen for immigrants.

"I'll never forget it. Some woman who spoke very little English came up to Sparky, and he introduces himself, and the woman nods and smiles and then asks him to draw Popeye. So he did."

Bill Mauldin is to Sparky Schulz as north is to south. One cherishes sobriety, the other Swedish gin. One is reticent and proper, the other ebullient and occasionally profane. "My first recollection of this world," wrote Mauldin in his autobiography, *A Sort of a Saga,* "is of sitting on the bank of a little river in Parral, Chihuahua, Mexico, in 1924, at the age of three, finishing the last of a pack of Chesterfields, which, according to three witnesses, I'd smoked in a little more than an hour." Mauldin's childhood was as gypsylike and wild as Schulz's was simple.

But, like Schulz, Mauldin is self-educated; he never even graduated from high school, a personal footnote that did not keep him from writing more than a dozen splendid books and mastering the editorial-cartooning genre. Also like Schulz, he received his first art instruction through the mail, taking a twenty-dollar correspondence course offered by the Landon Institute of Cleveland. Later he would attend the Chicago Art Institute. A broke teenager, Mauldin had the confidence to travel from his Southwestern home to a strange, large city to study art. Schulz, plagued by shyness and self-doubt, mailed his lessons to an art school only a few miles from his home. Mauldin, like Schulz, is really without professional peers, the best war cartoonist ever. As one army historian said: "There will never be another Mauldin. The Pentagon will never let him happen again."

"Schulz and I know each other philosophically," declares Mauldin, "though we have never been buddy-buddy, close friends. We've only been eyeball to eyeball maybe three or four times." Mauldin has likewise said he doubted he could pick Schulz (whom he calls Charlie) out of a crowded room, "but I regard him as one of my dearest friends."

The plodding and slow start of Sparky as cartoonist contrasts with the prodigious debut of Mauldin, who won a Pulitzer Prize before he was twenty-three. When Mauldin read in *Stars and Stripes* he had won the award he wasn't really even sure what it was. As a young soldier, Schulz studied—with no small degree of envy—Mauldin's Willie and Joe cartoons, but he all but abandoned his own art during the war. "I just wasn't ready, and I think Mauldin's work made me realize it."

Mauldin contends Schulz made up for lost time. "The thing about Schulz's work is the soul behind it. That's why it's great. He's a preacher at heart. All good cartoonists are jackleg preachers. There is a very strong moral tone there.

"Another thing about Charlie. There are very few cartoonists good enough to be able to draw simply. I can't. Most people can't. Jules Feiffer is one. Schulz is one. Thurber was another."

Mauldin and his friend Milton Caniff used to live near one another. Together they spent many nights, all night, ostensibly working, but doing a fair share of coffee-drinking and philosophizing as well, the warm-up exercises of creative minds. It was during one of those predawn bull sessions that Caniff coined the disparaging term *rivet man* to describe literal artists obsessed with detail, so that every rivet in the locomotive, every nail in the fence, every brick in the wall showed. "They never graduated from being art students," explains Mauldin. "It's so much better when you simply *suggest* it. That's what Schulz does."

The Schulz style was so radically different from anything then on the market when it appeared in 1950 that it is no wonder his strip built slowly. "And, of course, he had one helluva time selling that strip," notes Mauldin. "But that was because of the stupid editors and even stupider publishers. I've never known a publisher with enough sense to pour sand out of a boot. They don't understand strips. All they care about is 'Will it sell?' "

Mauldin started his syndicated career with United Feature Syndicate, too, after its superstar Ernie Pyle convinced the corporate father, Scripps Howard, it should enlist the young artist. After the war, Mauldin eventually left the syndicate in a huff after being treated, as he describes it, "like chattel." The trenchant commentary of Willie and Joe as it had been in Europe was too downbeat for a peacetime America that wanted to hear only the best about itself. So UFS routinely "softened" the views and comment of the incisive feature it had marketed as a comics-page feature to make it more palatable. "It was selling like hotcakes, because I had become famous. But then I lost newspapers as fast as I gained them." Mauldin had originally wanted Willie and Joe to be killed the day the war ended, but was discouraged from taking their potentially lucrative lives. So they died, instead, as civilians, from syndicate cowardice.

Mauldin, of course, went on to become a renowned editorial cartoonist, winning a second Pulitzer and excelling in the field that Schulz now rues. He won't even take issue with his friend Schulz on that. "I agree with Schulz about editorial cartooning. I suspect his opinion is about the same as mine, and I think it's a decaying profession. The whole thing has gone schlock. It has slipped into what I call the Comic Valentine School, with lots of words, word after word after word. Editorial cartoonists are nothing but letterers anymore. The editors prefer it. They don't like cartoonists or cartoons anyway. They don't understand them. So they like to stifle cartoonists. They make it their business to stifle them."

At any rate, Snoopy invariably imbibes his root beer "over at Bill Mauldin's house" each Veterans Day, sitting up all night and telling war stories. And Mauldin basks in the glory of bending an elbow with a beagle. "Sooner or later I'm going to spend a few days with Schulz and talk cartooning," Mauldin promises himself. Will they drink root beer? "Oh, hell no, I'll have a vodka."

Mort Walker sold *Beetle Bailey* the same year Schulz sold *Peanuts,* and he, too, had an enormous success on his hands. The men are exactly the same age, World War II veterans, and former magazine cartoonists. There the similarities end. *Beetle Bailey* did better faster than *Peanuts,* for one thing, climbing to 100 newspapers soon after Walker drafted his hero, who was to remain in the army for good. Hank Ketcham's *Dennis the Menace,* begun the next year, 1951, also grew faster than *Peanuts,* causing Schulz great consternation in those lean early years. Adding to his concern were two other strips. When *Peanuts* appeared in 45 papers, *Pogo* was in 80 and *Nancy* in 400.

Like Mauldin, the Kansas-born Walker was professionally precocious, selling his first cartoon by the time he was thirteen and working as a prolific artist for Hallmark Greeting Cards while he attended college.

And, over the years, Walker could never quit coming up with ideas for new strips. He eventually found himself head of a virtual production line of artists and writers who execute his ideas and contribute their own. He was the first, probably, to make a cottage industry of cartooning. Among his brainchildren: *Beetle Bailey,* its spin-off *Hi and Lois, Boner's Ark, Sam's Strip.* Other Walker strips have been started and abandoned for one reason or another, the most recent being *Gamin and Patches,* which featured a contemporary sort of Huck Finn, a streetwise, ragged urchin roaming the cruel streets. Readers complained to editors the strip made fun of the homeless. "I thought of him as a more classic character. At any rate, I was relieved when the thing died," Walker says. Walker has mastered the art of collaboration, delegating work and accepting success and failure with businesslike aplomb.

Schulz's experiences with the C word have been different. He detests collaborating. After one exception, Schulz has been creatively content to stick with *Peanuts,* mostly because producing more than one cartoon would necessitate collaborating, which Schulz cannot abide. His one attempt was in 1957, producing that Sunday page called *It's Only a Game,* with Minnesota artist Jim Sasseville handling the artwork. The feature, signed only by Schulz, consisted of several independent single-panel gags dealing with pool, fishing, or whatever sport was in season. One panel was always devoted to bridge. It started with only thirty-three client newspapers and after about a year had thirty.

During this period the Schulz family made its final move from Minnesota, to Sebastopol, California. Sasseville moved to Sebastopol, too, to continue his work on *It's Only a Game.*

The feature's lack of acceptance was not encouraging, but Schulz and his collaborator ran into other difficulties.

"Jim could really draw, but he began to suggest ideas. We even used a couple of them. But that was one of the sore points." Schulz simply is incapable of sharing or delegating conceptual responsibility for his work.

When Sasseville moved again, to nearby San Francisco, the two artists took the opportunity to abandon the struggling feature. They parted friends, but the experience taught Schulz a lesson about himself. Professionally, he is a loner.

"I have too much pride to use anyone else's ideas," Schulz says. Since then he has been content to explore new worlds only within the context of his one proven strip.

"I don't like 'trying my ideas out' on someone else," Schulz says, "or 'running it up the flagpole.' I'd rather live or die on my own." He has never bought a gag; he had just as soon rob a bank.

Early in his career Schulz collaborated with advertising artists on Ford commercials, "which gave me a terrible time. There were these long, difficult meetings, and everybody had their own idea. I can't work like that."

Despite their drastically different artistic approaches, Walker raves about Schulz, calling him "the Daniel Boone of modern cartooning," one who "modernized the comic pages with his economy of dialogue and openness of drawing."

Schulz has "broken just about every record there is," Walker notes. "Longevity, you name it." In the early days, when *Beetle* was growing like kudzu and *Peanuts* seemed stuck at forty-five or so newspapers, Walker casually followed Schulz's strip in the New York *World Telegram.*

"One day somebody brought in a *Peanuts* book to me, and I thought, 'This guy has a book?' I read it and was so impressed. Something about seeing all the strips together made much more of an impact than they had in daily installments. I think that still is true. You see a collection, and it's even better than it was day by day."

Walker acknowledges that Schulz is a private man, not prone to the almost-communal lifestyle within the cartoonist conclave Walker himself relishes. By noon each day, Walker usually has telephoned half a dozen cartoonist friends, always chatting about new projects, quizzing them about ideas that are invariably cooking on one mental burner or another. Whereas Walker thrives on feedback, Schulz avoids it. The opinions of others are just that. "What if they are wrong?" he says.

Walker sees Schulz as smooth socially, however. "He's very

gregarious at gatherings, very good on his feet. Of course, cartoonists won't let anybody be a loner. But I do remember once when the
cartoonists were in Washington, D.C., and we'd had a big day and
were sitting around talking and having a drink, and all of a sudden
somebody said, 'Hey, where's Schulz?' He had disappeared, gone on
one of those bus tour things all by himself."

Walker has weathered his share of controversies involving his
strips, not really intended to be controversial. Black and white readers alike have objected to his aptly named Lieutenant Flap, the hip
black soldier with an Afro, who wears flamboyant civvies to town
and who in 1970 (two years after Schulz introduced Franklin) effectively integrated what he called "this honky outfit." Walker caught
it from both sides. A few Southern newspapers even dropped the
strip until reader protests forced them to return it; then some blacks
objected to the character. Women's groups have loudly deplored
Walker's Miss Buxley, the bimbo-turned-serious-career-girl. She
serves mostly as a visual outlet for General Halftrack's lust. Critics
charge Walker with dealing in stereotypical characterizations.

"Schulz, on the other hand, has that rare quality of never having offended anyone," Walker says. And it is true: Schulz somehow
has managed to be poignant without being political, funny without
offending. He even integrated the strip without causing a ripple. The
Teflon cartoonist.

"I bet I lean further over backwards to keep from offending
anyone than any other cartoonist," acknowledges Schulz.

Elliott Caplin, who for twenty-three years wrote the strip *Abbie
an' Slats* and who is the brother of cartooning legend Al Capp,
downplays any differences his famous brother and Schulz might
have had. There were a few tart written exchanges between the two
of them in 1968, after Capp parodied *Peanuts* in *Li'l Abner*. Schulz
says Capp let him know beforehand the episodes mocking *Peanuts*
were to appear. It was a Capp custom to parody the strips of both
friends and foes; witness the Fearless Fosdick episodes that poked
fun at his buddy Chester Gould's *Dick Tracy*.

Schulz shrugs. "After they ran I just wrote and told him I didn't
think they were all that funny." That response, of course, infuriated
Capp, who reacted angrily.

"Whenever I was around Al Capp, I always enjoyed his company," says Schulz. "He was always pleasant. I probably wouldn't have responded to those strips at all if it hadn't been for a secretary I had working for me at the time. She was incensed. I remember once visiting him in his New York hotel, and the Lerner half of the Lerner and Loewe musical team was there. We had a good time. He said to me 'Nobody tells me they like the things I do now.' I know how he feels."

"I think Al admired Charles Schulz enormously in an academic way," says Caplin. "They weren't close friends, and they were extremely different personalities. Schulz's star was ascending and Al's was not. But still, my remark for the record would have to be that Al was a great admirer of Charles Schulz."

Indeed, Capp said only positive things about the strip in 1965, when interviewed by *Time:* "The 'Peanuts' characters are good, mean little bastards, eager to hurt each other. That's why they are so delicious. They wound each other with the greatest enthusiasm. Anybody who sees theology in them is a devil worshiper."

Elliott Caplin met Schulz years ago at an elementary school in New York State. After Schulz's speech was over, United Feature sales manager Harry Gilburt introduced the two cartoonists. "Oh, I admire you," said Schulz, "because you're doing the real writing."

"Here he was, the best writer in the trade, telling me that," Caplin laughs. *Abbie an' Slats* was a serialized strip set in fictional Crabtree Corners. It had lengthy, realistic dialogue.

Sparky's closest friend within the trade, Lynn Johnston *(For Better or Worse),* is an elegant woman whose own private sensibilities are hinted at through her cartoon heroine Ellie. "I was sitting at home one day, minding my own business, when the phone rang. 'This is Charles Schulz,' a strange voice said. I thought it was a friend joking. I had only been in the business for two or three years at the time. 'Who is this, did you say?' And he said, again, 'This is Charles Schulz. I draw *Peanuts.*' Like I wouldn't know who Charles Schulz was."

She knew, all right, having admired his writing above any other cartoonist's.

"I had admired the artwork of a lot of people, probably very subliminally had incorporated a little bit of everyone's drawing style whom I had admired. But his writing was the best. So tender and warm. You sense you know him very well."

They met soon afterward, at a Reuben dinner in Washington. "I looked across the room and there he was, this smiling, handsome fellow with his arms open for a big hug. . . . There are no pretensions about him, and it's as if we've known each other a long, long while. I find myself telling him things I normally would keep deep down inside.

"Know what I really love?" Lynn asked Sparky in writing, shortly after she paid him a visit. "It's the rare and fleeting times we sit and actually talk about drawing! On the way to San Francisco, our friend wondered why the drawing of the strip was so important, and I told him that the pen wasn't just an extension of the hand and that the pressure on the paper wasn't just a means of transferring ink to board, but our way of actually touching the character. Drawing has saved my sanity and meant more to me in my life than most things. If I couldn't draw, it would be devastating. Your work. . .has always been a benchmark for me. There are times when I work, with you in mind, wondering if what I'm doing is good enough! I know that it annoys you when people write and ask you to go back to the old stuff. The sarcastic philosophizing and the stark observations. You said you'd rather do something new. What I see in your work is something new—it's a softness and a story line that almost goes back to the past, but, just ever so carefully touches on what you really want to do. I don't think you're doing that yet. One's most insightful work comes from the innermost feelings that are occurring at the time. I suspect that you're not quite yet willing or ready to explore the thoughts that preoccupy you now. It's not so much the unrequited love or the sense of fair play that's on your mind. But, your health, your children's futures, death, and looking in the mirror, wondering why and how the years went by so fast and what to accomplish with the experience and expertise you've gained, in the future. Now and then when Charlie Brown or Linus expounds on what 'Grandpa says,' I see a hint of it."

Lynn won the Reuben the year she met Schulz, and, on returning to her home, promptly hid the trophy in her basement.

"I didn't want to look at it. I kept thinking, 'I don't deserve it. I'll never be able to live up to it. I'll never draw as well again. It came too soon in my career.' Most people would put it on the mantel and stare at it and show it off to their friends, but not me. I hid it. I decided Sparky was the only one who would understand my reaction. So I sat down and wrote him a letter. 'Everything looks different in my studio this morning,' I wrote to him.

"I went and put the letter in the mailbox, and the phone rang. It was Sparky, who said, 'Well, does everything look different in your studio this morning?' "

Perhaps because she is one of the few successful women in the profession, Lynn is mindful of how other cartoonists portray women in their strips. "Sparky really gives tremendous credit to women. Lucy was a strong character when she came along. A fussbudget, but at least not a wimpy kid. And Peppermint Patty is strong, full of ideas. And Marcie. She's a bright kid. The boys all tend to be weaker. Schroeder is totally absorbed in his own world, and Linus is introspective. And, of course, there's Charlie Brown. . . ."

During the National Cartoonists Society meeting in Washington, Lynn and Sparky visited the Vietnam War Memorial. "Sparky is very much aware of the futility of war. He doesn't like to talk about it. At the memorial, which is so beautiful, so emotionally taxing, he couldn't even speak for a few minutes. Then he said, 'This was such a good idea I'm surprised it was done. So often good ideas don't ever happen. And it was done by a woman.' "

Another day in Santa Rosa, as Sparky and his guest Lynn made the short walk from his studio to the Snoopy gift shop, Sparky was making the point, rather passionately, that women should "allow men to be the gallant gentlemen" of yesteryear. "He was using his hands to talk, speaking very emphatically," remembers Lynn. "And when we got to the gift shop, he kept talking and gesturing, and I opened the door and held it for both of us. We got inside, and he stopped, suddenly realizing what he'd just done."

Even with good friends like Lynn, Sparky Schulz lacks the confidence to bank on that friendship's continuing. One night, driving home from dinner, Sparky turned to Lynn and asked, point-blank, "Do you like me?"

Startled, Lynn assured him she did. "People always like Jeannie, but they never like me," Sparky said.

Another evening Lynn dined with Jim Davis *(Garfield)* and his wife. "Jim is really a connoisseur of fine wines, and the rest of us were just a bunch of bumbling sots who might as well have been drinking Night Train Express. I think Jim finally noticed we were swilling it back without checking its bouquet or anything, and so he cleaned the rest of it off himself. He got a bit mellow after that, and when Jim gets mellow he gets sweet, real quiet and romantic." Jim Davis told the group he rarely ever remembered dreams, but "one from the other night" had caused him to wake in a sweat. "I dreamed Sparky told me he was quitting, and it scared me to death. I'm not ready to be the Old Guard just yet. I want to continue to have someone to look up to."

Davis later told Johnston: "You know, when we're the Old Guard and the young cartoonists come up to us, we'll be able to say 'We knew Sparky Schulz.' "

Before he drew a comic strip, Jerry Scott, who is thirty-three, used to drive five hours from his central California home to a Bay Area meeting of cartoonists, just hoping to meet and talk to some flesh-and-blood professionals. At one such meeting he hit the mother lode. "Sparky Schulz was there. I couldn't believe it. I got one of the organization's officers to introduce me, and it was like talking to God. I have all these black-and-white pictures of me standing with my hands in my pockets, meeting Sparky Schulz."

Jerry Scott now draws and writes *Nancy,* the old Ernie Bushmiller comic strip that holds the distinction of starring the industry's ugliest little folks. Scott has breathed new life into the old strip—a harder job, really, than starting from scratch. "I've been at it six years and I'm still fighting a huge deficit. There are still people who come up to me and say, 'I haven't read that strip since I was a kid.' It's discouraging."

Scott used to, in fact, urge the United Feature Syndicate editors to drop that "terrible old strip" and replace it with one of his. "Sid Goldberg would say to me, 'You're wrong about this strip. It's going to make a comeback.' Then one day they called and asked me to draw it."

The actuality of drawing a daily strip only increased his regard for Schulz.

"Even now that I do a strip of more renown (previously Scott had inherited a panel called *Gumdrop*), you cannot imagine how good it feels to walk into a room and have Charles Schulz say 'Hello, Jerry. How's it going?'

"This sounds corny. Most people live their lives trying to please their parents. With me, it's Sparky. Every time I do a strip I wonder if Sparky would like this gag. It's sort of a measure I use."

Scott has no patience with those who say *Peanuts* has slipped in quality or popularity. "Those are usually people who didn't read the comics then and don't read them now. They cannot possibly appreciate the contributions this guy made to our language and to our culture. Any strip reaches plateaus of creativity, but consistency has been Sparky's hallmark. And then there are those flashes of incredible creativity.

"Sparky has told me often how important characterization is. He believes the trouble with most strips nowadays is that they are mainly jokes and gag lines that could be delivered by anybody. Lucy could never deliver a Charlie Brown line. Charlie Brown could never deliver a Snoopy line. Characterization is such an exact art, and he does it beautifully.

"I model myself after him professionally. Cartooning is everything to me. I'm a dull person outside of my drawing. I love it, and yet I grow sick of it. Still, it's my hobby, my job, my mistress.

"And when I'm feeling low is when I do my best work, for some reason. Listening to sad music helps, even. You just don't realize that there's such a strong tie between depression and humor. The two are closely tied in emotional strength."

Berke Breathed, whose *Bloom County* early owed much to *Doonesbury* but soon took on a rollicking direction all its own, claims, "I have not been, and I am not now, a comic reader. There is nothing on those comics pages, including my own strip, that would draw me there."

Not known for diplomacy, Breathed nonetheless professes an uncharacteristic warmness for Charles Schulz and *Peanuts*.

"When I got into the comics business, I made a point to educate myself in *Peanuts,* especially the work done in the 1950s and sixties. It completely enchanted me. I was surprised at the warmness and comfort that strip made me feel. Even old cynical me."

The difference between those early strips and the *Peanuts* episodes now? "Well, I'm a firm believer a comic strip, not unlike a television show, has a predetermined run. Not that all of them should last the same length of time, yet the end of the strip should not necessarily correspond with the end of a cartoonist's life. A system of repetition will creep in if the strip runs too long. I think Sparky knows that he is repeating himself.

"I see a difference in the last ten years. I don't think many strips any older than ten years work. Schulz lasted a lot longer than most. *Peanuts* remains on the front pages of most Sunday comics sections more for the reason of legacy than the impact it has, I think.

"Most importantly to me, I think *Peanuts* taught me you don't necessarily have to be an extraordinarily accomplished artist or writer to be a comic stripper. The art, the writing is different than any other. Sparky showed that brilliantly.

"Not that bad art and writing is the idea, certainly. There's a lot of that on the comics pages, and you see how badly it goes wrong.

"Whatever he had, that undefinable element of warmth, all I know for sure is Charlie Brown's face had more personality than anything, anything—and I include my own work—being drawn today."

Breathed readily acknowledges the vast differences between his own approach—political, sometimes profane, often earthy—and that of Charles Schulz.

"Well, *Bloom County* doesn't try to make everybody happy. Because of that, I know that sooner or later I'll wear out my welcome, and my own strip will be history. I'm more aware of that than anybody."

Breathed claims "not to be as much of a purist as Bill Watterson *(Calvin and Hobbes)*" when it comes to the question that lately divides the ranks of successful cartoonists: to license or not to license. Breathed has allowed reprint books, a line of stuffed toys, T-shirts, and calendars, leaving himself less room to criticize than before.

"I decry the attack on the product itself that I think is implicit in a line of three thousand licensing items. There's no way to keep a strip from becoming an advertisement for a product when you have that many licensing things. The strip itself is compromised. *Garfield* has certainly crossed the line. *Peanuts,* I don't know. . . .

"You do have to wonder when you see the characters selling life insurance. Why do they need to do that? How does that help the strip? The line of where to cut off licensing is blurry. Everyone has to decide for himself."

Sparky and Berke Breathed have met, but only briefly. When the younger cartoonist broke his back in an ultralight-airplane crash, he opened his mail in the hospital one day to find a Snoopy, drawn by Sparky in his inimitable style. "He was one of the few cartoonists I heard from after the accident," says Breathed. "He offered to help keep the strip going if I needed him. That meant more to me than almost anything."

Breathed expresses amazement at the simple lifestyle of Sparky Schulz. "These guys who have been at it so long. All they want to do is sit and draw the strip. They don't enjoy anything else. I don't have any trouble finding ways to spend my money."

23

Epilogue

*M*ore methodical than your garden-variety artist, too creative to be anything else, Charles Schulz is a peculiarly successful hybrid, a poet who prospers. A sensitive soul who beats every deadline.

Guinness has duly recognized his mammoth readership at 90 million; yet the one person he most wanted to please with his drawing, his mother, did not live to see anything her son published.

He has dined with presidents, been marshal of a Rose Parade, been live with Larry King, fielded the questions of David Brinkley,and blinked into the camera of Yousuf Karsh. But his favorite mealtime companion, outside his immediate family, is a bright housewife named Mollie Boice, who sometimes keeps him waiting. Mollie writes plays in her spare time and does the dead-on Katharine Hepburn. Another of his best friends is Raul Diez, a teacher-turned-carpenter who makes him think and laugh.

"Other people have been kind to me, done things for me," says

Diez, "but you heard about it later. Sparky always acted like I was doing him the favor."

The art of Charles Schulz inspires both grandiloquence and belly laughs. Serious art museums have done tony exhibitions of his work, complete with slick catalog. In one, Italian author Umberto Eco summed up the *Peanuts* gang as "the monstrous infantile reductions of all the neuroses of a modern citizen of the industrial civilization." That's serious!

His one wish in life, Sparky says, is for people to like him as much as they did his father. Carl Schulz could play "Redwing" on the mouth organ and was so beloved as a barber, businessman, and St. Paul fixture that the community gave him a festive dinner in 1959 and toasted his imminent retirement. Customers sometimes called him Senator, and it was frequently suggested he should have been a public official. Carl's barbershop anchored the same corner for forty-two years, and if he had had a dollar for every time he swept it Carl would have been rich as his son Sparky.

"My father dropped out of school after the third grade and later paid his own way through barber school. He became a leader. He accomplished more than I have. That's all I want. For people to like me like they did my father."

Toward that end he labors, "charming the socks off of reporters," as he likes to say, accepting newspaper interviews in the most democratic fashion, not really caring if circulation is ten thousand or ten million or if it's Brinkley or a cub reporter still green as his editor's eyeshade. (David Brinkley's was the least inspired interview he has been subjected to, Schulz says. It may not have been the famed newscaster's fault: Brinkley was scheduled for gallbladder surgery.) Visiting journalists all get the same cola in a Snoopy glass and the same tour of the ice arena and the same, well-spoken message of how sad things, not happy ones, inspire the best cartoons.

People do like him. Violinist Robert McDuffie composed a serenade to Schulz. The local Boy Scouts named him the Distinguished Citizen of Sonoma County and later the national organization hung the ultimate merit badge, the Silver Buffalo, around his neck. "All this and I was never even a Boy Scout," he marvels. At the height of

Snoopymania, in 1966, an enterprising Florida rock group called the Royal Guardsmen sold three million copies of a Top-40 song called "Snoopy versus the Red Baron," at first without asking permission. Lawyers live to correct such oversights, however, and the group went on to make an authorized career of Snoopy: "Return of Snoopy versus the Red Baron," "Snoopy and His Friends," and "Snoopy for President."

The tributes to *Peanuts* over the years have been both secular and sacred. In Buffalo's Westminster Presbyterian Church there is a Schroeder in stained glass, sharing his pane with no less than Albert Schweitzer, also at a piano, in a window designed to the glory of music. Two sets of bereaved parents have asked for and received permission for a *Peanuts* character to be used on a child's tombstone. There are probably more dogs named Snoopy in America than fat women named Bertha. Grunts coming out of the bush in Vietnam were assaulted with pornographic renderings of the *Peanuts* characters stamped on cigarette lighters and caps and playing cards—items certainly not approved by Creative Associates.

Oh, they like him all right! Fans send him bad paintings and sweet valentines and hundreds of letters weekly; they press relentlessly toward him with chewing-gum wrappers and stuffed dogs and ticket stubs on which he should sign his name. He must also provide the pen.

He can be petty and irritable and self-centered and vain. Some of his favorite pets are peeves. He grouses about people who have unlisted telephone numbers. If he can manage with a listed number, why can't everyone else? Why in the world would a golf pro need an unlisted number, for heaven's sake? He cannot abide fans who introduce him to their children as "Snoopy's father" or the misperception that comic strips, namely his own, are for children only.

"I hate it when an adult comes up to me in a bookstore and says 'Our daughter is nineteen and still reads your strip. Will you sign this book for her?' " Fanatical sports fans bug him. "I hate it when those guys paint their chests red and scream for the television cameras 'We're Number One!' They are not Number One. They are nothing." In self-defense he now limits to the exact minute the amount of time he will sign books after a speech. If there is a line when the allotted time is up, too bad. Otherwise, he says, people will chase him onto the elevator and out to his car waving Flairs and matchbook covers. "I don't mind so much signing a book they have bought. But it's always some scrap of paper. . . ."

He is not above a good feud. Years ago, the venerable *San Francisco Chronicle* columnist Herb Caen assigned an assistant to query Schulz on his separation from his first wife, Joyce. "Is it true," the researcher wanted to know, "that divorce is imminent?"

"Not that I know of," Sparky truthfully replied. Unbeknownst to him, Joyce had begun divorce proceedings that day. The Caen lieutenant called back the next day, accused Sparky of lying, and then hung up on him. Schulz has never forgotten the incident.

It bugs him that *The New York Times* does not carry comic strips in its hallowed pages. He considers it ironic, at the least, that a few years back, when *The Times'* newspaper chain bought the Santa Rosa newspaper, *The Press-Democrat,* he was the one who sold *The Times* the land on which to put its press. "I shouldn't have done it," says Sparky.

Sometimes his outlook is downright prudish. A pretty girl is ruined for him the moment she lights a cigarette. "I'll never forget when I was coaching the girls' softball team at Art Instruction Schools. This cute girl came trotting in between innings, and I smiled at her and said 'You're doing great!' Then she went over to the side and smoked a cigarette, and the bottom dropped out of the attraction."

He likes people around who compare him to Freud and his strip to *Alice in Wonderland* and who compliment him on his newest sweater and his latest strip. And while he can say, with sincerity, "Aw, shucks, forty years of comic strips is not the same thing as writing a Beethoven concerto," he'd just as soon someone else not say it.

On the other hand, he can be generous and loving and unassuming. He hangs up his own clothes in a home that is not in the least ostentatious. He is exceedingly quiet about his philanthropy, preferring to give anonymous gifts. Sonoma County certainly has benefited from his residence there. So have numerous individuals. "I never loan money. I give it."

He does not hoard his humor for the strip. One day he telephoned a friend who continually teases him about the long, epic books the children in the strip are forced to read. The friend was not at home but had left his answering machine on for messages. At the sound of the tone, Sparky, in a measured voice, began reading *War and Peace.*

He loves his children unceasingly and without reservation. At the request of his stepdaughter Lisa, the preeminent cartoonist of our time took great care in painting the alphabet around the wall in his grandchild's nursery. When his children were in grammar school he was president of the PTA and personally wrote the entire monthly newsletter. When Joyce was head of the women's bowling league, he illustrated her newsletter.

While he has nothing against money, Schulz is thrifty and not really materialistic. Splurging is simply no fun for him.

"I go into a bookstore and find a book I want and say 'Charge it!' and get home and find out it costs thirty-five dollars!" For a child of the Great Depression, even a multimillionaire child, that's a lot of money for one book.

Even in the 1960s, when Snoopy was a demigod and the Schulz bank account was growing faster than the Japanese export market, he managed to keep his home life relatively simple and normal. "I didn't even know we had a lot of money until I was about eighteen," says Amy. "I remember that whenever they'd ask us at school to fill out a form that listed our father's occupation, I'd be kind of embarrassed. I always wished he were a banker or something or had a title. 'Cartoonist' just sounded like he didn't really have a job."

The children got a dollar weekly allowance, with sometimes an extra quarter thrown in for feeding the cat. They never wanted for anything, it's true. And thanks to their mother Joyce's penchant for building things, the ranch called Coffee Grounds, the place they grew up near Sebastopol, California, resembled a scaled-down amusement park. There was that much-described artificial waterfall and a miniature golf course. "But when it came to money, as far as I can remember, it was never talked about," says Amy. "Not even once. I'm very uncomfortable talking about money now."

It was a wholesome yet privileged world of rolling hills and apple orchards, horses and dogs, ducks and bass, and a Mercedes in which to escape all that utopia for the city if things got boring. The kids managed a four-story treehouse and played ball on their own private diamond. Jill Schulz remembers waking up to the smell and sound of the lawn sprinklers misting the green grass. Like Amy, she was a teenager before she realized the implications of being Charles Schulz's daughter.

"Everyone assumed we lived in a big white house and had servants. They thought you were a snob before they gave you a chance to show you were not."

Like their father, the kids all thought of the strip's characters as a second family, brothers and sisters who were in and out of trouble on a daily basis. The comic strip children talked like the rest of them, indulged in the same mild oaths as their father, and were an unremarkable part of life.

"People say to me now 'I don't think you realize what a genius you have for a father,' " says Amy, "and I feel bad. They are right. I have trouble seeing it like that. Dad never made a big deal about himself. How can I see the strip as ingenious when he thinks and talks just like that?

"To tell you the truth, I don't like comic strips. His is the only one I read, and sometimes I wonder if I'd read it if it wasn't his. I like the action ones, where Snoopy is flying down the hill in his dog bowl. And of course I always watch the television shows."

Monte Schulz remembers being astounded at a sixth-grade friend who was a *Peanuts* aficionado. "For some reason that was shocking to me, that someone my age could be that interested in something my dad did. I guess I knew intellectually people read him, but the other kids never made a big deal of it." Monte has always gotten his dosage of *Peanuts* from the reprint books "because I don't like waiting until the next day to see how things would come out. I don't like reading it in the newspaper."

Prophet Schulz definitely was unsung in his own land. So today it thrills him no end when one of his children even thinks about the strip. "Monte said to me the other day, 'Dad, I've been thinking about it, and I think Charlie Brown is the smartest of all the kids.' Monte will go along and not say anything, and then he'll come up with something like that that lets me know he's been thinking." Schulz beams.

Nobody could be expected to be as preoccupied with the strip as its creator, of course. What devil of determination settled so early in his Twin Cities psyche? Schulz doesn't know. Even as a small child, he never wanted to be anything but a cartoonist. Well, there was that brief, addled moment of adolescence when he imagined a life on the golf links, but cartooning was his first passion, his prevailing wind. When, as a teenager, he worked briefly for a direct-mail advertising company, he spent all of his first paycheck on a book about cartoons. His friends looked at him incredulously and probably twirled their index fingers around their ears. What manner of boy is this who would waste an entire paycheck on a book?

So what if, just supposing, he had had no talent, no predilection for somehow making funny a simple drawing of two children standing behind a wall, talking? Or, if he had the talent and not the driving desire? What made him what he is—an artist who draws funny pictures and takes it all so seriously? A soldier to endure the regimen of daily production? An artist to boot? He has said he's not Picasso, but quickly adds Picasso probably would not have had the stamina to produce a daily comic strip.

He was a child of the city. Those who want to paint him as the simple rube are wrong. It was enough of an occasion when Sparky first saw cows to warrant a photograph for the family album. There he stood, resplendent in slacks and cowlick, enjoying a bovine experience. He knew street hockey and streetcars, not tractors and hoedowns. With his first wife he moved to the ranch, but Sparky made it his business to stay off the horses. He has never really been at home on the range.

Some say his popularity peaked. How can they tell, when newspapers kept buying the feature until there were virtually no

newspaper markets without it? With the sale of *Peanuts* to the newspaper in Needles, a promotional arrangement, really, with Spike's
hometown paper, he acquired his two thousandth customer, the
first syndicated cartoonist to reach the plateau.

He has not burned out or dropped out or quit. He draws seven
installments weekly, rain, shine, intestinal flu, or writer's block, and
an unplanned, unsought, and mostly peripheral empire grew like
Topsy without his doing anything differently than he had from the
beginning. For the first month's work he made ninety dollars; for
the same work forty years later he would make a million.

He became not worldlier, but simpler, more reluctant to travel,
a prisoner of his own talent and familiar surroundings. He would
leave airplanes at the last possible moment before take-off, cancel
engagements time and again. He would refuse to travel alone.

You cannot fathom Charles Schulz without understanding that
his genius is both a blessing and a burden. He is a hostage of unrelenting fame, fortune, and the unyielding desire to create a quality
strip. Many of the opportunities his success and money open up to
him are wasted, really, on a man who has little inclination and less
time to take advantage of them.

He has created a commercial success while pursuing an aesthet-
ic end. Forty years after beginning, he still is in dogged pursuit of
that same end, undistracted by and distrusting of his success so far.
He draws every picture and writes every word himself, unlike all
other cartoonists who have approached his standing. He does not
want someone in the next room, waiting to execute his ideas. He
wants the credit. He accepts the blame.

Whatever he has achieved, he has done by himself.

"I have been dismayed at the many people who, meeting me
for the first time, express amazement that I am still drawing the
strip. They remark that they were sure I had others doing all the
work by this time. Why, I ask myself, work so hard when they can't
tell the difference?"

He has defined his job this way: "A cartoonist is someone who
has to draw the same thing every day without repeating himself."
For nearly forty years he has done so. Filling in little squares with

his little folks, he has become a giant in a competitive, brutally de-manding industry that accepts no excuses, offers no sick days. With a shaking hand he draws a steady stream of funny pictures. Presi-dents and professors of divinity, waitresses and world leaders all read *Peanuts* and laugh. It has more levels than Macy's. Theologians and theater denizens debate his relevance and adopt his language.

If, as they say, good writing is only a future cliché, then Schulz has written well.

He wrote the book on happiness. It was a best-seller, yet. He de-fined happiness dozens of ways: warm puppies, piles of leaves, find-ing the little puzzle piece with the pink edge and part of the sky and the top of the sailboat, a piece of fudge caught on the first bounce. He can define it quite brilliantly, but he cannot seem to find it. He frets about past losses, past loves, the past in general, until even his friends and those who love him the most want to say, "Wake up, man! You have it all. You have earned the laurels. Take a load off!"

Only his misfortune is the world's gain. Because of his fretful, queasy, depressed personality, we all have *Peanuts.* We have the harpings of Lucy, the fantasies of Snoopy, the ponderings of Linus, the ultimate, sad wisdom of Charlie Brown. Our cost is small. Even with the inflated price of newspapers, we pay two bits or thirty-five cents for a bit of brilliance, a corner on wisdom, each day. That bit of brilliance cost Schulz more.

They honor him, now. Everyone with a rubber chicken feels obligated to hang him with an honorary title or degree, as if by asso-ciation they buy a share in the unique mind and talent of Charles Monroe Schulz. He dismisses the honors, each and every one, this way:

"Oh, well. Just another small thing to show the little red-haired girl's mother she was wrong about me."

Selected Bibliography

Books

Arieti, Silvano *American Handbook of Psychiatry* New York: Basic Books, Inc. 1974

Brown,Charlie *A Book of Good Grief* St. Paul, Minnesota: Entheo 1985

Eisenhower, Dwight D. *Crusade In Europe* New York: Doubleday and Company 1948

Mauldin, Bill *A Sort of a Saga* New York: William Sloane Associates 1949

Morris, Willie *North Toward Home* Boston: Houghton-Mifflin 1967

Orr-Cahall, Christina *The Graphic Art of Charles Schulz* Oakland, California: The Oakland Museum Art Department 1985

Robinson, Jerry *The Comics* New York: G.P. Putnam's Sons 1974

Schonberg, Harold C. *The Lives of the Great Composers* New York: W.W. Norton & Company 1970

Schulz, Charles M. *Charlie Brown, Snoopy and Me* Garden City, New Jersey: Doubleday and Company 1980

Schulz, Charles M. *Peanuts Jubilee: My Life and Art with Charlie Brown and Others* New York: Holt, Rinehart and Winston 1974

Schulz, Charles M. *You Don't Look 35, Charlie Brown!* New York: Holt, Rinehart and Winston 1985

Short, Robert *The Gospel According to Peanuts* Richmond, Virginia: John Knox Press 1965

Short, Robert *Parables of Peanuts* New York: Harper and Row 1968

Twerski, Abraham J., M.D. *When Do the Good Things Start?* New York: Topper Books 1988

Articles

Borgzinner, Jon *"A Leaf, a Lemon Drop, a Cartoon is Born"* Life March 17,1967

Pauer, Frank *"A Conversation With Charles Schulz"* Dayton Daily News-Journal Herald May 3,1987

Ruby, Michael *"Good Grief, $150 Million"* Newsweek vol.78 December 27,1971

Steinberg, Neil *"Penpal"* Mature Outlook September/October,1987

Tebbel, John *"The Not -So Peanuts World of Charles M. Schulz"* Saturday Review vol. 52 April 12,1969

"The World According to Peanuts" Time vol. 85 April 9,1965

Witt, Linda *"The Soul of Peanuts: Will the Real Charlie Brown Please Stand Up?"* The Chicago Tribune, Sunday Magazine January 2, 1986